LABORING FOR JUSTICE

Laboring for Justice

The Fight Against Wage Theft in an American City

REBECCA BERKE GALEMBA

STANFORD UNIVERSITY PRESS
Stanford, California

Stanford University Press
Stanford, California

Printed in the United States of America on acid-free, archival-quality paper

Library of Congress Cataloging-in-Publication Data available on request.

Library of Congress Control Number: 2022027844
ISBN 9781503613454 (cloth)
ISBN 9781503635203 (paper)
ISBN 9781503635210 (ebook)

Front cover art and design: Gia Giasullo
Typeset by Elliott Beard in Minion Pro 10/14.4

Dedicated to Centro Humanitario para los Trabajadores, the Direct Action Team, and the workers, students, and community partners who participated in this project

The author will donate all royalties from the book and associated speaking fees to Centro Humanitario para los Trabajadores and the Direct Action Team

Contents

List of Illustrations

Acknowledgments

I acknowledge that much of the research and writing for this book occurred on land held in stewardship by the Cheyenne and Arapaho Nations, as well as the brutal history of genocide, violent eviction, and theft in which the University of Denver, where I work, was historically implicated. These forms of forced dispossession and erasure are not confined to history, but continue to infuse dynamics of racial capitalism, settler colonialism, gentrification, and eviction in the name of progress. As I align myself with the struggle for immigrant and workers' rights, I recognize my position as a settler on stolen lands. I acknowledge that I contributed to the very dynamics of gentrification and displacement as I moved to Colorado during the post–Great Recession construction boom I began to study. I hope this book is an invitation, and can also serve as a pedagogical model, to discuss issues of escalating inequality, histories of theft and dispossession, and racial and immigrant justice to stimulate innovative types of solidarity, relationship building, and social change across multiple axes of difference.

This project was ignited by my growing involvement with the immigrant rights movement and my desire to apply what I learned about borders and migration from my prior work at the Mexico-Guatemala border to my own community. I am grateful that I found Centro Humanitario para los Trabajadores (Centro), Denver's worker center, as a result of a recommendation from a former connection in Boston with the American Friends Service Committee. What began as a classroom partnership spawned not only a multiyear collaborative activist research project, but an organization, colleagues, and friends who will continue to be part of my life, work, political commitments, and community.

I relied on many people who appear in this book to teach me about immigrant and labor rights. With their permission, I use their real names to credit them for their time, intellectual contributions, and the ongoing work they commit each day to the struggle for immigrant and worker justice. A book about wage theft cannot be written without underscoring the social relationships, labor, and time that others put into this project at various stages. Students at the University of Denver were critical collaborators through their work as paid research assistants, outreach volunteers, or students in my courses. They helped push my thinking forward, especially as many of them went on to work in the fields of immigrant and labor rights and even, in some instances, became community partners.

I especially thank Camden Bowman, who helped me initiate the research and wrote his master's thesis using some of the early data. Kendra Allen, Max Spiro, and Morgan Brokob were instrumental as lead research assistants and helped supervise other students in the field. Morgan and Kendra helped with early coding, and Max, through his independent study, helped map out the sites and provided data that helped us later construct the survey sampling design.

I will be eternally grateful to Amy Czulada (coauthor of Chapter 7), who continues to push me to embrace a broader lens of economic justice and is a natural organizer. Amy came to the project to help translate for attorney Raja Raghunath's student law clinic and joined me and my students to talk with day laborers on the corners where they waited to find jobs. Amy soon became a lead research assistant on the project, helped me develop the survey manual and train surveyors, ran know-your-rights workshops, and became a co-conspirator in all things wage theft. During her time as a student, she took on a leading role coordinating Centro's Direct Action Team (DAT) as she also organized students on campus around immigrant rights and student debt. I am indebted to and continued to be inspired by Amy. Diego Bleifuss Prados (another coauthor of Chapter 7), who began as a surveyor on the project, was an integral collaborator, especially when he went on to serve as the coordinator of the DAT after Amy graduated. Diego helped connect the wage theft struggle to a larger politics of change, infusing the group with his connections from the Democratic Socialists of

America, immigrant rights groups, and unions when he went on to work for the Service Employees International Unit after graduation. Abbey Vogel (another coauthor of Chapter 7) aligned with Diego on these tasks while bringing an organizing sensibility to the project. Abbey started as a student in my Qualitative Methods course, whose student group joined the project for an academic quarter to focus on the sense of community day laborers cultivate at the corners. Abbey quickly became hooked on direct action and sustained involvement until after she moved away from Denver after graduation. Abbey connected easily with workers, other researchers, and DAT volunteers; brought keen theoretical insights to the project; and always encouraged me and others to look for the sparks even when they were difficult to see. She became a critical thought partner for this book, and I hired her after graduation to help me with literature reviews and organization and editorial assistance while she also served as the lead author for the coauthored chapter. I am certain I could not have written this book without her editorial assistance, strong organizational abilities, and her encouragement for me to sometimes step away from critique and embrace the wins, the possibilities, and the relationships forged in the process.

Former students Claudia Castillo, Yessenia Prodero, and Samantha McGinnis played key roles not only in the wage theft research, but in broader attempts to connect to the immigrant rights movement. I learned from the work of students like Amy, Diego, and Yessenia. Yessenia took my methods class, worked as a surveyor, continued to volunteer with the DAT before moving away from Denver, and currently works as an immigrant rights organizer with Massachusetts Jobs with Justice. All three helped organize day laborers through know-your-rights sessions and with the DAT while they volunteered to assist immigrants in sanctuary. Other students were involved with Abolish ICE and volunteered with Colorado's rapid response network to notify and prepare when raids occurred, all of which ramped up during the Trump administration. In 2017, I spearheaded a group called the DU Immigrant and Refugee Rights Colectivo (Colectivo) to help structure the organizing work in which students were already engaged.

A Facebook site began by Katie Dingeman, a former colleague, worked to connect the DU and wider community on immigrant rights, but it largely operated virtually. Colectivo sought to provide a grounded presence while building up connections between DU and the community to share resources and spur collaborations around immigrant rights. Claudia and Samantha were critical to providing structure to the group and developed a model that I lacked the organizational experience to even envision. Samantha and Claudia, and other students, helped provide the seeds for what eventually became the DU Center for Immigration Policy and Research, which I launched with my colleague Lisa Martínez in 2020 when it was selected for funding from a competitive Knowledge Bridge process at the University of Denver launched by Corinne Lengsfeld.

I am grateful to Samantha McGinnis for helping me bring the project more into the public sphere, including her help with social media materials, the Wordpress site, and communications when DU selected this project to run a crowdfunding campaign through the DU Good Campaign. Stephanie Renteria-Perez, who worked with the DAT through my methods course, helped me produce public reports and translate them into Spanish to share with Centro members. She, as well as Nathanial Kern (who also originally became involved through the methods course), helped systematize the DAT's database. Ariadma Segura provided additional literature review support and Chloe Thomas assisted with reformatting and checking the endnotes.

Mark McCarthy, one of the most impressive undergraduates I have ever met, volunteered and interned with Centro, helped code data from my database to identify patterns, and coded Centro's own data to produce a demographic report about its membership. I continue to seek out his expertise as he has gone on to work with the International Organization for Migration and the International Labor Organization.

I am grateful for the DU student surveyors: Eloy Chavez, Diego Bleifuss Prados, Amy Czulada, Claudia Castillo, Yessenia Prodero, Cristal Torres, Andrea Mártires Abelenda, David Feuerbach, Jazmin Bustillos, Blake Linehan, and Estefan Hernández Escoto (Regis University student). Daniel Olmos, a postdoctoral fellow at DU during this time, helped during the first survey phase and shared insights from his own work on immigrant labor. While many of these students also led know-your-rights workshops at hiring sites, I appreciate additional assistance from students Mariel Hernández and Ana Gutiérrez. For data assistance for the survey, I appreciate DU student Jordyn Dinwiddie's work with data entry and Randall

Kuhn's UCLA students: Rosario Majano, Alexis Cooke, Brian Kim, Michael Tzen, and Anny Rodriguez-Viloria.

Many students contributed to this project through my Qualitative Methods course at the Josef Korbel School of International Studies at DU, whether they interviewed day laborers; volunteered with the DAT; interviewed nonprofits, attorneys, employers, and Department of Labor staff; or attended Wage Theft Task Force meetings with me. Some of them appear throughout this book. I thank the additional students who contributed to this project from the methods course (I apologize for any omissions and do not include those already credited above): Danyah Al Jadaani, Sierra Amon, Kaley Anderson, Cecily Bacon, Jo Beletic, Haven Campbell, Michelle Carrere-Seizer, Kate Castenson, Jeanne Crump, Sarah Davis, Chelsea Dillane, Kaylee Dolen, Kate Douglass, Anne Dunlop, Pamela Encinas, Kat Englert, Otilia Enica, Bri Erger, Sarah Friend, Patrick Garrett, Ryan Goehrung, Ashley Greve, Avalon Guarino, Julia Hanby, Ayesha Hamza, Laurel Hayden, Savannah Hildebrand, Kenny Hood, Becky Hostetler, Christina Ibanez, Sarah Johnson, Andrew Johnson, Rachel Kerstein, Brianna Klipp, Zorana Knezevic, Mary Kohrman, David Koppers, Tyler Kozole, Stellah Kwasi, Caitlin Long, Ryan Lowry, Nikky Mades, Sarah May, Elayna McCall, Kara Napolitano, Alexander Nasserjah, Aaron Nilson, Meg O'Brien, Monica Peterson, Brittny Parsells-Johnson, Sarala Pradhan, Ann Rogers, Laura Scharmer, Andrew Scott, Liz Shaw, Marissa Shoback, Stacy Shomo, Kendra Snelson, Natalie Southwick, Laura Tilley, Rougui Toure, Caitlin Trent, Arianne Williams, Ashley Williamson, and Jennifer Zavala. I thank Chelsea Montes de Oca, Stephanie Renteria-Perez, Feleg Tesema, Sam Colvett, and Bianca Garcia for assisting with organizing the community partnerships for this class with the support of the DU Center for Community Engagement to Advance Scholarship and Learning (CCESL) Public Good fellow program.

This project enjoyed support for numerous internal funding sources at the University of Denver, including the Korbel Research Fund and grants from the Interdisciplinary Research Institute for the Study of (In)Equality (IRISE) and a Public Good Grant from CCESL with Raja Raghunath from the DU law school. CCESL generously supported the community-engaged components of my course that allowed me to sustain the project over time.

Raja and I also received funding from the Labor Research and Action Network. Since 2017, the Michael and Alice Kuhn Foundation has generously provided a yearly collaborative grant between my research, the DAT's work, and Centro's workers' rights programs. Since the first year, this grant has been led and administered by Centro. I also thank Einstein Bros. Bagels and Kaladi Coffee Roasters, who donated the bagels and coffee that we shared with workers.

Numerous community partners were instrumental to this research, as well as becoming partners in advocacy and information sharing. Marco Nuñez and Sarah Shikes served as partners through Centro, where I was grateful to learn from other staff including Nancy Rosas, Tony Lemus, Sarahy Plazola, and Alan Muñoz, as well as worker leaders. At Towards Justice—a nonprofit law firm dedicated to worker and economic justice—I appreciate my collaboration with David Seligman, Nina DiSalvo, Lindsay Fallon, and Jesus Loayza. I benefited from conversations with Ron Ojeda in the Office of Financial Empowerment & Protection within the City of Denver; Scott Moss and Liz Funk from the Colorado Department of Labor and Employment; Minsun Ji, the founder of Centro; and Jim Gleason and Joe Deras from the Carpenters' and Painters' unions, respectively. Mateos Alvarez generously opened the doors of the Dayton Street Day Labor Center for students to learn and speak with workers. Chris Wheeler inspired me and many students through his commitment to the DAT, whether teaching us about wage theft delegations, bringing fruit salad to meetings, or in committing much of his retirement time to workers and immigrants. Chris continuously provided feedback on my work and invitations to community events, and he patiently supported my students whether they pursued a long-term collaboration with the DAT or just the ten-week academic quarter.

At the DU Sturm College of Law, I appreciate the brilliant collaboration of Raja Raghunath and Tammy Kuennen. Tammy, also a coauthor of Chapter 7, motivated me to think about the law in new ways as we endeavored to train our students and came to learn from each other. Meeting attorney Matthew Fritz-Mauer, who also holds a PhD in criminology, law and society, virtually over the course of the pandemic pushed my analysis deeper as we talked about cases and read each other's work. Alex Sanchez, a coauthor of Chapter 7, became a collaborator on many levels. Starting as a student at CU Denver in Jim Walsh's class, she showed up at the DAT to volunteer for the semester. Alex went on to become the DAT coordinator after Diego, worked for Centro, and was instrumental to my research by helping to organize and analyze case data. Many volunteers gave their time and energy to the DAT over the years, but Davor stands out for his commitment to the group, fellow workers, and his readiness to accompany my students.

I am especially indebted to Sarah Horton, whose scholarship I not only draw on throughout this book but who also partnered with me for various parts of this project. She and her students participated in early fieldwork and collaborated with Towards Justice to help workers file wage claims. Sarah helped co-organize a Wage Theft Summit with me in November 2016 through the Scholars Strategy Network, which brought together stakeholders to discuss the policy climate, share research, organize workers, and educate employers. At this event, I was lucky to learn from Kim Bobo, even if briefly. I am also grateful to the participants of the Wage Theft Task Force, whose list has swelled from a small circle to over 140 members. Through this task force, I shared my research, learned strategies from partners, developed research connections, and learned from experts they brought in from the Restaurant Opportunities Center United to Terri Gerstein. By sharing my research in public, policy, and academic forums, I moved from providing social critique to the advocacy conversation. I appreciated spaces to share research and provide support to nonprofits in Denver, Denver Public Schools Family and Community Engagement (with Raja Raghunath), local town halls, and an invited talk at the UCLA Labor Center thanks to Randall Kuhn, Abel Valenzuela, and Tia Koonse. I am thankful to have met Cecilia Menjívar, who helped me broaden my circles and supported my ongoing development as an immigration scholar. At workshops through the Colorado Immigration Scholars Network, I benefited from general conversations and more explicit feedback from Daniel Olmos, Sarah Horton, Edelina Burciaga, Lisa Martínez, Cesar García Cuauhtémoc Hernández, Chris Lasch, Ming Chen, Whitney Duncan, Fernando Riosmena, Evin Rodkey, and Jessica Garrick, among others. I appreciate additional feedback from other immigration and labor scholars, including Josiah McHeyman and Ruth Gomberg-Muñoz, at earlier stages of the project.

At the Korbel School, I benefited from feedback and support from the Latin America Center and colleagues. I am particularly grateful to Aaron

Schneider and Marie Berry for their unconditional support in many aspects of my life and generous feedback on parts of the manuscript. Marie Berry inspired me to dig deeper into relational forms of care and solidarity, critique my own position, and turn a broader critical lens onto capitalism, and also shared a lot of child care and wine during difficult and more joyful times. Colleagues like Lynn Holland, Oliver Kaplan, Kate Tennis, Singumbe Muyeba, George DeMartino, and Ilene Graebel championed my work in various ways and made me feel at home as somewhat of a disciplinary outsider. Tricia Olsen provided a much-needed writing partner as we supported one another to meet our respective deadlines and not overedit.

My partnership with Randall Kuhn pushed me to put my training as an anthropological demographer to the test, revealing to both of us the challenges and rewards of mixed-methods work. Although this project was somewhat outside his own comfort zone, Randall took a leap of faith, for which I am grateful. He designed the sampling strategy, helped with survey design, and performed the weights and statistical analysis of the survey results. Randall generously connected me to others to support my work and solicit additional feedback for our cowritten work from Fernando Riosmena, Ruben Rumbaut, Erin Hamilton, Victor Agadjanian, Abel Valenzuela, and Roger Waldinger. I thank Randall for being patient with the style and time line of an ethnographer compared to demographers and public health scholars!

Writing a book at the height of the pandemic would not have been possible without a deep support network. I appreciated writing groups organized by the University of Denver to keep me on track, as well as support from other academic mamas, many of whom were also dealing with managing remote schooling and care for their children while schools were closed and loved ones became ill or quarantined. The group also functioned as a space for solidarity, sharing, and care. I appreciate the support of Kate Centellas, Sarah Osten, Emily Yates-Doerr, Betsey Brada, and Julia Young. Kate Centellas especially provided useful comments on parts of the manuscript. I also appreciate the feedback of Abigail Andrews and David Trouille: we formed a virtual writing group as we all struggled to write our second books about issues related to immigration while managing child care with the pandemic.

My family provided invaluable support. When I became responsible for daily care and remote schooling, my spouse, Dan, took over weekends and nights, including teaching my kids how to become good skiers on weekends so that I could write. My mother-in-law watched my children from our porch when we were nervous to go inside, and my daughters became curious about the book as they tried to be as independent as they could. I took turns with my neighbors Kevin and Theresa watching our kids play out front at a distance as we worked outside. I was lucky to have my parents move nearby in fall 2021, as well as support once lockdown subsided from our long-time sitter, Maddy Solimando. As I wrote, I asked my mother more about my grandmother, Rose, who I knew had been an advocate for women's and workers' rights. As a daughter of Jewish immigrants with a budding interest in organizing to which her parents disapproved, she would sneak out to labor organizing meetings. She became an educator, vice principal, and advocate for Title IX; especially for women within the teachers' union at a time when women faced significant barriers. I now wish I had asked her more questions.

I appreciate the support of the Korbel Research Fund in funding a book workshop so that I could gather additional feedback from scholars and community partners. Angela Stuesse and Sarah Horton provided detailed feedback on the manuscript, helping me reach broader audiences of anthropologists, immigration scholars, and those interested in community-based research. The book workshop was also an opportunity to share the work with partners David Seligman, Sarah Shikes, and Matt Fritz-Mauer, who devoted time to providing comments as the workshop evolved into a productive space to discuss future partnerships, organizing ideas, and policies.

As my book revisions progressed and I searched for photos to include, I became unsettled with images of workers that seemed to trap them in space and time at the corners. Although I had oral consent to take the photos and some even relished the opportunity to have their photo taken, such depictions seemed to distill workers' more diverse identities and experiences into particular days they waited for work. I worried that such images perpetuated stereotypical images of day laborers, for which they would be imprinted to represent. Inspired by muralists around Denver and artwork used by the National Day Labor Organizing Network in some of their outreach materials, I decided to do my own artistic depictions of three images. For this effort, I am enormously grateful for the guidance of Anna Wall at the Art Barn and her connections to Leslie Judy, who helped me cut the glass for the windows of the collage of Centro, and Nate Phelan, who photographed the art pieces. When I approached Anna, who had taught my daughter, for some guidance and materials to help with the collage of Centro, we had no idea the process that lay ahead and I thank her for her extraordinary patience. I made the collage of Centro on a table that Anna procured from Habitat for Humanity, and I collected the majority of the materials from magazines, outreach brochures I accumulated throughout the research, and materials from around Centro, including rocks, glass, wire, wrappers, cans, and bottles. My older daughter, Lanie, helped with sanding, drawing the outline, and some of the early collage and painting work. With the assistance of Leslie Judy to seal the table with resin, I hope to exhibit it to partners and donate it when Centro finds a new home. When I learned that Diego Bleifuss Prados was a talented watercolor artist, I commissioned a piece from him of the Aurora corner. Art fostered the kinds of solidarity and creativity that words could not always capture.

Some of the survey analysis, tables, charts, images, and cases that appear throughout this book can be found in Rebecca B. Galemba, " 'They Steal Our Work': Wage Theft and the Criminalization of Immigrant Day Laborers in Colorado, USA." *European Journal on Criminal Policy and Research* 27 (1): 91–112, March 2021; Rebecca Galemba and Randall Kuhn, " 'No Place for Old Men': Immigrant Duration, Wage Theft, and Economic Mobility Among Day Laborers in Denver, Colorado," *International Migration Review* 55 (4): 1201–1230, April 2021; and Rebecca Galemba, "Anthropology of Wage Theft in Colorado," *Anthropology News, Society for Economic Anthropology*, May 22, 2020. I thank Springer Nature, Sage, and the American Anthropological Association for allowing me to reprint some of this material, as well as TEDx for giving me permission to use a case featured in my TedxMileHigh talk.

I appreciate the constructive feedback from the anonymous reviewers, Michelle Lipinski for initially endorsing this project, and Stanford University Press for having patience for the time it took to complete. At Stanford, I appreciate the editorial assistance and eye of Dylan Kyung-lim White, Bev Miller for copyediting, Gigi Mark, and the entire editorial, marketing, and production team. I would also like to Matthew John Phillips for his meticulous work constructing the index and his assistance with proofreading.

LABORING FOR JUSTICE

INTRODUCTION
STOLEN WAGES ON STOLEN LAND

Yes, indeed, it is a bit strange, complicated, curious. Because, before, all this was Mexican land. Colorado, New Mexico, Texas. And now afterward, because of some greedy people, some money, we lost everything . . . so much land. If not, just imagine: today, Mexico would be much, much, much bigger.

—*Severiano A. interview with Abbey Vogel*

CLAUDIO WORE A LONG BRAID down his back with a red cap perched on top.[1] He was waiting to find day labor employment at the intersection of Federal Boulevard and 19th Street in West Denver, Colorado, when I met him in August 2015 (Figure 1). The sleek metal curves of the Denver Broncos stadium hovered in the background of the informal hiring site as the August sun pierced through the stadium's upper rungs. It was early in the morning, and I had just arrived at the corner with graduate student Max Spiro and an attorney, Raja Raghunath, to talk to day laborers about their work experiences and help conduct intakes for Raja's wage theft clinic.[2]

Claudio was a 53-year-old undocumented immigrant from Veracruz, Mexico, who had lived in Denver since 2003. He was nursing a work-related foot injury sustained a few months earlier. He never asked his employer for assistance because he wanted to avoid problems, although his mounting

FIGURE 1: Day laborer waiting for work at the Federal and 19th Street hiring site. Author's artistic interpretation of photo. Photo of artwork by N.A.P. @ pHactory8.

medical expenses worried him. In need of income, Claudio even returned to work for this same employer. That time, the employer shortchanged him $350 for his work. Why would Claudio return to work for a boss from whom he was still seeking payment for medical expenses? Claudio directed his gaze at me, his answer obvious: "There is not much work. You think that people are good and sometimes it is not true." After not being able to work for months because of his injury, Claudio was back at the corner soliciting employment. He hoped that his injury would not prevent employers from hiring him.[3]

Most day laborers like Claudio are immigrants from Latin America who seek daily work for cash; nationwide, about three-quarters are undocumented.[4] Day laborers are usually hired by lower-level subcontractors, labor brokers, and home owners.[5] Day labor was previously mostly limited to large, traditional immigrant gateway cities like Chicago, Los Angeles, and New York, but day labor hiring sites have expanded across the United Stated alongside the wider informalization of employment, economic restructuring, and rise in immigration from Latin America in the 1990s.[6] Day laborers may solicit employment at a street corner like Claudio, outside a home improvement store, or at one of the growing network of nonprofit worker centers around the country. They tend to work in industries associated with residential construction—masonry, painting, roofing, cleaning, and demolition—as well as in moving and landscaping.[7]

On a typical day at a street corner hiring site, a truck screeches to a halt, the driver rolls down the window, and yells out how many workers they need for the day (Figure 2). One man waiting at the corner, Javier, explained, "Sometimes the employer will stick out his fingers . . . 1, 2, 3" to indicate their preferences. Workers rush to the passenger side window as they jockey with one another to get the job while they also attempt to assess the nature of the work, hours, and wages. Accordingly, Javier asserted, "We fish too. . . . We are the piranhas. We will say, 'Take me, I'm tougher, stronger, more experienced.'" Still, day laborers often have just a few minutes to negotiate with the employer before getting into the vehicle. "If the employer chooses you," Javier added, "you go. Many times the *patrones* [bosses] choose, the short one, the thin one . . ."

Day laborers in the Denver area dub street corner hiring sites *liebres*—jackrabbits in Spanish—because landing a job requires a mix of cunning

FIGURE 2: Day laborers hanging out by a truck at the Kentucky and Sheridan site. Author's artistic interpretation of photo. Photo of artwork by N.A.P. @ pHactory8.

and speed. Ivan, a man from El Salvador whose peers nicknamed him "the jewelry man" because of his multiple chain necklaces, explained the term *liebre*: "You have to run to the job . . . to grab the job first. The quickest wins." The race to compete for limited work exists in tension with solidarity that develops as workers wait together for work, sometimes for hours and day after day. Ivan commented: "There is competition, [but] others work in solidarity. I am *solidario* [supportive/in solidarity] and respectful."

"A day worked is a day paid," day laborers assert, meaning that they expect to be paid for their work at the end of each day. They fear employers who string them along, promising to pay later or even disappearing. Wage theft—what occurs when employers underpay workers like Claudio or refuse to pay them at all—is rampant in day labor markets. The rapid, competitive, and unregulated nature of day labor makes workers vulnerable to low pay, insecure employment, discrimination, victimization, hazardous working conditions, and labor violations like wage theft.[8] Desperation for work, fear of immigration consequences, and lack of alternatives motivate workers like Claudio to work through injuries, not complain, and sometimes chance risky job offers even when they know better. Despite the odds, Claudio had faith that his luck would improve.

THE CATCH-22 OF WAGE THEFT

Wage theft occurs when individuals do not receive their legally owed wages and benefits. Legal status should not technically matter because wage-and-hour laws apply to all employees who have performed work in the United States regardless of their immigration status. Yet the inclusion of unauthorized immigrant workers into these protections was not designed to benefit them. Instead, it is intended to deter employers from hiring unauthorized workers so that they do not receive an undue competitive advantage. Nevertheless, US labor laws offer some of the few tools that unauthorized workers can draw on to address a subset of the kinds of exploitation they endure.

Labor laws stand as an exception to a US legal system that provides few forms of protection or relief to unauthorized immigrants and is otherwise largely dedicated to policing and removing them. Unauthorized immigrants are legally prohibited from living and working in the United States. But if they do the work, wage and hour laws entitle them to minimum wage, overtime, and the right to bring a wage claim against employers who violate these laws. Because they often work in the shadows, unauthorized immigrants who seek protections under US labor laws find themselves in a catch-22: they need to make their exploitation visible to pursue legal remedies when their labor rights are violated, but there is usually little to no record of their employment or presence. Scant record of their employment and their potential for removal are precisely what make unauthorized workers lucrative to employers and easy to exploit. Although laws prohibit employers from wielding immigration status to threaten workers who attempt to exercise their labor rights, employers frequently get away with it. The fear of immigration consequences, employers' relative positions of power, informal hiring arrangements, and restricted employment options make unauthorized immigrants hesitant to assert the limited labor rights they are afforded. This catch-22 makes wage theft a productive site from which to analyze how changing immigration enforcement patterns affect labor rights, as well as the possibilities for developing legal and organizing strategies to advance the rights of immigrant workers.[9]

LABORING FOR JUSTICE

Laboring for Justice brings together over seven years of engaged anthropological research to explore day laborers' experiences with wage theft in Denver and how advocates have supported workers to navigate courts and labor agencies, improve worker protections, and accompany workers to pursue justice. Latino immigrant day laborers like Claudio are not uniquely susceptible to wage theft, but their precarious legal and economic position combined with racial discrimination make them especially vulnerable.[10] Yet their predicament is also portending for growing numbers of workers in advanced capitalist economies as work has become increasingly precarious and insecure.[11]

This introduction outlines the book's theoretical arguments, which draw from the experiences of Latino immigrant day laborers and advocates to highlight how wage theft is more than an individual or even an immigrant problem. By centering the plight of day laborers, I argue that wage theft is a broader systemic and structural problem that is produced by, and a wider symptom of, the informalization and growing insecurity of work, weak labor standards enforcement, deepening interior racialized immigration surveillance, more militarized national borders, and systemic racism.[12] The same factors that condition wage theft impede the ability of workers to protect themselves, confront their employers, or request assistance when they weigh trade-offs of scarce work opportunities, the low likelihood of wage recovery, and retaliatory threats. I explore the challenges of policy advocacy, legal assistance, and accompaniment. While legal and policy reforms have improved access to justice and accountability, I consider how regulatory approaches can risk cordoning off social problems about escalating inequality to the legal realm and deflecting them out of political debate and public engagement. Despite the obstacles, I highlight how day laborers devise creative strategies to promote worker justice, resist, and assert their dignity in the face of precarity. After setting out the theoretical contributions, I detail the Colorado and Denver contexts, the local advocacy landscape around wage theft, the day labor hiring sites in the Denver metropolitan area, my methodological and community-engaged approach, and the organization of the chapters.

The concept of wage theft began to provide allies with a useful organizing and advocacy tool to reframe discourses that criminalize immigrants to redirect the gaze at the criminal behavior of employers who exploit them. Policymakers also started to pay more attention to wage theft, recognizing that wage theft investigations could reveal graver types of criminal employer behavior such as labor trafficking.[13] Yet wage theft is indicative of subtler forms of theft that are widely accepted as exploitative labor practices become routine across low-wage industries.[14] These labor practices often blur the line between "routine exploitation and criminal behavior" but decimate working conditions, subject low-wage workers to disproportionate rates of workplace illness, mistreatment and injuries, and erode wages amid rising costs of living.[15]

From a Marxist perspective, the capitalist concept of wages intrinsically constitutes a form of theft. Capitalist relations divorce the performance of work from its later payment, making workers rely on debt or savings while they await compensation and employers benefit from their labor as "credit."[16] Wages obscure the power dynamics of "unequal exchange between a class that possesses money and another that is compelled to work for free . . . to continue to exist" and the surplus value from wage labor that employers enjoy even after wages are paid.[17]

I argue that wage theft is not an exceptional aberration, but instead inheres in how the economy is increasingly organized. Wage theft is a "structural crime,"[18] meaning that it is enabled by prevailing power dynamics and social, economic, and racial hierarchies. This form of theft can provide a window into the wider structural factors under advanced capitalism that degrade employment and increasingly normalize stagnant and low wages, job insecurity, and lack of benefits and protections.[19]

This book also offers pedagogical reflections on community-engaged research and teaching, starting from a place of *convivencia*—or standing alongside and listening to workers. Throughout the book, I interrogate the process of accompanying workers and pushing for policy changes in my own city, including negotiating my position and the roles of my students who worked on this project under my supervision.

THEORETICAL INTERVENTIONS

The book makes three related theoretical interventions. First, the reason that immigrant day laborers are vulnerable to wage theft and hesitant to seek redress is not because they are excluded from US society or labor protections. US immigration laws prohibit, but in practice do not necessarily prevent, unauthorized immigrants from living or working in the United States. Instead of exclusion, unauthorized immigrants experience subordinate inclusion.[20] Lack of legal status guarantees their subordinate position in the labor market as low-wage workers who are wary of exercising their limited rights, which benefits employers and a variety of other actors and industries.[21]

Second, wage theft is not an exceptional or solely individual crime. Most existing legal remedies are overly individualistic and reactive, meaning that they rely on individuals to come forward to seek restitution after their rights are violated. Treating wage theft as an individualized incident or dispute can distract attention from the power discrepancies and structural factors that render it systemic. Wage theft is a symptom of how decimated labor standards enforcement, unaccountable contracting arrangements, the decline of organized labor, and the devaluation of immigrants have degraded employment and normalized increasingly unjust wages and widening economic inequality.[22] By examining how immigrant day laborers experience, seek recourse to, and aim to prevent wage theft, I show how this theft is just one outcome of the trajectory of neoliberal racial capitalism, which appropriates value from immigrants, racial and ethnic minorities, and workers to advance processes of accumulation. By policing citizenship and granting differential forms of inclusion, the state delivers a "subsidy to corporate capital" by segmenting the labor force, its value, and rights based on immigration status and national origins.[23] Thus wage theft committed against immigrant workers is structurally guaranteed through the US state itself.

Third, *Laboring for Justice* contributes to scholarship on forms of structural, symbolic, and legal violence by showing how day laborers and advocates reconfigure what justice looks like in the face of precarious work. Scholars have described Latino immigrant day laborers as a structurally vulnerable population.[24] This term refers to populations that are individually and as a social group exposed to structural violence, or the patterned forms of harm and suffering baked into the social structure.[25] To counter explanations that blame the vulnerable for their suffering, structural violence directs attention to the forces that limit individual choice and agency.[26] Specifically, poverty, racial discrimination, and lack of immigration status structure immigrant day laborers' marginal position in society, which is aggravated by the nature of contingent work.[27] Cecilia Menjívar and Leisy Abrego add the barrier of legal violence as the violence of immigration law seeps into the work and home lives of the unauthorized to instill fear and curtail their mobility, resources, and opportunities.[28]

Day laborers' structural vulnerability makes them especially prone to labor violations and illness and injury, as well as stress, social isolation, substance abuse, homelessness, and depression.[29] Because their vulnerability is produced through the social structure, marginalized groups and individuals like day laborers may internalize the social order and the roots of their oppression as individual failings; scholars call this process of internalization "symbolic violence."[30] Symbolic violence refers to how individuals misperceive the exploitative social order as natural, as well as how they shape their behavior in ways that inadvertently reproduce the oppressive social order.[31]

In a rich literature that details how structural, symbolic, and legal violence make immigrant day laborers vulnerable to low wages, wage theft, and injury, wary to report workplace violations and organize,[32] and even likely to internalize suffering as their own individual failings, I contribute to this discussion by drawing attention to the diverse tactics workers draw on to endure, contest, and prevent exploitation.[33] While it is important to understand the structural factors that constrain day laborers' choices, depictions of structural violence can risk portraying it as all-encompassing and defeating, leaving little room for transformation or resistance.[34]

Structural vulnerability does not preclude worker organizing or solidarity. However, day laborers' strategies often do not meet advocates' preconceived notions of social justice activism. I show that day laborers' more nuanced forms of social action or even nonaction—doing nothing, claiming that only God can exact justice for their suffering—may be misrecognized as symbolic violence. Instead, I point to how comments that may otherwise signal futility can be read as constituting restrained forms of agency in a context of extreme marginalization.

Day laborers draw on what James Scott calls "weapons of the weak" as they resist undignified working conditions while simultaneously submitting to them in order to acquire work.[35] For example, day laborers' "hidden" and more overt "transcripts," or ways of interacting at the hiring sites, serve to warn others of unscrupulous employers.[36] Workers yell out "don't go" or simply remain quiet when employers with bad reputations solicit workers. They informally organize to upgrade the wage floor at the *liebre*, creating an unspoken understanding to reject low offers. At worksites, workers speed up or slow down work to maximize income and push back on employers who attempt to manipulate hours and payment agreements or request unpaid extra tasks. Although many day laborers prefer to move on rather than expend more time chasing unpaid wages, some do directly confront their employers, take them to court, or even attempt more violent tactics, including threats to steal tools. However, their actions also defy understandings of resistance. For example, workers often bend to employers' whims to curry favor so they will be asked to perform more work, even though these behaviors can increase their risk of exploitation. As Javier explained, workers assert a sense of agency by acting as "piranhas" to fish for employers, but these behaviors reinforce the competitive nature of informal hiring sites that make workers susceptible to exploitation.

Throughout the book, I highlight the subtle, silent, and sometimes violent ways workers struggle to make their labor and lives visible, assert a place for themselves in US society, and articulate alternative visions of justice, even if their tactics are not organized, do not necessarily yield beneficial results, or are not readily recognizable to advocates.[37] I attune to how day laborers develop strategies to *convivir* [coexist, get along, or be alongside] with other workers as a way to keep going, but also to establish human connections in a society that tends to devalue low-wage Latino immigrant workers. As Ivan noted, workers balance desires for solidarity with the realities of a competitive and informal hiring field. By establishing relationships based on *convivencia*, they shield themselves from fuller forms of trust and friendship that may pose risks in a competitive and unregulated market. Workers may also extend a guarded solidarity to researchers and advocates, with whom they seek camaraderie, support, and sometimes direct assistance, although this is distinct from their relationships with one another. They are aware that these relationships are often temporary, advocates may be unable to help, and they usually occupy vastly distinct positions in society.

At the start of this research, workers were silent when student interviewers asked about "wage theft." The term connoted stigma, victimization, and shame. For some, it implied they had been duped. Even when workers wanted to report cases, their experiences were not reducible to incidences of victimhood.[38] Workers' experiences with wage theft were more complex than acquiescence, resistance, or even refusal. While scholarship on social and structural violence redirects blame away from marginalized populations to hold the power structure, as well as powerful actors, accountable, Eve Tuck warns that research that centers suffering can inflict harm by reproducing one-dimensional depictions of marginalized communities as "broken."[39]

By spending time with workers to learn about their work experiences, migration histories, and lives in the United States and accompanying workers who decide to pursue their unpaid wages, I sought to understand their lives more holistically. As I did, I became more unsettled when I used the term *day laborer* or even *worker*. These individuals were already overly defined by a society that largely values them for their (cheap and temporary) labor rather than as complex human beings.[40] I have not resolved this dilemma, but throughout this book, I tried to avoid directly labeling individuals with such modifiers when using pseudonyms, but I sometimes use these terms when referring to groups more broadly.

LABOR AND IMMIGRATION IN THE WILD WEST

Many studies that explore the impact of immigration enforcement on labor rights are based in localities with relatively strong histories of labor and immigrant rights organizing, notably California, Chicago, and New York,[41] or in traditional border reception sites like Texas.[42] Alternatively, a growing body of scholarship focuses on newer immigrant destinations, notably states in the South and Southeast with more virulent anti-immigrant policies,[43] dismal labor protections, and histories of anti–Black racism, such as

Angela Stuesse's ethnography of Latino immigrant poultry workers in Mississippi,[44] or studies of reconstruction in post–Hurricane Katrina New Orleans.[45] Colorado, as a reemerging immigrant destination with a relatively weak but improving labor rights infrastructure, offers a window into how the local reception context shapes immigrant workers' lived experiences. In particular, the state has straddled disparate positions on immigration and labor since the mid-2000s.

Colorado is a state of contrasts. According to 2019 US Census data, Colorado has the tenth to eleventh highest median household income in the country and is among the most educated states.[46] Yet it sits near the bottom in K–12 and higher educational spending, state and local taxes, and Medicaid spending.[47] Colorado has swung between having some of the most restrictive *and* most progressive state-level immigration policies. The state passed a flurry of anti-immigrant bills in the 2006–2007 legislation session including SB90, one of the nation's first show-me-your papers bills and a predecessor to Arizona's infamous SB1070 in 2010, which was the most expansive and stringent anti-immigrant law at the time. Colorado's Representative Tom Tancredo was a major player in introducing anti-immigrant legislation at the national level, such as the draconian Mass Immigration Reduction Act (2001 and 2003), during his tenure in the US House of Representatives from 1999 to 2009. In the mid-2000s, Colorado had some of the most anti-immigrant policies in the country.[48]

However, the state began to change after the 2008 Obama election, especially as the demographic composition of the state shifted.[49] In response to laws like SB90 and galvanized by immigrant rights mobilizations occurring around the country in 2006, more grassroots immigrant rights organizations emerged in the state and intensified organizing efforts.[50] As a result of political change and pro-immigrant organizing and advocacy, Colorado's state-level measures made it one of the most "welcoming" for immigrants by 2013.[51]

The state's labor policies have also varied. Colorado has a tense labor history, especially because of its historical dependence on mining. The state witnessed two of US labor history's most violent manifestations of employer retaliation in response to workers striking to protest poor working conditions and attempting to organize: the 1903–1904 Colorado Labor Laws and the 1913–1914 Colorado Coalfield War, including the 1914 Ludlow massacre of twenty-one men, women, and children occupying a tent labor camp.[52]

Currently, Colorado's Labor Peace Act suspends Colorado somewhere between union and right-to-work states by applying higher standards before a workplace can become a union shop.[53] Progressive policy pushes to spend are frequently restrained by Colorado's regressive tax policies. In 1992, Colorado voters approved the Taxpayer's Bill of Rights (TABOR) via ballot initiative. TABOR severely restrains the legislature's taxation and spending power and has led Colorado to have "the most restrictive tax and expenditure limitations" in the country.[54]

Colorado historically served as the gateway to the Mountain West. Denver's emergence as a financial, transportation, and communications hub is closely associated with the discovery of gold in 1858 and drives for westward expansion.[55] It developed an early reputation as a city of newcomers, from miners in the nineteenth century to health migrants after World War II, who came to Colorado for its "dry climate, high elevation, clean air, mild weather, and abundant sunshine," which they believed was therapeutic for tuberculosis.[56] Colorado also attracted a significant portion of the Mexican immigrant flow in the 1920s, but its importance waned as the bracero temporary labor exchange program concentrated Mexican laborers in California and Texas even though some came to Colorado to work in the sugar beet fields.[57]

In the 1970s and 1980s, Colorado, much like other regions in the West, South, and Sunbelt, began to attract new populations from cities in the Northeast, not only because of their hospitable climates but also in response to economic restructuring as firms were attracted to these states' probusiness climates, cheaper energy costs, and lower union density.[58] In the 1990s, Mexican immigration to the state regained importance and Colorado became considered a "reemerging" or "renewed historical destination."[59] By 2000, Colorado was seventh of the top ten destinations for Mexican immigrants.[60] Its Hispanic population grew from 12.9 percent of the population in 1990 to 21 percent by 2014.[61]

In recent years, Colorado has surged to become one of the four fastest-growing states in the country, largely fueled by interstate moves by millennials, retirees, students, and outdoor enthusiasts, which has created tensions around growth, development, gentrification, resources, affordability, transportation, and sustainability.[62] Colorado stands out as a state of newcomers: the majority of residents originate from other states.[63] These changes began to lead the state to lose its swing-state moniker as it shifted more to the left but also incited nativist backlash; for example, the popularity of seemingly innocuous "Colorado Native" bumper stickers.[64] Alongside progressive shifts in cities like Denver and even within the state legislature, individuals like gun-rights advocate Lauren Boebert were elected to represent Colorado's Third Congressional District in 2021. Boebert introduced two anti-immigrant bills, the No Amnesty Act and Secure the Southern Border Act.[65]

Colorado's identity as a state of newcomers not only fueled nativist retrenchment, but belies the state's character as a frontier of western expansion led by pioneers. Immigrant workers' experiences with wage theft must be considered from an alternate rendering of the state's settler-colonial foundations. As Gledhill insists, "The mode of insertion of Mexican labor into U.S. capitalism has always been overdetermined by the colonial constructions of a nation-state founded on military expansion and the racist social imaginary of 'whiteness.'"[66] Modern Colorado was built on the theft of land and labor from Native Americans and Mexico. The western quarter of the state was part of Mexico before the Treaty of Guadalupe ceded it to the United States after the Mexican-American War in 1848. Colorado also has a historic Hispano population, used to refer to descendants of Spanish settlers residing in the Southwest prior to US annexation.[67]

In the mid- to late 1800s, rapid growth and resource exploitation of the hinterlands, notably through mining, to fuel Denver's development were accomplished via racist narratives that framed Native Americans as "obstacles of progress."[68] When Denver was founded in 1858, northeastern Colorado was largely Cheyenne and Arapaho territory, and its west belonged to the Ute Nation.[69] Settlers and troops, under the direction of territorial Governor John Evans, violently expropriated land from, and exterminated, the state's Native populations, most viscerally through the Sand Creek Massacre when US Army Colonel John Chivington led a massacre of "over 160 Cheyenne and Arapaho, mostly women and children" in 1864.[70] The University of Denver, where I work, sits on stolen Cheyenne and Arapaho land. Only recently, after an investigation and report authored by multiple faculty in 2014, has the university begun to come to terms with its ties to John Evans and slowly rename titles and buildings bearing his name. As of this writing, however, it retains the racist "Pioneer" mascot.[71]

Denver's twentieth-century development additionally benefited from the constrained mobility of African Americans, racist housing policies, and urban renewal projects in the name of progress that disproportionately displaced communities of color.[72] The Ku Klux Klan exerted strong influence in Denver—its Colorado epicenter—in the 1920s; it played an outsized role in Colorado politics and "no other state in the Rocky Mountain West compared in membership or political clout."[73]

However, such narratives of progress that have obscured processes of racial capitalism and dispossession have also been valiantly resisted through community organizing. For instance, Colorado became an important front "far out of proportion to the size of its Mexican-origin population" in the Chicano movement in the 1960s until its decline in the mid 1970s.[74] In Colorado, the movement was led by the Crusade for Justice, founded by professional boxer and politician Rodolfo "Corky" Gonzales to restore Chicano pride, combat systemic discrimination, and advocate for self-determination.[75] Another notable outcome of tireless resistance by activists was the official renaming of a neighborhood named for former mayor and Klan supporter Ben Stapleton as Central Park in August 2020.[76]

In recent years, redevelopment efforts to expand Colorado's Central 70 highway continue legacies of theft in the largely Latino and immigrant neighborhoods of Globeville and Elyria-Swansea by pressuring residents to sell their homes by invoking eminent domain, and in some cases even blighting neighborhoods to drive down home prices when residents were reluctant to sell. Yet vocal activist Candi CdeBaca beat the two-term incumbent to become the first Democratic Socialist and LGBTQ Latina on Denver City Council in 2019. As the representative of District 9 where her family has lived for five generations, she continued the legacy of her relatives who organized when highway expansion first sliced the community in half in the 1960s. Her family members also helped file one of the first lawsuits against the smelting plant that led to a designation of a Superfund site.[77] The area is one of the most polluted residential zip codes in the country, with high rates of childhood asthma, certain kinds of cancer, and cardiac disease.[78]

This history goes far beyond the scope of the book, but these brief sketches demonstrate the continuity of tensions among theft normalized by racial capitalism, the imprint of racism and settler colonialism, and strides of resistance and revival. The main point of this book is that wage theft is not new or exceptional, but foundational and routine. It is deeply embedded in a US history of violent settler colonialism and racial capitalism built on, and maintained through, theft of land, labor, and bodies deemed expendable.

COLORADO'S WAGE THEFT ADVOCACY LANDSCAPE

Colorado is a productive site to examine wage theft advocacy from the local level. When Daniel Galvin scored all fifty states and Washington, DC, on the strength of their wage protection laws in 2013, Colorado was in the bottom third.[79] Policymakers in Colorado began to pay more attention when a 2014 report by the Colorado Fiscal Institute estimated that half a million Coloradans experience wage theft each year, losing $750 million in lost wages and benefits, which was also undercutting state and local governments, resulting in $25 million to $42 million in cheated revenue.[80] The report revealed that workers of color were more likely to be employed in industries prone to wage theft and were disproportionately at risk.[81] In 2015, when I started this research, Colorado was beginning to join a growing list of states, cities, and localities striving to bolster their wage protection laws. Many of these local efforts emerged in response to gaps in coverage that low-wage workers experience under federal wage-and-hour protections that focus on larger enterprises, as well as weakening federal labor rights enforcement over the past few decades.

Advocates have been critical to helping Colorado, and especially the cities of Denver and Boulder, achieve significant progress on worker protections where it was unlikely just a few years prior. More recent legislation has sought to acknowledge wage theft as a crime that disproportionately impacts Colorado's most vulnerable workers, as well as to marshal more public enforcement entities to join the fight against wage theft. The nonprofit and union landscape has been critical to improving worker justice in Colorado in terms of direct worker assistance, organizing, and policy advocacy.

Centro Humanitario para los Trabajadores (Centro), founded in 2002, is Denver's worker center, which has mostly catered to immigrant day laborers and domestic workers. Some say that the term *wage theft*, and models for addressing it, even originated in Denver from advocates like Chris Newman, now the Legal Director and General Counsel at the National Day Laborer Organizing Network (NDLON).[82] As a law student at the Sturm College of Law at DU in the early 2000s, and with support from mentors like Christine Cimini and Doug Smith, Chris helped Centro's founder, Minsun Ji, start Centro by creating its first wage clinic.

Centro has been at the forefront of addressing wage theft in Colorado through worker organizing and empowerment, its employment program, and policy advocacy. The Direct Action Team (DAT), a group of volunteers loosely affiliated with Centro, uses direct action strategies to accompany workers to confront, shame, and hold employers accountable for unpaid wages. Although union membership in Colorado is relatively weak, the Southwest Regional Council of Carpenters and International Union of Allied Painters and Trades in Colorado have been especially active in organizing workers, pointing out widespread wage theft and employee misclassification, and advocating for more worker-friendly policies.

Towards Justice, founded in 2014, is a nonprofit legal services organization dedicated to expanding access to justice and creating systemic change around workers' rights. It offers free legal intakes on wage theft cases, with advice on next steps and referrals; provides community and legal education; and has built a pro bono collaborating attorney network. Its staff attorneys pursue impact litigation to incite systemic shifts, including notable wage theft cases against au pair agencies, sheepherders on Colorado's western slope, a class action lawsuit against SkyHouse apartment complex in downtown Denver for $800,000 in unpaid wages to drywall workers, and a forced labor suit against the GEO Group, which runs the immigrant detention facility in Aurora, Colorado. Towards Justice is a major player in policy advocacy around wage theft, building worker power, and economic justice more broadly.

In 2015 and 2016, Towards Justice and Centro reconvened the Colorado Wage Theft Task Force, which was critical to spearheading and passing the state's 2014 amendment to the Wage Protection Act, discussed in Chapter 5. The task force is a coalition of nonprofit advocates, attorneys, academics, labor unions, high-road employers committed to enforcing wage laws and investing in their workers and job quality, and faith-based and labor organizations that collaborates to hold current wage theft laws accountable, organize policy advocacy, educate the public and policymakers, learn from advocates across the country, and devise strategies to enhance worker justice.

DAY LABOR HIRING SITES

The research sought to cover all day labor hiring sites in the Denver metropolitan area. The sites included the worker center Centro in Denver's Five Points neighborhood; Stout Street across a parking lot from Centro; Federal and 19th in West Denver; Dayton and Colfax in Aurora; and Kentucky and Sheridan on the border between Denver and suburban Lakewood (Map 1).[83]

The Federal and 19th hiring site is located near the Broncos football stadium in a historic Latino neighborhood. The area quickly shifts from

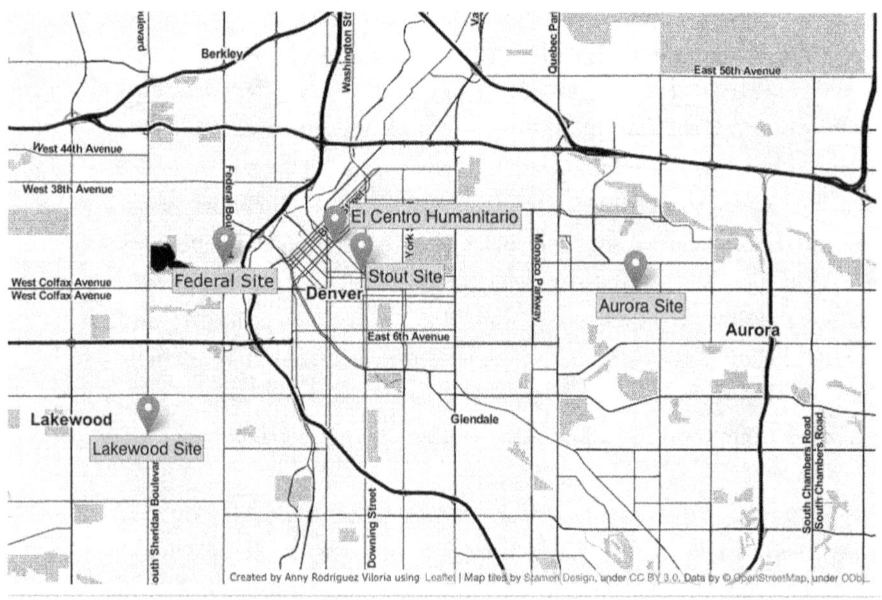

MAP 1: Map of day labor hiring sites (*liebres*) in the Denver metropolitan area. Map by Anny Rodriguez Viloria. Reprinted with permission from Rebecca Galemba and Randall Kuhn (2021).

Vietnamese- to Latino-serving restaurants and grocers. The area, like many other Denver neighborhoods, is rapidly gentrifying. When I first visited the site in 2015, I learned that a temporary employment agency across the street had been recently replaced by a CrossFit studio.

The intersection of Dayton and Colfax is the largest of the hiring sites. It sits around the block from the bustling center of Aurora, one of the most diverse cities in the country—20 percent foreign-born, and home to speakers of about 120 languages.[84] The establishments surrounding the hiring site include a Salvadoran *panaderia* with a money wiring service, an African hair-braiding salon, an Ethiopian grocer, a Nepali grocer, a Mexican restaurant, a barber shop offering *tintes y cortes*, and a Jumping Jack Cash next to a store advertising *seguros*, or a range of insurance products. Where the men stand to wait for work is bracketed by a pawnshop and an evangelical church, Iglesia Evangelica Jesucristo es Rey. In 2016, a small grocer across the street, where workers often bought cigarettes, sodas, and lotto tickets, began to be retrofitted to construct a new worker center with partial financial support from the Aurora city council. It is now the Dayton Street Day Labor Center. The Lakewood site at Kentucky and Sheridan is nestled in a parking lot between a church and a school in a historic Latino area.

Centro and Stout Street are located in the historic Five Points neighborhood, which was once the center of Denver's Black community.[85] Centro was founded in 2002 but officially opened its doors in 2006, although the organizing work had started earlier (Figure 3). Its founder, Minsun Ji, herself a recent immigrant and labor organizer from South Korea, worked for the American Friends Service Committee (AFSC) when she moved to Denver. AFSC tasked her with organizing day laborers, which brought her out to the street corners as she rapidly learned Spanish while still working on English. The founding of Centro addressed two problems Minsun identified through her conversations with day laborers: antiloitering ordinances and pervasive wage theft. Community support for a safe space was galvanized after a worker fell from a roof on a job, suffering debilitating injuries, and the employer was nowhere to be found.[86] Thanks to advocacy from Minsun, AFSC, and their coalition building with labor, faith-based, and other progressive groups, they built support for Centro and secured a small grant from the mayor to pay the first year's rent. The workers themselves, supported by donations, transformed the worn-down warehouse into the space

FIGURE 3: Centro Humanitario para los Trabajadores in Denver, Colorado. Collage interpretation by author with assistance from Elena Galemba, Anna Wall at the Art Barn, and glass cutting assistance from Leslie Judy. The author gathered some of the materials from around the building site of Centro and from brochures collected throughout the research. The surface is a wooden table procured by Anna Wall from Habitat for Humanity. Photo of artwork by N.A.P. @ pHactory8.

it became. Centro is now one of more than fifty organizations affiliated with the National Day Labor Organizing Network (NDLON).

Worker centers are community-based organizations that usually offer a mix of direct services, advocacy, and organizing, education, and leadership development to empower low-wage workers. Most, but not all, cater to immigrants.[87] Centro sees its direct services, leadership development, organizing, and advocacy as interconnected. Although workers may initially come to Centro to find a job or to address an immediate problem like wage theft, discussing these problems with others can pave the way to building worker leadership and organizing campaigns.[88] Worker centers provide a safe and warm place to wait for work, but their wider goals involve instilling transparency into the hiring process, upgrading wages and working conditions, preventing and redressing worker mistreatment, and developing leadership and organizing skills.[89] Centro does not directly offer jobs or employ workers, but its employment program connects worker members to employers who register with the employment program in a dignified employment relationship by "promoting fair wages and safe working environments."[90]

Workers themselves helped design Centro's employment program. Each morning, staff use a lottery ball to assign each worker member who arrives a number to prioritize them for jobs when employers arrive. Employers register with Centro and guarantee a minimum wage and hours, agree to Centro's principles, and provide contact information. This process prevents wage theft by slowing the hiring process and deliberately insisting on the accountability and transparency lacking at street corner hiring sites. Workers devised a system whereby employers must wait behind a line as staff negotiate the hours, working conditions, work, and pay before they can access workers.

Centro hosts know-your-rights, worker safety, skills, and leadership and workforce development training. It has had a Women's Program since 2004, including a green cleaning cooperative, a catering collective, child care provision, and training on leadership, job skills, and domestic workers' rights.[91] Centro identifies as a member-led organization, dedicated to developing worker leaders. It is also active in local organizing and wider political advocacy around immigrant and labor rights. As Chris Newman, Legal Director and General Counsel at NDLON, told me, across the country many organizations that became "pillars of the immigrant rights movements started out as day labor organizations." They first addressed urgent crises and then built toward the larger movement as they grew.[92]

Across the parking lot from Centro is the Stout Street site, where workers previously congregated prior to Centro's opening. A concentration of nearby social services and homeless shelters blurs the day labor and homeless populations that congregate there. The area was a natural reception site for immigrant arrivals. Notably, a bus service, Los Limousines, is located across the street from Centro, offering direct services to El Paso.

As the Five Points neighborhood has gentrified, many Latino immigrant day laborers have moved out of the area, mostly to North and West Denver. A microbrewery, upscale lounge, and an "escape room" opened a few doors down from Centro in 2019, frequented by residents of newly built midrises and the downtown professional class. The changing nature of the neighborhood and maintenance expenses prompted Centro to sell the building, which closed on October 15, 2021, and consider new options.[93]

METHODOLOGICAL APPROACH

My interest in wage theft was motivated by my classroom community partnership with Centro. In spring 2013, I started collaborating with Centro through a master's-level qualitative research methods course that I teach at the Josef Korbel School of International Studies at the University of Denver (DU). The course pursues a hands-on approach as students combine ethnographic research with service-learning. Centro has been a constant partner for this course, although the research focus has evolved as we continually reevaluate our mutual goals and interests.

In 2014, Centro's staff became interested in understanding day laborers' experiences with wage theft. Our partnership spawned a larger collaborative project, including one year of qualitative interviews with 170 day laborers at street corner hiring sites and Centro from 2015 to 2016; a follow-up survey of 411 workers (393 in weighted sample) from October 2016 to August 2017 at the same sites; and over sixty-five interviews with attorneys, nonprofit personnel, staff from the Department of Labor, union representatives, employers, politicians, city officials, and law enforcement. I have conducted ongoing participant observation and direct collaboration with policy working groups and the Colorado Wage Theft Task Force, and I have volunteered as a participant activist with the Wage Theft Direct Action Team (DAT). From 2015 to 2017, I directly collaborated with Raja Raghunath from the DU Sturm College of Law and his Workplace Rights Clinic as it took on pro bono wage theft cases. Raja and I often took our students to the corners together, my research team referred cases to his clinic, we shared insights, and some of my students worked for his clinic as translators (Figure 4).[94] I foresaw few of these collaborations at the outset. Instead, my teaching and community partnership opened new connections and leads that I followed as I came to map out the landscape of stakeholders.

Since 2015, over ninety students have worked on this project as students in my methods course, paid research assistants, surveyors, outreach work-

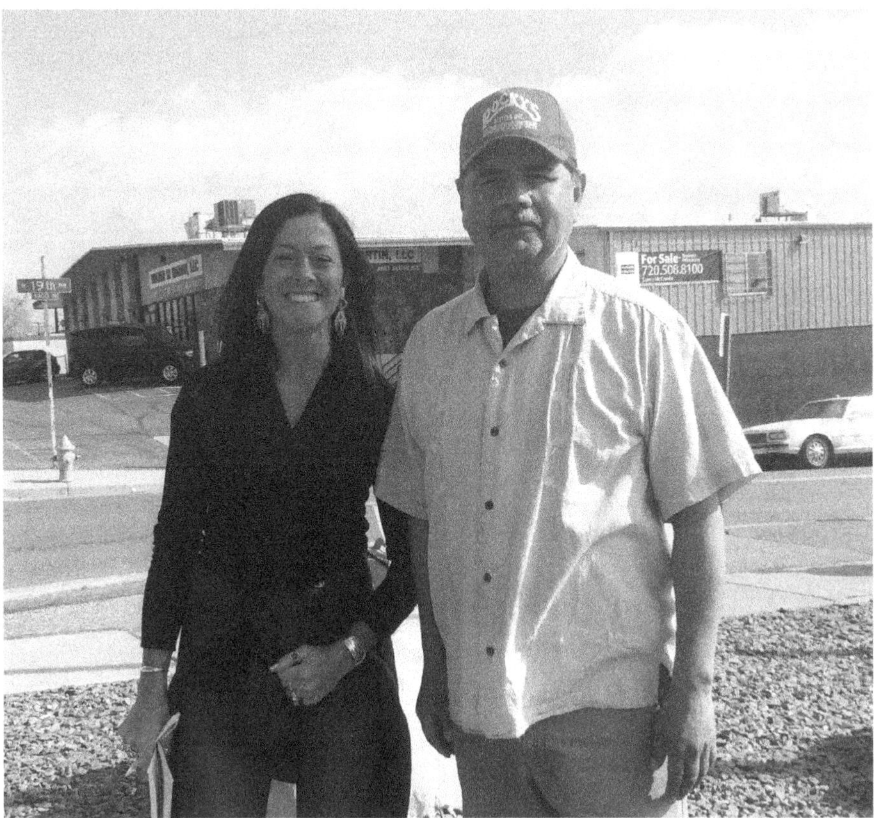

FIGURE 4: Worker with graduate student Kara Napolitano at the Federal and 19th hiring site. Photo by Author.

ers, and volunteers with the DAT. With their permission, I include students' participation throughout this book and cite their work and field notes when applicable. As participant activists with the DAT, my students and I accompanied workers to pursue their unpaid wages using direct action tactics as we took field notes and reflected on the process (Figure 5). Direct action techniques include calling employers to negotiate; conducting delegations (group visits to accompany a worker to an employer's home or business to demand unpaid wages); preparing workers for small claims court, call campaigns, and protests. The DAT shared case data to help evaluate their strategies, and I shared insights from my broader research with them. The Colorado Department of Labor and Employment (CDLE) provided access

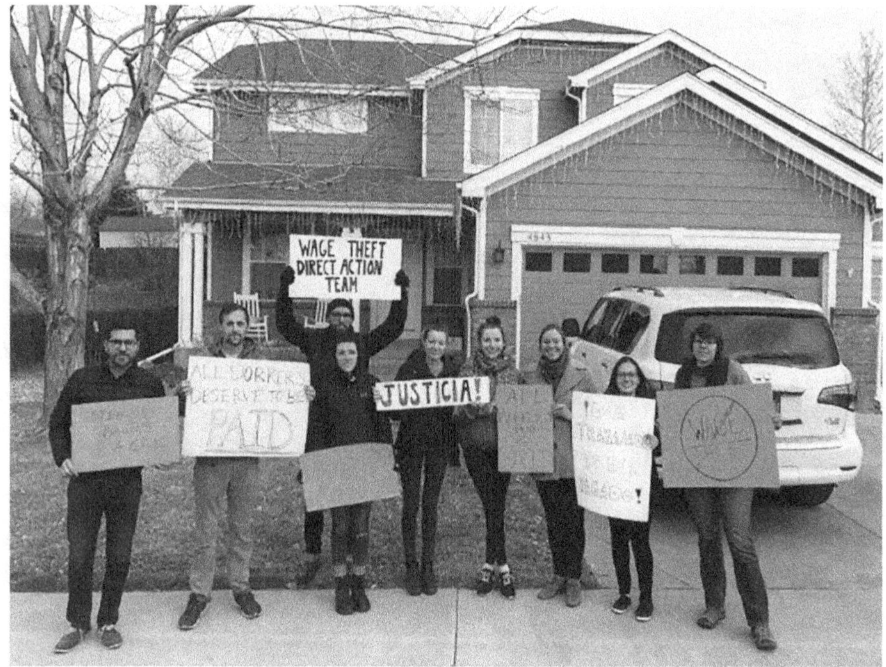

FIGURE 5: DAT protest at an employer's home. Photo by David Feuerbach.

for students to interview staff and regularly shared data. As the research progressed, I discussed results with city officials, policy working groups, and district and city attorney offices in Boulder and Denver as they pursued bolder approaches to wage theft.

CONVIVIR AS A FORM OF ENGAGED RESEARCH

Setha Low and Sally Engle Merry's hallmark 2010 article details different trajectories for engaged anthropological research, which can range from more detached forms of research involvement that offer social critique—which advocates, policymakers, and communities can apply to inform their own efforts—to more direct forms of advocacy and activism.[95]Activist anthropologists push the involvement of the ethnographer further by embracing a shared commitment to the struggle they are studying.[96] However, even when researchers attempt to align themselves with a particular struggle or pursue community-engaged research partnerships, they often fail to account for how the power dynamics of knowledge production appoint researchers a privileged role in determining what partnership, solidarity, and even activism look like.[97]

My research process started from the task of *convivir*, to stand alongside, listen, and learn from workers at the *liebres* and at Centro. Before asking any questions, we spent time with individuals as they waited for work to learn about their migratory histories, work experiences, lives, and general concerns; shared coffee and bagels; and explained the research. A methodological approach that centers *convivencia* troubles the hallmark anthropological method of participant observation, which can mute the power inequities between participants to be observed and researchers who interpret such observations into analysis. Indigenous and decolonial feminists show how such approaches to knowledge reproduce a hierarchical binary between what Dakota scholar Kim TallBear describes as the "researcher and researched—between knowledge inquirer and who are what are considered to be the resources or grounds for knowledge production."[98] TallBear eloquently recommends "think[ing] creatively about the research process as a relationship-building process. . . . A researcher who is willing to learn how to 'stand with' a community of subjects is willing to be altered, to revise her stakes in the knowledge to be produced."[99] My attempt to build relationships with day laborers from my position as a researcher, as well as from a social location distinct from theirs, meant reconsidering my own preconceptions of what might concern workers and understanding their broader aspirations beyond incidences of labor exploitation.

Convivencia draws on but complicates researchers' attempts to "stand with" participants, especially when they occupy distinct positions in society, by making the power dynamics that infuse the social production of knowledge transparent.[100] The more tenuous sense of solidarity invoked by *convivir* acknowledges the intersectional forms of power that infuse research encounters. Day laborers have been both over-researched and underserved, and as a result often hold researchers and advocates at a distance as they seek out their solidarity and even assistance. Still, *convivencia* underscores how embracing relational encounters can build solidarity and trust and raise collective consciousness across difference over time. Even so, these relationships are constantly forged in relation to power dynamics that threaten to sow division and suspicion between workers themselves as well as with those who claim to support them. Learning to *convivir*—or standing with and in community with workers—can offer a theoretical and ethical orientation from which new meanings of justice and solidarity can emerge so long as researchers critically interrogate their own position in the process.

I adapted the research design through an iterative process of data collection, analysis, worker accompaniment, and reflections and discussions with students, community partners, policymakers, and workers over seven years, including soliciting their feedback on my findings.[101] My research was inspired by Centro's concerns, but in contrast to much activist anthropology, I designed the questions and methodology, albeit with their input. I aligned with the struggle to tackle wage theft as an activist ethnographer, but workers, advocates, unions, policymakers, government agencies, and attorneys sometimes had distinct priorities, perceptions of the obstacles, and potential solutions even when they mostly sat on the same side. For example, my relationship with Centro helped me access and understand members' and advocates concerns while my independence as a researcher allowed me to reach workers waiting for work at street corners who were more reticent to organize or even speak with center personnel. Working alongside my students also opened educational opportunities to interview, and learn from, stakeholders on different sides of the issue.

The long-term, community-based nature for the research provided opportunities to validate insights over time and ensure that what I was learning resonated with the workers and advocates working to advance worker justice every day. As I learned more, I applied my research to help inform new legislation and policy changes at the city and state levels, whether through sharing ideas in working groups with stakeholders, writing a brief with Towards Justice and the Carpenters Union,[102] or submitting research and comments to the CDLE's rule-making processes. I saw recommendations applied through these initiatives, collaborators commented on my findings, and I interviewed stakeholders about how policy changes continued to unfold. This iterative process worked to strengthen rapport, accuracy, and validity as I incorporated feedback and new developments.[103] By inviting some of the community partners to comment on this book through a virtual workshop, I not only sought to correct errors and improve the material, but also to facilitate a space where we could learn from our different approaches to strategize steps forward in our collaboration.

Each year, students in my methods course continue to work on this research. They conduct interviews with workers at street corners, volunteer with the DAT to assist with wage theft cases, and have expanded their interests to examine the impacts of the pandemic and the gendered contours of wage theft.[104] When pursuing their class projects, students work under my larger research program but also carve out their own spaces. Each year, some students publish their work through the DU Just Wages blog.[105]

As the research progressed, I recognized that I needed to expand my tool kit. My inductive and iterative approach helped me understand the challenges workers and advocates faced, but I could not convince policymakers how pervasive the problem was. I partnered with demographer Randall Kuhn as our methods classes worked together to design a survey sampling frame and design based on my qualitative data and site scouting; the Methodological Supplement provides more detail on the qualitative and quantitative research processes.

ORGANIZATION AND SUMMARY OF CHAPTERS

This book details the sociostructural factors that make day laborers vulnerable to wage theft and the challenges that workers and advocates face preventing wage theft, deterring unscrupulous employers, recovering unpaid wages, and pursuing justice. Different studies of day laborers have debated their potential to organize, but their conclusions potentially reflect their methodological focus on workers' centers (more optimistic) versus street corners (more hesitant).[106] Or, as in Shannon Gleeson's research on low-wage workers, they focus on the minority of workers who *do* come forward to make legal claims, albeit their obstacles are instructive of the barriers.[107] I contribute to a growing literature on immigrant labor rights by exploring day laborers' experiences at Centro, at street corners where the majority of day laborers in Denver solicit work, and inside and outside the legal claims process. I further ethnographically trace how various stakeholders and advocates, including my students and I, contribute to the landscape of worker justice as they negotiate their own positions. I narrow existing studies of day labor to workers' nuanced understandings and struggles around wage theft, while also using day labor and wage theft to broaden understandings of worker and immigrant justice and the role of community-based research.

Chapter 1 explores the scope of wage theft as a product and symptom of the informalization of work, border imperialism, declining labor standards enforcement, and a history of racially devaluing and stealing the labor of Mexican immigrants. Chapter 2 describes the day labor population in Denver while situating their plight within Denver's postrecession residential construction boom. The chapter demonstrates how changes in construction labor practices and immigration laws structure racial and citizenship hierarchies in the industry, as well as the precarious position of day labor. It explores how pervasive subcontracting and labor brokerage arrangements and heightened interior immigration enforcement have combined to limit immigrant workers' employment options, instill fear into workers, degrade working conditions in the industry, and exert pressure on workers' social networks. Immigrant day laborers did not benefit from the construction bonanza. Instead, the climate was conducive to rampant labor violations.

Chapter 3 examines how employers take advantage of vast and unaccountable subcontracting chains and immigrant workers' desperation for work and precarious legal status to deny wages and sometimes cloak their own illegal labor practices.[108] The chapter widens considerations of wage theft to understand the graver problems of work and income insecurity, as well as harmful employer actions that fail to reach any legal threshold.

Chapter 4 explores what day laborers do to prevent wage theft and seek redress and how they envision better protecting themselves in the future. It argues that the same factors that make day laborers vulnerable to wage theft, as discussed in Chapter 3, constrain their ability to avail themselves of street strategies and legal options. When day laborers lose more money from lack of work than from wage theft, it becomes rational for them to continue to test their luck in dubious employment situations even when they know the risks.

Chapter 5 ethnographically examines the CDLE administrative wage claims procedure in its first few years. The chapter demonstrates how the labor rights enforcement system reflects, rather than offers a way to remedy, the dominant social structure that continues to exploit low-wage, minority, and immigrant workers. The largest portion of CDLE closed claims analyzed were categorized as "failure to pursue," which meant that the worker failed to continue the case or could not be reached. I argue that failure to pursue cannot be purely remedied by educating workers or improving agency processes. Instead, I show how failure to pursue is produced by bureaucratic power and unauthorized immigrant workers' catch-22: the paradoxical position they occupy in the United States as unauthorized workers with underdocumented work arrangements. The chapter discusses the limits of existing legal and regulatory approaches to uphold the labor rights of unauthorized immigrants while highlighting the potential of recent policies that respond to some of these critiques.

Chapter 6 focuses on workers who do not come forward, may appear resigned to wage theft, say that "nothing" can be done, and express faith in an alternative form of justice. Many workers claim that only God will make justice, they need to have faith, or that karma will punish offending employers. Although resorting to faith does little to prevent wage theft, I show how these beliefs provide a sense of comfort, hope for the future, and a grammar to articulate a moral order that revalues immigrant workers. Workers also cultivate a sense of *convivir* that stimulates human connectedness at the corners while protecting them from the risks that can ensue from placing too much trust in their *compañeros* or even in well-intentioned researchers and advocates.

Chapter 7 pursues an experimental coauthored format with collaborators involved with the DAT. As I was writing this book, I recognized that the activists most involved in the work of direct action were best positioned to tell these stories. As we engaged with one another through the writing process, we began to co-theorize patterns in our experiences that framed the analysis and organization of the chapter.[109] We offer that the tensions we experienced between the team's different approaches and our own roles in our struggles alongside workers can be productive in informing a reflective praxis and theorization of justice. Coauthors include Abbey Vogel, a former DU student who began volunteering with the DAT through my methods class and continued volunteering until she graduated; Diego Bleifuss Prados, a former DU student who worked as a surveyor and subsequently as the DAT's coordinator; Amy Czulada, a former DU student who started on the project as a translator for Raja's legal clinic and then went on to be the lead research assistant for the survey, the first student coordinator of the DAT, and worked temporarily for Centro before moving to the East Coast; Tamara (henceforth Tammy) Kuennen, a professor at Sturm College of Law, the supervisor of the Sturm Civil Litigation Clinic, and a current DAT volunteer; and Alexsis (henceforth Alex) Sanchez, who came to the DAT through a class at the University of Colorado, Denver, served as a coordinator of the DAT, worked at Centro, and continues to volunteer with the DAT. While many of my students, other activists, and workers have collaborated with the DAT, the coauthors stand out for their leadership roles on the team, particular life experiences, and desire to stay engaged with the project and contribute to the chapter. Many other students, workers, advocates, and volunteers contributed to the stories and analysis that appear throughout the book and I note and credit them accordingly.

The Conclusion returns to my first wage theft delegation to an employer's home alongside a worker to recover unpaid wages. I use this case to open critical scrutiny into the ethical challenges and power dynamics raised by conducting community-engaged research in my own city, as well as the labor politics undergirding the production of this book. The conclusion begins with an example of what appeared to be a successful example of strategic collaboration between stakeholders. In this particular case, a combination of research, street outreach, and collaboration among Towards Justice, the DAT, and the Sturm Civil Litigation Clinic produced a court victory for four workers against their employer. The workers and advocates publicized the success, only to eventually realize that the workers could never collect their money. These two examples illustrate the ambivalent praxis of community-engaged research, as well as the challenges of pursuing justice in the face of persistent systemic injustice.

Interlaced with the chapters, I include two worker interviews. Abbey Vogel and Alex Sanchez interviewed Severiano A. and Diana A., whom they respectively assisted with wage theft cases with the DAT.[110] The interviews appear as conversations as the workers reflect on their experiences. Abbey translated and transcribed both interviews. I insert these interludes before and after the coauthored Chapter 7 to illustrate themes raised in the book although they are disconnected from the central narrative. As an ethnographer, I struggled throughout this book to draw on interviews, participant observation, survey data, and workers' stories to illustrate broader theoretical points about immigrant worker justice with the recognition that the process of abstraction threatens to extract and reduce workers' stories in ways all too similar to what they experience in their interactions with courts, judges, and sometimes advocates.[111] The interludes do not resolve the power dynamics that continue to plague academic research but strive to provide a more honest account of them.[112] They offer a space for the kinds of relationships cultivated between workers and volunteers to continue to grow after their claims are closed.

Although the book advocates for a broader structural approach to advance worker and immigrant justice, there are also policies that can dramatically improve workers' rights and access to justice and begin to tilt the power dynamics that facilitate wage theft, especially at the state and local levels. These initiatives, and their benefits, opportunities, and shortcomings, also appear throughout the book.

1 STEALING IMMIGRANT WORK

WHEN I BEGAN STUDYING WAGE theft in 2013, I had never before heard of the term, nor had many day laborers or my students. When I mentioned the term to employers, they argued that "wage theft" occurred when their employees stole from *them*. This sentiment reflects a wider public discourse that blames immigrants for "stealing American jobs," especially during economic contraction. This chapter explains the concept of wage theft, its scope, and how it indexes the wider degradation and informalization of work. While the problem of wage theft extends beyond immigrants, the chapter focuses on how the historical devaluation and criminalization of Latino—and especially Mexican—immigrants make them exceptionally vulnerable. Latino immigrants' experiences with wage theft in the United States are built on a longer history of appropriating immigrants' labor value. I also show how wage theft, and other forms of racialized labor exploitation, are globally produced and locally fortified through the conjuncture of neoliberal restructuring, militarized borders, and intensified interior immigration enforcement.

According to the Economic Policy Institute, workers in the United States may be losing as much as $50 billion a year to wage theft.[1] This may even be an underestimate because the problem is underinvestigated, many workers and the public are unaware it is happening, and even when workers are aware, they fear retaliation from their employers if they report it. Wage theft also costs the federal and state government in the form of shirked income, social security, Medicare, unemployment taxes, workers' compensation insurance, and other benefit funds. This revenue is undercut when employers engage in payroll fraud by misclassifying workers or hiring them off the books, in addition to lost consumer dollars that would otherwise enter local economies.[2] When wage theft becomes rampant in particular industries, it incentivizes a race to the bottom that places honest operators at a competitive disadvantage.[3]

When the public thinks about theft, people tend to mention personal property theft, burglary, or armed robbery. Yet yearly economic losses to robbery, burglary, and auto theft amount to about $14 billion per year combined, much less than what workers lose each year for their unpaid work.[4] Wage theft can take many forms: paying below the minimum wage; underpayment; withholding earned benefits, tips, overtime, or breaks; improper deductions; misclassifying employees as independent contractors; and what day laborers most frequently experience: outright nonpayment.

Wage theft not only benefits offending employers; it can erode wages in entire workplaces and industries when exploitative labor practices become routine.[5] Wage theft punishes employers who play by the rules by giving unscrupulous actors who undercut their workers a cost-savings advantage. Wage theft is increasingly prevalent across many industries, but it is no coincidence that it is especially concentrated in deregulated and restructured industries that rely heavily on the labor of women, people of color, immigrants, and other low-wage workers.[6] The Unregulated Work Survey of over four thousand low-wage workers in New York City, Chicago, and Los Angeles found that foreign-born Latinos suffered particularly egregious rates of wage theft; their exposure to minimum wage violations was twice that of US-born Latinos and six times higher than US-born whites.[7] Wage theft is especially endemic in construction, agriculture, poultry plants, garment factories, nursing homes and home care work, and day labor.[8] Unpaid wages further translate into money that workers cannot spend as consumers and tax dollars that are not filtering into cities and states when employers dodge labor laws and associated insurance and tax obligations.

GLOBAL PRODUCTION OF WAGE THEFT

Wage theft is not just a problem in the United States; it has become pervasive across other advanced economies alongside global economic integration and neoliberal restructuring. The rise in precarious work, attenuating workers' rights, and diminishing pay and benefits has proceeded alongside global economic changes that propel firms to search for a more flexible and cheaper labor force abroad and incentivize states to dismantle regulations, worker protections, and social safety nets to cultivate investment.[9] Meanwhile, neoliberal reforms in developing countries decimated real wages, benefits, and public sector employment and increased economic insecurity motivating migrants to seek work abroad. The global informalization of work proceeded alongside a rise in transnational labor flows as vulnerable migrant workers were disproportionately relegated to industries where nonstandard work arrangements were common and regulations and worker protections were weak, such as in "construction, domestic work; and low-end retail, sales, and service."[10]

Over the past few decades, advanced capitalist economies have increasingly fortified their national borders and more actively surveilled migrants who reside in their interiors, which has allowed employers to insulate the benefits of a precarious and rightless migrant workforce while subjecting migrants to heightened forms of fear and exploitation.[11] Harsha Walia calls this a system of border imperialism, showing how migrants are displaced "as a result of the violences of capitalism and empire, and subsequently segmented into precarious labor as a result of border restrictions, state illegalization, and systemic social hierarchies" of race, class, gender, sexuality, and ability wielded by exclusionary nation-states.[12] Migrants enrolled in legal temporary worker programs also find their presence and rights curtailed by state-sanctioned arrangements that tie, and subject them to, to the whims of their employers.[13] The transnational parallels in the rise of wage theft, insecure work, and unsafe working conditions are the natural products of border imperialism and racial capitalism, which combine to guarantee a global precariat with limited rights.

The precarious working conditions of many Latino immigrant workers in the United States are not just a local issue; this structural vulnerability to low wages and wage theft is globally produced.[14] In 1994, Mexico, the United

States, and Canada signed onto the North American Free Trade Agreement (NAFTA), which compelled deeper privatization of the Mexican economy and land while its liberalization components encouraged Mexico to remove agricultural subsidies and social protections that were critical to sustaining the poor. It is no coincidence that the Clinton administration accelerated the militarization of the US-Mexico border at the same time.[15] The administration was aware that NAFTA would generate displacement and stress—at least in the short term and especially in Mexico's rural areas—and fortified the border accordingly.[16] Dispossession in Mexico, which especially devastated its rural and indigenous south, combined with militarized border controls, did not deter migrants from crossing or employers from hiring them. Instead, they made crossing the border riskier and more costly and constrained migrants' rights once they arrived.[17] These dynamics delivered a cheapened pool of excess racialized and illegalized labor on which employers and restructured, low-wage industries could benefit with relative impunity.[18]

ERODING LABOR STANDARDS IN THE UNITED STATES

In the United States, wage theft thrives in the spaces between weakened labor standards enforcement, the evisceration of organized labor, and the rise in racialized anti-immigrant policing. The US Fair Labor Standards Act (FLSA), part of a suite of New Deal legislation passed in 1938, provides the foundational architecture to regulate workers' wages, hours, and working conditions. Yet labor protections are intrinsically undermined by a history of racialized exclusions, antilabor and antiregulation assaults since the 1980s, and the changing nature of work.

At their inception, compromises were incorporated into the FLSA and other New Deal legislation to appease southern congressmen to maintain "the social and racial plantation system in the South—a system resting on the subjugation of blacks and other minorities."[19] After the end of slavery, Jim Crow exclusions kept African Americans out of higher-paying jobs with occupational mobility, pushing them into low-paying industries like domestic and agricultural work that also enjoyed fewer protections under labor laws.[20] When the FLSA emerged out of the New Deal in 1938, it excluded farm, domestic, and home care workers, sectors dominated by African Americans. "Occupational classification" cloaked racially derived exclusions of minority workers who were concentrated in these sectors, thereby guaranteeing a source of cheap, underprotected labor.[21] The exclusion of farmworkers from the National Labor Relations Act (NLRA), which protects the right to organize and engage in concerted activity to improve working conditions, and the FLSA, also benefited the consolidation of agribusiness in the South and Southwest and helped condition its reliance on importing Mexican laborers, ensuring that growers would "continue to have free rein over [their] workforce."[22]

Agricultural and domestic workers are still not covered under the NLRA. They are underprotected and underpaid not because of the nature of the work, but because of the racialized devaluation of the minority groups who have historically performed it.[23] Work that was once performed by African American men and women, like agriculture and home care, was increasingly relegated to Latino immigrant men and women once racist mobility and employment restrictions relaxed and migration from Latin America increased after 1965.[24] Labor protections that appear neutral or industry-based have deep connections to and continue to reinforce inequality across interlocking identity differences, including race, gender, class, and citizenship.

Many of the New Deal's original racialized exclusions persist under the guise of classificatory carve-outs and exemptions. Only workers legally classified as "employees" are covered under the FLSA; contract workers are excluded. However, in the past few decades, the changing nature of work has cast more workers out of employee status. These exclusions correspond closely with the minority and immigrant populations that labor protections historically excluded. Immigrants, women, and people of color disproportionately labor in this expanding economy of precarious and underprotected work, including temporary, day labor, contract, gig, and part-time employment.[25]

The New Deal consensus around labor regulations and protections also began to unravel in the 1970s and 1980s. Firms and business interests went on the offensive to dismantle unions and regulations and restructure employment relations to control wages amid economic stagnation and rising international competition. Firms began to outsource operations abroad where labor costs and regulations were lower. In contrast, place-bound industries like construction, trucking, and janitorial services, which could not be simply relocated abroad, were restructured or relocated to regions of the country with lower labor costs and unionization rates.[26]

Economic restructuring from the late 1970s through the mid-1990s involved a transition away from manufacturing towards "service-producing industries . . . [which tended to offer] lower pay and fewer opportunities for upward advancement."[27] Jobs that previously offered decent wages, economic mobility, and benefits, "largely as a result of unionization—were either outsourced to other countries or transformed into nonunion, low-wage, precarious jobs" with few benefits and little job security.[28] Instead of hiring workers as employees, firms cut costs and increased their agility by hiring workers in temporary, involuntary part-time, contingent, contract, piece-rate, and independent contracting capacities.[29] Such nonstandard work arrangements enabled them to attenuate responsibilities to their workers, increase flexibility, and decrease fixed labor costs.[30] In the past few decades, firms facing competitive pressures also deployed strategies such as "subcontracting, franchising, and third-party management" to break off parts of their operations and shift them onto other enterprises—what David Weil calls "workplace fissuring."[31] Workplace fissuring allowed firms to lower costs, limit liabilities for their employees, and offload responsibility for various activities related to their core outcomes while maintaining many of the benefits.[32] As a result, the number of small workplaces has ballooned, making them harder to monitor and identify responsibility.[33] For example, Weil notes, customers staying at a hotel chain may perceive the hotel as the sole provider of their stay, but the hotel may actually subcontract, or delegate to various third-party entities or even a temporary staffing agency, cleaning and food services.[34] David Seligman, executive director of Towards Justice, observed that these practices have exploded, proliferating in industries as varied as food service, farmwork, and meatpacking. The unregulated, insecure nature of day labor employment now characterizes growing sectors of the economy and populations of workers.

The antiregulation fervor sweeping the 1980s not only decimated unions; it also gutted labor standards enforcement. The US Department of Labor (DoL) is a relatively small federal agency, but its resources and personnel have been aggressively curtailed since the 1980s.[35] The number of its investigators dropped 31 percent between 1980 and 2007.[36] Drastic cuts proceeded alongside an expansion in the number of workplaces to monitor—the number of workplaces and employees both rose about 11 percent from 1998 to 2007[37]—and new laws to enforce.[38] The DoL had jurisdiction over 7.3 million workplace and 130 million workers, but had only 700 investigators when President Barack Obama took office in 2008.[39] Although the Obama administration boosted staffing to 1,000, this level was just below the 1980 numbers.[40] The decline in investigations coupled with the increase in workplaces led David Weil to estimate the annual probability of a workplace being investigated at about 0.3 percent.[41]

Lack of sufficient capacity makes the DoL largely "passive and complaint-driven," meaning that it largely depends on individuals to come forward with complaints.[42] It previously pursued more proactive investigations. Between 1998 and 2008, more than three-quarters of investigations emerged from workers' complaints in contrast to 60 percent being investigations driven in 1960.[43] Because there is low capacity for agency-driven investigations and low-wage workers face high hurdles mobilizing the law for themselves, the majority of labor violations are never discovered. In 2008, the Government Accountability Office issued a report that the DoL "routinely failed workers," citing a drop in enforcement actions from 47,000 in 1997 to fewer than 30,000 by 2008, as well as the agency's failure to take and respond to complaints and levy penalties on willful and repeat offenders.[44] Similarly, although the FLSA prohibits retaliation for lodging complaints about labor conditions, "the Wage and Hour Division has pursued very few retaliation cases."[45]

Still, the FLSA, enforced under the DoL's Wage and Hour Division, covers only employees who work for businesses with two or more employees that have "annual gross sales or business involving at least $500,000 per year" or are engaged in interstate commerce. This limitation excludes many employees of such small and fissured enterprises. It also omits the growing numbers of workers reclassified from employee status into a host of nonstandard, temporary, and independent contracting arrangements that carve them out of these protections.[46] Because most low-wage immigrant workers work for small enterprises or employers, they are unlikely to find recourse through the DoL's Wage and Hour Division. Similarly, when individuals do not have sufficient coworkers and are owed small dollar amounts, their cases become uneconomical for most attorneys. In many states like Colorado, where minimum wage and wage theft laws are stronger than they are at the federal level, state-level departments of labor and pro bono attorneys, nonprofit legal services organizations, and worker centers, unions, and other advocacy organizations become important avenues for low-wage workers.

Unauthorized Latino immigrant workers disproportionately work in precarious sectors of the labor market that remain underprotected by labor laws. The complicated historical importation of Mexican immigrants into the US labor market as racialized low-wage laborers workers has also devalued and institutionalized the theft of their labor.

STEALING MEXICAN IMMIGRANT LABOR

As detailed in the Introduction, the United States usurped over half of Mexico's territory on the signing of the Treaty of Guadalupe in 1848. Although the United States granted citizenship to Mexicans residing in the annexed territories, the dogma of manifest destiny and the fact that citizenship was granted through conquest subjected them to "systemic racial discrimination and segregation."[47] The appropriation of Hispanic land influenced economic and land disparities between Mexican Americans and whites in the Southwest that still persist.[48] Mexicans were racialized as "other" within their own land as they experienced discrimination and Jim Crow–like (or "Juan Crow") segregation in the Southwest.[49] Mae Ngai thus labels the reliance on temporary Mexican laborers a form of "imported colonialism," based on the "subordination of racialized foreign bodies who work in the United States [on Mexican land usurped by conquest] but who remain excluded from the polity."[50]

The regulation of Mexican migration historically served the interests of US employers and established a history of theft.[51] The prominent role that Mexicans laborers played in agriculture and railway expansion in the Southwest in the early twentieth century grew out of racist immigration quotas between 1924 and 1965 that barred Asian and limited southern European immigration. Although there was no quota restriction on immigration from Mexico during this period, border enforcement practices—notably a head tax to be paid upon entry, humiliating medical inspections and toxic delousing baths that treated Mexicans as disease vectors, visa requirements, and entry control through the creation of the Border Patrol in 1924—not only led to the construction of Mexicans as the "largest group of illegal aliens by the late 1920s" but set in motion a conflation between unauthorized migration, the Southwest border, and the racialization of Mexicans as foreign others.[52]

In the 1920s and 1930s, private agencies used the *enganche*, translated literally as "hooking" system, to recruit Mexican laborers, especially along the border. By placing recruitment, transportation, and labor management in the hands of private actors and agencies, this system led to "unfair contracts, eternal indebtedness, miserable life conditions, child labor, private police and recruitment agencies."[53] This exploitative system, coupled with mass deportation drives and growing anti-Mexican racism in the 1920s and 1930s, further commoditized Mexican labor and devalued it as "foreign . . . disposable . . . in addition to being cheap."[54]

The bracero program, a binational agreement between Mexico and the United States from 1942 to 1964, led to the total importation of roughly 4.6 million Mexican laborers.[55] Braceros provided US growers with a low-cost solution to war-induced agricultural worker shortages and offered a palliative to unemployment in Mexico.[56] Still, even at that time, some objected that growers manufactured the perception of a labor shortage to avoid paying decent wages.[57] The bracero program was also a response to the abuses of the *enganche* system, which it intended to curb by regulating contracting through bilateral coordination between the US and Mexican governments.[58] In the United States, the authorization of the bracero program entailed overturning existing prohibitions on contract labor in place since 1885, largely because Americans associated contract labor with slavery because laborers were not free to negotiate their wages, working conditions, or employers.[59]

The bracero program categorized Mexican workers as contract workers, which deliberately positioned them outside the free market system, depressed their ability to garner market wages, and tied them to their employers as unfree wage labor according to employers' proclivities.[60] Labor contractors also provided employers with further insulation from responsibility over braceros, which presage labor brokerage and subcontracting practices that exist today.[61] Still, to address the potential for abuse, the program attempted to institute conditions that much of the agricultural workforce lacked: protection against discrimination, a minimum wage, a process to investigate contract violations, and the ability for braceros to choose representatives to help advocate on their behalf with their employers.[62] In practice, however, payment below contract rates was common, braceros were hesitant to report violations, which were seldom punished, and conditions were often substandard.[63] Nevertheless, even as some braceros were willing to "endure difficult conditions . . . to get their families ahead," others spread knowledge among their networks, lodged complaints, or skipped contracts to find better opportunities—but then they risked apprehension as illegal laborers.[64]

The bracero program was also repeatedly threatened during times of economic downturn and racialized anxiety, including raids and mass deportation drives that removed US citizens of Mexican origin, braceros, and unauthorized Mexicans alike, notably including the Immigration and Naturalization Service's (INS's) highly militarized 1954 Operation Wetback.[65] Moreover, while advocates argued that the bracero program would decrease unauthorized migration, the opposite occurred: growers preferred informal recruitment near the border, demand on both sides was greater than allotted by the program, growers in states that Mexico barred from the program because of their segregation dynamics recruited "illegal workers," braceros' social and kinship networks often followed them, and other braceros left exploitative conditions to take a risk as illegal laborers.[66] Growers incurred scant liability for hiring unauthorized workers because they were shielded by the Texas Proviso.[67] Under pressure from growers, the INS even helped "legalize" workers by paroling them directly to growers after arresting them, a process known as "drying out wetbacks," which made distinguishing legal from illegal recruitment a farce and undermined the stated ethos of the program.[68] The implementation of new measures that allowed braceros to be recontracted pending employer satisfaction further insulated employers from complaints and incentivized braceros to please them.[69]

Although the bracero program ostensibly claimed to formalize labor contracting, diminish unauthorized migration, and safeguard laborers, the program reinforced "industrial farm production as a low-wage enterprise" excluded from worker protections and cemented the racial construction of Mexicans as cheap and disposable labor.[70] It also set a precedent for the blurring of immigration and labor policy and selective enforcement of immigration laws that favor employer interests and encourage workers to remain silent about exploitation. Compounding the bracero program's legacy of devaluing Mexican labor, the program deposited a portion of braceros' wages in accounts in Mexico to be recovered once they returned. Now, over half a century later, many former braceros are still fighting for these unpaid wages.[71] Not only did braceros suffer exploitation in the fields and have their labor power undercut; the Mexican government even directly stole their hard-earned money.[72]

The bracero program's termination in 1964 did not end employers' appetite for Mexican labor or Mexicans' desires to work in the United States. Instead, Mexican migration became increasingly governed through its "illegality," which carried strong racial undertones.[73] Not only had growers become accustomed to Mexican labor, but those born in the United States came to racialize and reject agricultural work as "foreign."[74]

In 1965, the United States passed the Hart-Cellar Act, which was celebrated for removing racist national origins quotas and liberalizing the immigration system. However, for the first time, it applied immigration quotas to the Western Hemisphere and allotted the same number of visas to all countries, regardless of their size or proximity and depth of migratory ties to the United States. As a result, migratory flows from Mexico were increasingly "illegalized" because of the new quota on immigration from Mexico, which coincided with the termination of the bracero program.[75] Illegalization did not prevent Mexican migration, but it restricted and channeled the work opportunities of a Mexican immigrant population that would increasingly be unauthorized owing to the new cap. Nicholas De Genova thus argues that Mexican "illegality" is legally produced.[76]

IMMIGRATION LAW AND THEFT: PROFITING FROM ILLEGALITY

Immigrant illegality is not just punitive or exclusionary; it is also productive and profitable.[77] In particular, it provides a subsidy to employers and particular industries that benefit from lower labor costs, a labor force that is unlikely to complain about wages and working conditions, and sometimes the pure profit of not paying its employees at all.[78] Writing about the experiences of Filipino immigrants in the United States, Yen Le Espiritu argues that immigrants experience "differential inclusion" rather than mere exclusion or inclusion.[79] Specifically, the United States considers particular immigrant and minority groups to be valuable precisely because of their subordinate position, and, for many, their illegality.

The Immigration Reform and Control Act (IRCA 1986) is a key example of how immigration law enforcement has shaped precarious working conditions, undercut immigrant labor, and transferred the value of unauthorized immigrant labor to employers. IRCA's provision on employer sanctions intended to make employers—not workers—liable for potential civil or criminal penalties for knowingly hiring unauthorized workers, requiring employers to check employment eligibility by completing the Employment Eligibility Verification (I-9) form and to retain other kinds of documentation.[80] However, loopholes around IRCA's "knowingly" clause provided employers with a good-faith excuse to largely evade punishment.[81] The costs of the criminalization of unauthorized work were transferred from employers to unauthorized workers; employers turned a blind eye as long as workers were compliant, but could easily "selectively apply the I-9 documentation process" to suppress complaints and organizing efforts.[82]

IRCA encouraged employers to rely more on subcontractors and brokers to access undocumented workers so they could avoid the associated legal liabilities.[83] In effect, IRCA submerged markets further underground, where workplace violations were harder to monitor, and stimulated a market for false documents.[84] Instead of deterring employers from hiring unauthorized workers, IRCA shifted the costs and risks onto workers in the form of reduced wages.[85] After IRCA, the wage gap between documented and undocumented Latinos, as well as immigrants who were hired by subcontractors,[86] began to more sharply diverge.[87] Yet IRCA also depressed the wages and bargaining position of authorized Mexican immigrants and the US-born who occupied similar market niches as they increasingly labored alongside workers with limited rights.[88]

IRCA did not hold employers accountable, and the risk of penalties was low; instead, it delivered them a subsidy in the form of a compliant workforce. Instead of sanctions, it gave employers a "sword" that "empowers [them] to terrorize their workers" and selectively weaponize immigration laws in the workplace.[89] IRCA did not intend to undercut labor protections or punish unauthorized workers, but its loopholes and selective enforcement basically guaranteed it.[90]

Recent legal decisions have compounded the impacts of IRCA to weaken unauthorized immigrants' coverage under labor laws and undercut their due earnings. The US Supreme Court case *Sure-Tan, Inc. v. NLRB* (1984) established "undocumented workers as 'employees' under the National Labor Relations Act (NLRA)," which protects the right to organize and collectively bargain.[91] However, in *Hoffman Plastics Compounds, Inc. v. National Labor Relations Board (NLRB)*, the US Supreme Court addressed the case of a worker who used false papers to obtain employment and then was dismissed after joining a union, which constituted a violation of the NLRA. The 2002 decision argued that unauthorized workers were not entitled to back pay for work that would have been performed as restitution for unfair labor practices because IRCA legally precluded them being eligible to work in the first place.[92] The ruling thus shifted the gaze from the employer's violation of the NLRA and twisted the intentions of IRCA to focus on the immigrant worker's status to deprive him of back pay.[93] Prior to the ruling, unauthorized immigrants enjoyed similar NLRA protections to citizens. After *Hoffman*, unauthorized workers retained the right to organize to improve their labor conditions under the NLRA, but with inherent risks that threatened their livelihoods. Lung argues, "By depriving undocumented workers of the right to back pay under the NLRA, *Hoffman* empowered employers to violate the NLRA and other employment laws with impunity."[94] Although firing workers for organizing constitutes an unfair labor practice regardless of immigration status, *Hoffman* sent a clear message to employers that they could selectively manipulate immigration and labor laws at little cost because they did not have to award back pay or reinstate these workers.[95]

Immigrant illegality establishes a "hierarchy of rights" such that unauthorized immigrants are incorporated into the United States for their cheap labor while their precarious legal position and the threat of removal inherently limit their access to more protective parts of the legal system, facilitate exploitation, and make their claims and even very existence invisible.[96] Their subordinate inclusion and legal vulnerability make unauthorized immigrants simultaneously lucrative to employers and fuzzy to labor agencies that otherwise attempt to assist workers regardless of immigration status.

LABOR RIGHTS FORECLOSED

The mandates of US labor and immigration enforcement agencies are intended to be kept separate to prevent unscrupulous employers from obtaining a "perverse incentive" to underpay and exploit immigrant workers.[97] However, immigration enforcement has become increasingly entangled in the workplace. By 2018 the Immigration and Customs Enforcement (ICE) budget had surged to $24 billion, eleven times higher than the labor standards enforcement budget.[98] It is difficult for unauthorized immigrant workers to prove they exist: they fear employer retaliation, and immigration enforcement threatens to pose harsh consequences for working illegally. Despite the fact that employers should be the ones held criminally liable for hiring unauthorized workers, few have been prosecuted.[99]

ICE has even used the pretext of worker mistreatment to justify workplace enforcement operations. By investigating cases of worker mistreatment, "uncovering such violations," and criminally prosecuting "employers who knowingly break the law," ICE contends that it "can send a strong deterrent message to other employers who knowingly employ illegal aliens."[100] ICE workplace investigations and warrants are frequently prompted by suspicions that employers are harboring and employing unauthorized immigrants, as well as by reports of workplace violations. ICE states that the goal is to punish employers who violate the law, but the results tell a different story: immigrant workers are disproportionately punished while employers continue to operate with relative impunity. Meanwhile, the specter of enforcement silences future complaints and attempts to organize in the workplace. Instead of removing the "perverse" incentive to hire unauthorized immigrants, enforcement practices reward it.[101]

The punitive nature of immigration enforcement and more protective elements of labor law do not necessarily clash. Instead, they operate in tandem to structure the subordinate inclusion of unauthorized immigrant workers as a low-wage, pliant labor force with limited rights that are even less actionable.[102] Immigrant illegality does not prevent the unauthorized from working or employers from hiring them, but it becomes more likely that workers will not complain, cheapens their labor, and disproportionately segments them into the sectors of the labor market least protected by labor laws, from where it is even more difficult to seek recourse as they face heightened ICE interference.

CONCLUSION

The availability of Mexican migrant workers as a labor reserve for US capital has long been, and continues to be, structured by the racialized devaluation and illegalization of Mexican labor.[103] Dating back to the US conquest of the Southwest and the delineation of the modern US–Mexico border, the border and its extension to Latino immigrants more broadly have stood in for US racial anxieties.[104] US media and political discourse from both sides of the political spectrum reinforce this devaluation by depicting Latin American—often glossed as Mexican—immigrants as cheap labor. When employers pay immigrants less than US citizens or code particular jobs as "immigrant jobs" or jobs that US citizens do not want, this racist framing leaves capitalist relations that artificially create "bad jobs" unquestioned. In doing so, it further constitutes theft of immigrants' labor value. Mireya Loza argues, "Instead of reforming exploitative labor practices or addressing deplorable wages or work conditions," the United States has long courted Mexican migrants to fill such jobs.[105]

Wage theft thrives along a historical continuum whereby the United States has selectively incorporated Mexican immigrants into the United States as cheaper labor and scapegoated, criminalized, and expelled them during times of economic distress.[106] The same social hierarchies and racist notions that justify paying Latino immigrants less (e.g., they should not be here or should accept whatever they can get) make it less objectionable to steal from them. As Fernández-Esquer and colleagues write, "Wage theft is only possible because of racist beliefs that individuals who lack legal documentation are of interior status and therefore rightfully excluded from society."[107] The United States tolerates and values unauthorized immigrants for their productive potential rather than as people who deserve social and political membership; these discourses construct the trope of the young male Mexican migrant willing to work hard.[108] These discourses are shaped by, and continue to justify, the disposability, deportability, and replaceability of Latino immigrant workers

Moreover, wage theft is enabled by the proliferation of fissured workplaces as employers wield more power and enjoy relative impunity over their workers. The US labor rights enforcement system is not only ill equipped to deal with employment arrangements that increasingly informalize work and untether employers from accountability over their workers; it has long guarded these arrangements.[109]

2 BOOMTOWN

Construction and Immigration in the Mile High City

ONE MORNING AT THE FEDERAL and 19th hiring site, Hermelindo pointed to a light blue two-story home across the street, tucked behind the Family Dollar Store. The paint was chipping, but the building otherwise appeared well kept. Hermelindo was in his mid-60s and limped from an ankle injury suffered during a painting job. He never reported the injury to his employer because his son had worked hard to convince the boss to hire him. He didn't want his son to have any problems. At the time, Hermelindo was renting a room in this blue house, but he had to vacate by the end of the month. The house was going to be bulldozed to pave the way for a new duplex. In spring 2015, the construction flurry was palpable. Hermelindo ironically reflected that maybe he would get a job painting the very duplex that was rendering him homeless. Instead, he returned to Juárez in the fall.

In 2015, Denver's residential construction market was booming and struggling to keep pace with population expansion and demand for new units (Figure 6). The boom emerged in the wake of the market's collapse and the bust of the housing bubble leading up to the 2008–2009 Great Recession. Nationally, residential construction was hit hard by the Great Recession and experienced a 26.8 percent decline in employment between 2003 and 2013.[1] During the downturn, Colorado's construction industry lost 40 percent of trade positions and was slow to recover.[2] Upon recovery, the in-

FIGURE 6: Redevelopment around the Federal and 19th hiring site. Photo by author.

dustry faced a significant skilled worker shortage because skilled workers, many of whom had been laid off or discharged during the downturn, had fled the industry or even the state entirely.[3]

After the recession, Colorado surged to become one of the four fastest growing states in the United States.[4] The Denver metro area, in particular, was one of the top three fastest growing large urban areas from 2010–2016.[5] Construction was unable to keep pace with demand, leading prices to soar.[6] Rents in Denver were expected to rise faster than any other US city for 2015 as it became one of the country's hottest housing markets.[7]

I wondered if a construction boom would offer day laborers, who largely worked in the residential construction industry and associated jobs, leverage for better wages and working conditions. Many day laborers told us they came to Colorado from other states precisely because they heard that there was a glut of work and that contractors paid higher wages than in other cities, especially when compared to the South, Midwest, and Southeast. In Denver, day laborers could demand an hourly wage of $12.00 or $15.00, significantly higher than Colorado's $8.23 hourly minimum wage at the time. Contractors were even reportedly stealing subs from other sites.

Studies demonstrate that wage violations tend to follow unemployment trends; violations rose sharply during the Great Recession with disproportionate consequences for immigrants, women, and workers of color.[8] Perhaps in a postrecession upswing with a labor shortage, employers needed to be on better behavior. Despite the boom and recovery, we kept hearing that day laborers could stand for hours at the corner without landing a job, and they continued to experience wage theft and pervasive employer mistreatment.

Why could day laborers not leverage a construction bonanza to their advantage? This chapter explores why day laborers did not benefit from the construction surge. Instead, labor violations proliferated with relative impunity. First, the chapter situates the role of immigrant workers and day labor within the residential construction sector. I show how the changing nature of the industry, coupled with rising immigration from Latin America in the 1990s, led the construction industry to become increasingly bifurcated between skilled and unskilled labor pools, segmented by race, nationality, and citizenship, and to rely more heavily on labor contracting arrangements.[9] The chapter then explores how rising interior and workplace immigration enforcement in the mid-2000s coincided with the impacts of the Great Recession to more severely restrict and surveil the opportunities available to unauthorized immigrants. This context helps explain why economic recovery not only eluded day laborers but was also conducive to labor violations like wage theft.

IMMIGRATION, CONSTRUCTION, AND DAY LABOR

Day labor is one of the oldest forms of contingent and flexible work.[10] It occupies a historically close relationship with the construction industry, which a century ago was characterized by workers lining up daily for employment.[11] Residential construction long necessitated flexible labor; its seasonal nature and project fluctuations do not lend themselves well to maintaining a steady, permanent workforce.[12] The needs and skills required can vary within a project and from job to job.[13] However, with economic restructuring, day labor markets actually reemerged and expanded in the 2000s across the United States, as well as in other advanced capitalist countries.[14] Day labor markets are ideal for restructured industries like residential construction because they provide an excess, on-call labor reserve for employers, small firms, and homeowners seeking flexible and cheaper labor.[15]

When manufacturing firms struggled to compete amid rising global competition, inflation, and economic stagnation in the 1970s, they outsourced operations abroad to find lower labor costs and regulations.[16] Place-based industries like residential construction devised other strategies, including decimating unions and restructuring labor contracting arrangements.[17] Labor is the highest and most unpredictable cost in construction, but once union power was depleted, it became the easiest aspect of the industry to manipulate.[18]

Unions were previously major players in the construction industry and were critical to training workers through skill development, setting wage standards, and bargaining for better working conditions in the industry.[19] In the 1940s, 80 percent of construction workers had union representation, but representation plummeted to 22 percent by the 1990s and 13.4 percent in 2020.[20] Union losses were particularly concentrated in the residential sector, which largely converted into a bastion of nonunion contractors.[21] Firms' efforts to attack unions and pervasive contracting practices to cut labor costs decimated wages and working conditions in construction; real wages declined 17 percent from 1980 to 1992.[22]

Construction firms not only actively promoted nonunion subsidiaries but also restructured contracting arrangements to control costs. Employers long relied on subcontracting to fulfill disparate project needs[23] but had previously mostly employed a mix of their own crews, largely skilled union subcontractors for specialized tasks, and also performed a portion of the work themselves.[24] Instead, they pivoted away from a general contractor model toward a labor contracting or construction manager approach that resembled providing a "service" to firms.[25] Because contractors became more like service providers and worked for fees rather than a lump sum, they became more invested in lowering labor costs.[26]

When employers offload portions of projects to subcontractors, they benefit from not having to keep a stable roster of employees, which decreases fixed labor and insurance costs, lowers payroll tax obligations, and facilitates access to workers as needed.[27] Labor contracting practices also enable contractors to break projects into smaller pieces that require fewer skills, which decreases their need for skilled and more expensive union subcontractors. Contractors began to rely more on lower-tier subcontractors, who functioned more like labor brokers, to supply and manage crews on an as-needed basis for smaller projects and thus largely obviated the need for the skilled contracting firms of the past.[28]

Jim, a representative with the Southwest Regional Council of Carpenters, explained the transition: "If drywall contractors [had] a commercial project, say an apartment complex downtown, fifteen or twenty years ago they wouldn't even have a sub, you were it." The reliance on three and four tiers of subs and brokers began in the late 1990s. Jim explained that brokers "don't supply their own materials or bid a job . . . they just supply labor." He first heard about pervasive labor brokerage practices in Miami in the 2000s as contractors took advantage of an increase in Latino immigrant labor to build high rises on a cash basis. The model spread to become what he called an "exploitation niche": brokers bring in workers off-the-books and for cash and have networks throughout the country. With just a phone call, Jim told me, they can bring workers from Texas to Colorado for a short-term job. The labor costs and responsibilities shift to the labor broker, who profits from supplying no-strings-attached labor. There is little oversight of these arrangements as brokers and the workers they supply may both be here today and gone tomorrow.

Labor contracting not only brought labor cost savings but also insulated firms by transferring their liabilities for employees to subcontractors and labor brokers.[29] Residential construction became increasingly characterized by multiple small-level operators, tight profit margins, and strong cost competition.[30] A dizzying number of small-level operators in competition with one another thrust wages into more aggressive competition to squeeze labor to win bids. "Cutthroat competition among subcontractors and the intensive labor exploitation classically associated with it rapidly emerged,"[31] which led to an exponential rise in labor violations that were otherwise relatively uncommon in the industry.[32] Aggressive labor sweating, pervasive labor violations, and the "downgrading of employment conditions" created a race to the bottom that hit the entire industry, allowing low-road employers to accrue a competitive advantage and downgrade the labor market.[33]

Immigrants are often blamed for displacing US-born workers and undercutting wages in domestic industries like construction. However, Ruth

Milkman demonstrates that the case is the reverse. As wages and conditions in the residential sector plummeted, many US-born workers abandoned the industry or fled to its commercial side.[34] Firms began to more actively recruit immigrants to fill newly degraded jobs.[35] Growing numbers of unauthorized immigrants in the 1990s and early 2000s readily provided the supply the industry demanded. In the early 1980s, just 7 percent of residential construction workers were Latino; by 2001, this had grown to 16 percent, of whom over 70 percent were foreign-born.[36] The share of Latinos in the industry more than tripled from 1990 to 2015.[37] The growth of undocumented Latinos in the industry expanded to the point that they came to outnumber their documented counterparts.[38] In Colorado's construction workforce, 33.9 percent are Hispanic compared to 27.6 percent nationally (average across 2011 to 2019).[39]

However, Latino immigrants are not evenly spread across the industry. Undocumented Latinos may account for 30 percent of residential construction workers in the United States, but they are underrepresented in managerial roles, as well as in foreman and higher-skilled occupations like welding and electrical work.[40] Latino immigrant day laborers are concentrated in the most laborious, insecure, and dangerous segments of the industry, especially residential construction and remodeling.[41] Still, the majority of undocumented Latino construction workers are not day laborers; rather, they occupy a range of roles including working as subs, as labor brokers, for regular or repeat contractors and subcontractors, and in other forms of contingent work.[42]

Many labor brokers are entrepreneurs of a sort in the Latino community.[43] Some immigrants who cultivated a niche smuggling migrants across the border naturally extended their skills into labor brokerage as they began to also deliver migrant workers to employers.[44] Subcontractors, who are also often Latino, are more likely than day laborers to be born in the United States or have legal authorization and possess bilingual abilities. Day laborers mentioned that contractors often depended on such subs to translate and serve as intermediaries to monolingual Spanish-speaking workers. In contrast, firm executives, investors, owners, and general contractors are overwhelmingly white US citizens, many of them located out of state. According to data from the *Colorado Business Journal*, of the twenty-five top residential and commercial construction firms in Denver, all but two owners were white men.[45]

The racial and legal stratification of the industry reflects and works to reinforce the bifurcation between skilled (largely used to refer to union workers, who are more likely to be white and US-born) and unskilled workers, who are more likely to be Latino immigrants.[46] Aaron Schneider discusses how the industry is segmented between a primary and a secondary sector. The primary sector includes larger public and corporate infrastructure projects, which are considered to require skilled labor and expertise. The secondary sector, in contrast, is characterized by smaller residential jobs, which are considered to be unskilled.[47] Yet these trends have increasingly unraveled these distinctions—themselves manufactured by employer and industry actions—as the working conditions associated with primary jobs increasingly resemble the degraded working conditions once more characteristic of the secondary sector.[48]

Day laborers often cycle through different roles in the residential construction industry, but many of these positions are only slightly more secure. In a segmented market characterized by diffuse contracting arrangements, workers' attempts to organize, survive, or perhaps get ahead frequently pit them against their own social networks.

THE CHANGING PORTRAIT OF DAY LABOR

Day laborers increasingly look like Hermelindo. They are no longer the young, recently arrived migrants from Mexico attempting to gain a foothold in the US economy, as documented by studies in the early and mid-2000s.[49] The National Day Labor Survey (NDLS), conducted with a nationally representative sample of day laborers across the Untied States in 2004, found that day laborers were overwhelmingly male (98 percent); 93 percent were foreign-born, 59 percent were of Mexican origin, and 75 percent were undocumented.[50] They were also mostly recent immigrants; 60 percent of NDLS respondents had arrived in the past five years, and only 11 percent had lived in the country for twenty years or more.[51] Most day laborers had worked in day labor for only short periods of time, but it was the first job that the majority of respondents held when they arrived in the United States.[52] These findings suggested that day labor could provide a gateway for new immigrants into the economy as they gained experience and developed connections.[53]

Day laborers in the Denver area are still mostly male, Latino, foreign-born, undocumented, and from Mexico. Our survey of 393 day laborers found that respondents were exclusively male: 94 percent identified as Latino, 88 percent as foreign-born, 69 percent were from Mexico, and 42 percent possessed legal status. However, their profiles departed significantly from earlier studies in terms of age and time in the United States (among the foreign-born). They were older, had been in the United States for the long haul, and had long relied on day labor. Forty-six percent had arrived in the United States more than twenty years ago, and just 10 percent had arrived in the past five years.[54] Mean duration in the United States among foreign-born day laborers in Denver surveyed in 2016 and 2017 was 22.5 years versus just 6.4 years in the NDLS, while the mean age of day laborers in Denver was 45.5 years old, about eleven years older than the average NDLS respondent.[55]

These results are not unique to Colorado; they depict trends documented by other studies conducted since 2010 that also noted an aging and longer duration sample of day laborers in different regions of the country, including San Diego and San Francisco, Houston, Dallas, Arlington, and Central Texas.[56] The changing demographic composition of day laborers suggests that some individuals may risk becoming entrenched in day labor. Or they may churn in and out of various informal markets as they contend with low wages, job insecurity, and legal status barriers.[57] Other immigrant workers might return to day labor after being cast out of other jobs, rendering it a reserve for the more senior, injured, infirm, or merely unlucky.

Although day laborers in the Denver area earned relatively high hourly minimum wages in 2016 and 2017—an average of $15.60 per hour compared to the $10.00 per hour documented by the NDLS in 2004—they still suffered from insufficient work, which depressed overall earnings.[58] The average day laborer in Denver worked only 2.7 hours per reported day, which meant that they worked only 16 hours per week. When we accounted for lack of work, the average day laborer earned just $1,060 per twenty-five-day work month, no different from the low incomes documented by the NDLS in 2004 over a decade earlier.[59]

The difficulties day laborers face transitioning out of contingent work or becoming relegated to precarious work are visible in Miguel's story that follows. Like Miguel, many immigrant day laborers are increasingly foreclosed from economic mobility because of the lingering impacts of the Great Recession, greater interior immigration enforcement, and the segmented labor contracting structure of the residential construction industry.

MIGUEL'S STORY: CHANGING MIGRATION DYNAMICS AND THE GREAT RECESSION

One morning in mid-March 2015, Miguel was still hanging around Centro even though he had not found a job that day. Centro's morning employment lottery had ended two hours ago, and employers had stopped coming through the doors to solicit workers. Miguel commented, "Now I am resting because there is no work." In the past, he might have tried his luck across the street at the Stout Street site. Yet he was less concerned about needing to hustle, he said, because he no longer needed to send money to his wife or his children in Mexico as he had in the past: they had moved on. "My children are grown now, they don't need me anymore. They are married and can take care of themselves. . . . Now I am living for myself," he explained. Workers like Miguel often stuck around until Centro closed in the early afternoon to chat, pass the time, use the lockers or computers, stay warm, or cook a meal in the kitchenette.

Miguel first arrived in the United States in 2002; he was advancing in age, and immigration enforcement and the recession had altered both his migratory plans and employment prospects. In 2002, he migrated from Juárez, Mexico, just over the border from El Paso, Texas, to Denver. On this first trip, he worked for a roofing company for six years. For the past five years, however, he depended on searching for day labor jobs at Centro.

Miguel lost his job with the roofing company in 2008 as a result of the Great Recession. He recalled, "After, came the crisis. . . . They let me go . . . and so I went back to Mexico." Miguel spent a year back in Juárez, but quickly realized that there was little for him there: "For me, because I am already old. . . . There is no work [in Juárez] . . . just for the young people." Miguel was able to return to the United States in 2010 because his tourist visa was still current. However, the visa was valid for only six months and had since expired. "Now, I can no longer return," he mentioned. He was implying that if he returned to Mexico, it would be unlikely that he could ever come back to the United States because recrossing the border without documentation had become prohibitively expensive and dangerous.

In Denver, Miguel was living with a woman who was sort of his girlfriend, but it was more a relationship of convenience. He admitted, "It's just so that I am not suffering in the street here. . . . [And] she understands . . . because she doesn't want to be alone." He no longer had a relationship with his ex-wife in Juárez, who, he realized, had been "just spending and spending." He trusted only his mother, who also lived in Juárez, and he sent her money to save for his return. Miguel was planning to return to Juárez the following year. He commented wistfully, "Because I no longer want to be here [in the United States]. I came here to work, not to live. I don't like it. I am old [now] here."

When Miguel worked for the roofing company on his first migration trip, he had a regular salary that increased from $8.00 an hour to $14.50 by the time he was let go. He could no longer work for companies as he had in the past because he lacked immigration papers. He explained, "The rules have changed. . . . Before, when I entered with them [the roofing company in 2002] I had fake papers and with that, I looked for work. . . . You know there are new rules that they no longer accept these. You know this too, right?" He had noticed a change about three or four years ago; as he told me, "They [the US government] began to investigate the companies that [employed] people without papers." Miguel had few remaining options outside day labor or repeat informal employers who might call him.

Miguel's story highlights three changes that impinge on the economic prospects of unauthorized immigrant workers. These changes have led the "unauthorized immigrant population in the US to be increasingly . . . made up of longer-term residents" like Miguel.[60] First, the escalating militarization of the US-Mexico border since the 1990s, and especially after the terrorist attacks of September 11, 2001, raised the risks of crossing the border, which led migrants to increasingly rely on smugglers who charged higher fees.[61] These inflated costs motivated migrants who may have previously returned home after encountering low-wage, high-risk, insecure employment in US labor markets to remain longer to justify the migratory sacrifice and debts incurred. Like Miguel, as they prolonged their stays in the United

States, some of their emotional and financial ties to their families back home frayed.[62]

Even so, until relatively recently, the majority of US immigration enforcement resources were targeted at the US–Mexico border, with the chance of apprehension declining once immigrants settled in the interior.[63] However, a suite of laws in the 1980s and 1990s set the stage for interior and workplace immigration enforcement operations to intensify by the mid-2000s. The Immigration Reform and Control Act (IRCA) of 1986 imposed potential criminal and civil penalties on employers who "knowingly" hired authorized workers, but as described in Chapter 1, IRCA's loopholes and selective enforcement cast the burden on workers instead.

Under IRCA, employers have wide leeway to deny their complicity to use this information against workers. First, the IRCA did not prevent employers from accessing undocumented labor; rather, it incentivized them to shift hiring practices to ensure compliance and claim plausible deniability.[64] Employers increased their reliance on labor subcontracting, which allowed them to enjoy the benefits of unauthorized labor while they could distance themselves from the legal risks and responsibilities of being the employer of record.[65] IRCA ushered in a wave of documentation falsification, especially because employers could avoid punishment by claiming a good-faith effort instead of actually scrutinizing the veracity of the documents.[66] Miguel relied on false documents to work for the roofing company.

Yet the stakes of working without documentation or with false papers escalated in the late 1990s as a result of legislation that increasingly attached criminal consequences to unauthorized immigrant conduct and work-seeking practices.[67] The passage of the Illegal Immigration Reform and Responsibility Act and the Antiterrorism and Effective Death Penalty Act in 1996 intensified the mandate and funding for interior immigration enforcement, including measures that enabled local law enforcement to participate in immigration policing, merged the criminal justice and immigration systems closer, further curtailed avenues to adjust legal status or pursue removal relief, expanded categories of noncitizens who were considered deportable, and increased the range of offenses for which individuals could be deported.[68] Closer collaboration between local law enforcement and Immigration and Customs Enforcement (ICE) added the threat of what Sarah Horton calls "denounce-ability" to the fear of deportation.[69] Unauthorized immigrants feared not only deportation or losing their jobs for working without papers or procuring false documents but also possible incarceration.[70]

The enforcement of these laws took on renewed vigor after the terrorist attacks of September 11, 2001, as interior immigration enforcement was enmeshed into directives to address national security and received a massive resource infusion.[71] In 2002, the Immigration and Naturalization Service (INS) had an all-time-record budget of $6.2 billion,[72] but the Department of Homeland Security's (DHS's) funding reached $64 billion by 2016 with roughly half dedicated to immigration law enforcement.[73] In the mid-2000s, states and localities across the United States devised their own anti-immigrant laws and ordinances, many of which took advantage of components of the 1996 laws to equip local law enforcement to target unauthorized immigrants.[74] Whereas interior apprehensions represented 10 percent of all apprehensions in 2002, they climbed to constitute almost 50 percent by 2011.[75]

Immigration enforcement operations and the racialized policing of immigrants began to menace more deeply inward.[76] Since the mid-2000s, interior enforcement began to pose more ramifications for immigrants' daily and work lives, including a rise in home raids, workplace inspections and raids, and silent workplace raids—or the preventive implementation of Social Security no-match letters[77] and biometric technologies like E-Verify to verify employment eligibility.[78] The implementation of Secure Communities in 2008 (suspended in 2014 but restarted in 2017), which facilitated digital information sharing between local jails and ICE, further surveilled immigrants and made them hesitant to interact with law enforcement, collaborate with the criminal justice system, and even report crimes.[79]

The inward seepage of immigrant policing did not prevent immigrants from working, but it restricted their employment opportunities, infused fear into their workplaces, and pushed employment further underground to some of the least protected sectors of the labor market.[80] The fear of immigration consequences disciplined immigrants' conduct in the workplace by discouraging them from reporting violations and raising labor and safety concerns, which has undermined labor rights organizing in industries that employ significant populations of the unauthorized more broadly.[81] Some employers wielded tools like E-Verify and no-match Social Security letters to illegally threaten or fire workers, interrupt labor and safety investigations, and deter organizing in the workplace.[82] Unauthorized immigrants like Miguel started to worry that working with false documents could invite felony charges of identity theft and possible incarceration,[83] or they were relegated deeper into informal markets where such documents were not requested but workplace violations abounded and were more difficult to monitor.[84]

The economic contraction and racialized anxiety provoked by the Great Recession also strengthened the impacts of interior immigration enforcement for unauthorized Latino immigrants. Post-9/11 discourses that construed racialized men as objects of terror, combined with displaced economic anxieties from the Great Recession, conjured the fear of the criminal, jobless Latino man.[85] As the Great Recession entrenched more low-wage Latinos into precarious work late in the first decade of the 2000s, racialized interior immigration policing intensified in tandem fashion.[86] In 2008, employers in Colorado began to more widely adopt E-Verify technologies to screen employment eligibility. Claudio pointed to a CrossFit studio across the street from the Federal and 19th *liebre,* where a temporary employment agency once stood. It didn't matter, he noted, because after E-Verify, it was no longer an option. Another day laborer, who previously alternated day labor with stints at restaurants and temp agencies and in janitorial services, remarked of the altered employment landscape, "You can't even clean a toilet at Walmart anymore."

Latino male day laborers, because they wait in the open for informal work, are a particularly visible and vulnerable scapegoat for criminal and economic anxiety.[87] Centro and day laborers have frequently become targets for local anxieties around race, immigration, and "illegality." For example, in December 2005 the US House of Representatives passed the Border Protection, Anti-Terrorism, and Illegal Immigration Control Act (also known as the Sensenbrenner bill after its sponsor, Wisconsin Republican representative Jim Sensenbrenner), which would have more aggressively criminalized unauthorized immigrants, as well as organizations that assisted and served them.[88] The bill failed to pass the Senate, but in response, a wave of pro-immigrant organizing swept the country in 2006 and 2007 to demand immigrant rights.[89] However, the bill's failure also provoked intense anti-immigrant backlash, including states that passed their own anti-immigrant laws, a series of ICE workplace and home raids at the behest of the Bush administration, and organizing from vigilante groups. In Denver, Centro and day laborers were targeted by a Minuteman anti-immigrant protest in early January 2006. However, Minsun Ji, Centro's founder, had received a warning from NDLON. In response, Centro gathered over 150 allies to demonstrate support and counteract the small numbers of vigilantes who showed up.

Miguel was not unique in considering a return to Mexico as he found his options increasingly constrained. Due to changing demographic trends in Mexico (notably falling fertility rates) and the impacts of the Great Recession on reducing the pull for labor migration, new arrivals from Mexico began to drop after 2006.[90] For a decade, more Mexican immigrants were leaving than coming to the United States, a trend that began to turn positive again only from 2013 to 2018 but was still below earlier decades.[91] Still, the total number of Mexicans residing in the United States fell from 2007 to 2019.[92] Meanwhile, precarious work, life, and social relationships were interwoven. Miguel hung onto his relationship of convenience for companionship and to stave off homelessness.

UNSTABLE WORK: DAY LABORERS, SUBS, AND BROKERS

Although the residential construction industry is stratified by race, citizenship, and skilled and unskilled workers, workers do not necessarily occupy stable positions or lack mobility. They may be hired as day laborers on one job, independent contractors on the next, and sometimes act as subcontractors on others.[93] Because labor contracting arrangements pass off labor costs and responsibilities down the chain, workers at the bottom of the market weigh complex ethical decisions as they navigate and attempt to move out of contingent work. In doing so, they risk preying on their own more vulnerably positioned social networks.

Most day laborers relied solely on day labor for income, but others varied day labor with other on-and-off jobs with small firms, repeat employers, or small subcontractors. Many found jobs through their extended kinship and social networks. Workers referred to these jobs as more regular employment, but frequently they were anything but that. They were often back at the corner between contracts for supplemental income or when inclement weather led regular bosses to not call them for periods of time. One man explained that he held two relatively regular jobs in the summer in gardening and remodeling, but in the winter, he returned to the corner. Other men at the corner would approach us to inform us that they got a regular job, implying that we would be unlikely to see them on our next visit. These might be stints with a previous boss or even for a new company, but this work was often temporary. A few months later, we reencountered many of these same individuals back on the street looking for work.

Moreover, employment with small firms or contractors, or even owning a small business, was not much more stable. These regular jobs usually did not pay enough or offer sufficient security to rule out day labor. Or, given the unregulated nature of the residential construction sector, their working conditions looked a lot like day labor. Workers were summarily fired for having disagreements with employers, suspicions of drinking on the worksite, or simply when jobs ended. Many had frequent and unexpected unpaid days off. Or their regular jobs simply did not pay enough despite long, regular hours. One man explained that he had a "fixed construction job" Mondays through Fridays, but came to the corners on Saturdays for additional income. Some men who claimed they held regular jobs actually met their bosses at the corner to pick them up for the day. But sometimes their employers never arrived. Others had to call their employers to find out if they had work that day. If not, they went to the corner. One man told us that he had arrived at the corner at 8:00 a.m. that morning, but he wasn't looking for work. He was waiting for his *patrón* [boss] to call him to tell him what the work arrangement was and pick him up. But it was already late morning with no word.

Small subcontractors also suffered unpredictable work. When agreements with contractors dried up or projects ended, they attempted to string together multiple jobs and pursue relationships with other contractors. Because many small subs are also immigrants (some are also undocumented), they may work for an array of contractors and even other subcontractors without the security of a written contract. They had to fill out invoices, file taxes, and pay their workers regardless of their own instability. One subcontractor, for example, was still pursuing a month's wages from his regular contractor. He was trying to move on, but struggled to find new contracts because he had invested over a year working with the same contractor.

Some day laborers became, or occasionally performed roles as, labor brokers and subcontractors. When they got to know contractors and subcontractors and developed experience, these contractors began to rely on them to recruit other workers, who were often members of their social networks or fellow day laborers. Some workers tried to open small businesses to manage these relationships. When I asked Otilio at the Federal and 19th *liebre* how these arrangements worked, he asked to borrow a sheet of paper from my notebook. He drew a circle with radiating lines to illustrate contracting arrangements: "So a homeowner will contact a contractor because they want a fence. They say how they want the fence to be built. That person then arranges for various people," he continued as he outlined more radiating spokes. Perhaps, I wondered, these were the subcontractors? Otilio continued:

> [The contractor] arranges to pay that person for the job and then that person is responsible for bringing people by the hour or day to work. They will say, go and get these many people. . . . Sometimes [the contractor] gives them half [the money] before the job and half afterward. Then [these individuals] are responsible to pay [the workers] out of the money they get from the contractor. The contractor employs a lot of people like this to bring their own people because they [have many projects going on].

As Otilio explained, it was clear how the fissured workplace operated as the lines emanating from the circle multiplied and in turn had their own sub and sub-sub radiating spokes. These constellations made identifying the responsible employer, or even the individuals involved in the work process, more difficult the farther one traveled from the original node. Still, it was an arrangement to which he and many others aspired in order to achieve more control over their working arrangements and earn more money.

The racial segmentation of the residential construction industry and its reliance on referrals and informal recruitment means that subs, labor brokers, and workers often share social and kinship networks. Workers may therefore be exploited by the family members and social connections they relied on to get these jobs, who are frequently little better off than they are. Nico's experience demonstrates how day laborers can convert into subs, which positions them in troubling binds between their employers and their peers. Even as lower-tier subcontractors acquire more responsibility, they may attain little economic gain from these arrangements as they incur greater liabilities.

Nico migrated from Michoacán, Mexico to the United States in 1983. After twelve years in California, he came to Colorado because he heard there was more work. An employer recruited him at Federal and 19th with other men for a cement job, but none of them got paid the $2,000 owed them. Nico complained, "I spent money on materials and everything, and I didn't get my money. I want them to pay me because I put a lot of work into it."

When individuals like Nico are asked to bring their own materials and recruit other workers, they acquire more control over the work and can earn more; they may be paid a portion up front and the remainder on completion. But they also run more risks. Employers may claim that individuals in Nico's position are subs or brokers and thus charge them with responsibility over the workers although these employers still exert control. Based on these realities of control, the law stipulates that all of these workers including Nico should be considered employees. Yet employers deliberately muddle these arrangements to offload responsibility. The three men whom Nico recruited were friends of his, and he was unable to pay them. Nico saw himself as one of the several men who got cheated, but he also felt terrible that he owed money to his friends.[94]

Higher-up contractors who orchestrate such deals try to outsource their responsibility for workers by delegating it to subcontractors and even workers like Nico, who do not understand and are unlikely to question the legality of these arrangements.[95] Even when it is clear that the subs and contractors who make these arrangements should also be held responsible as employers, enforcement agencies rarely extend these liabilities.[96] Matthew Capece with the Carpenters Union argues that these arrangements disproportionately delegate risk to and incentivize the proliferation of labor brokers such that "the failure of accountability for the upper-tier contractors has given oxygen to the growing adoption of the labor-broker model."[97] Meanwhile, Nico not only felt responsible for the men who did not get paid, but he also became the face of this exploitation to his peers. Further down the chain, his peers probably did not know who hired Nico, let alone who hired that sub and so on. To these workers, the subs, brokers, or even fellow workers like Nico are "the boss." They come to embody the blame for violations deflected down the contracting chain's lowest rungs.

The segmentation of the residential construction industry by race, national origin, and citizenship imbues labor contracting arrangements with a racialized dimension that sets workers against one another. Miguel told us he had the most problems "with the *puros patrones Mexicanos* [just the Mexican employers]." He added, "La *misma raza*" [the same race] takes advantage of you." Because day laborers are more likely to directly work for labor brokers or subs, who are also more likely to also be Latino, race animates their perceptions of exploitation. Claudio concurred: "The Mexican screws over his fellow Mexican."

Legal status is also weaponized to squeeze profits down the chain. I followed up to ask Claudio why he thought that Mexicans were more likely to exploit other Mexicans. He laughed at my question: "It's difficult. I don't have papers. But what would happen if tomorrow morning I had papers and I became a *patrón*?" "Wouldn't you sympathize?" I asked. He responded, "You would think people would, but they don't. They don't consider [this] and want to get ahead themselves. . . . Mexicans are the people who work the most, Mexicans without papers work the hardest . . . are the most desperate. Necessity makes one this way. It is difficult."

Workers frequently lamented that their own slightly better-positioned social networks knew best how to exploit them in a segmented industry that exerts pressure downward. Doussard notes, "Immigrant workers often escaped the uncertainty of construction employment by converting themselves into labor barons" whose own mobility comes with "exercising a position of power over their peers."[98]

In contrast, day laborers had less exposure to higher-up contractors, who were more likely to be white and Anglo. They usually had scant knowledge of the employment chain beyond the person who hired them. When day laborers worked for gringos, glossed as white and US-born, these arrangements were less likely to be influenced by labor contracting—for example, when they were directly recruited by homeowners. However, day laborers often attributed these less exploitative relationships to race instead of the employment arrangement. When problems occurred, they were more likely to excuse the behavior of gringos. Miguel told me about an incident when a white woman underpaid him $50. He excused her behavior as an honest mistake: she had just counted wrong. Eventually the woman paid him an additional $30 after the staff at Centro brought up the issue the next time she came in to hire workers. Miguel defended the woman: "But I don't think it was intentional. It was an accident. As I told you, I don't have anything bad to say about the Americans. They have always paid me well."

Workers' racialized assessments of exploitation obscured the workings of labor contracting and encouraged them to replicate these exploitative structures as they depressed their own social networks. Yet these explanations insulate the roles of construction firms, investors, developers, and contractors in structuring these conditions and setting industry norms and expectations. Larger contactors, homeowners, and developers may be unaware of unscrupulous practices occurring down the employment chain, but they largely operate to their benefit while they make it difficult for honest small-level operators to compete. Even when other industry players claim not to know about these practices, there are clear red flags. Many developers told students, for example, that they were suspicious when subs listed no employees on their records.

Through pervasive labor contracting, risks are concentrated and profits whittled down—they may even completely vanish—along the industry's outermost spokes. Absent creative legal detective work and policies explicitly designed to target this problem, it is difficult to hold higher-up subs and contractors accountable for violations down the chain. These arrangements are not merely a matter of workers versus employers or even consumers, but instead index a climate where many businesses cannot survive.

CONCLUSION

When Marco Nuñez, a former director of Centro, went to street corners to engage workers in know-your-rights chats, he frequently began by pointing to the numerous cranes hovering at the horizon. The cranes signposted the rapid pace of construction enveloping the city. For Marco, this landscape signaled urgency:

> Because I knew it [wage theft] was happening, and each crane represented maybe 50 or 100 different contractors. They are not all violators, of course, but the exposure we had [through Centro] and the kinds of

> employers we had seen commit wage theft. . . . [This] led me believe that a lot of growth in Denver . . . from hotel rooms and corporate buildings, private homes, pop tops . . . rapid construction left and right. On one side you look at it as progress, but I interacted almost every day with people with stories of wage theft.

The skyline left Marco with a nagging question: Progress for whom? Many people driving into Denver might see fifteen to twenty cranes along the skyline as progress, but he saw wage theft.

Colorado's postrecession construction boom was clearly not for immigrant day laborers. A postrecession recovery was elusive to immigrant and workers of color more broadly across the United States.[99] The "jobless" postrecession recovery was more acute for minority, immigrant, and precarious workers.[100] Instead, Latino low-wage workers experienced rising unemployment, deteriorating wages, and overall declines in their wealth, which channeled more people into precarious work.[101] Rising racialized interior immigration policing exacerbated economic contraction and a stalled recovery to root more low-wage Latinos like Miguel and Claudio into contingent work with "more exploitative work arrangements."[102] One day laborer told graduate student Sarah Johnson about the recovery: "The economy is for them [employers, homeowners], not for us."

The mixed-use buildings going up around Centro, duplexes displacing workers like Hermelindo, and the proliferation of build-to-rent homes developed by out-of-state real estate firms are profitable for investors and lure lifestyle migrants and retirees to Colorado from other states.[103] But they make housing increasingly unaffordable for most Coloradans. Redevelopment and its twin racialized process of cleaning up urban blight are reminiscent of the Skyline Urban Renewal plan. Over half a century ago, Denver took advantage of federal dollars available through the US Housing Acts of 1949 and 1954 aided by "eminent domain to condemn 'blighted' areas of the city . . . to revitalize downtown areas" and to reverse white flight to the suburbs.[104] These efforts contributed to what some called the progress that converted Denver's downtown into gleaming office skyscrapers, parks, and condos, whereas working-class and minority communities experienced displacement that "reinforced . . . entrenched patterns of racial segregation" and destroyed historic parts of their communities.[105] The

Denver Urban Renewal Authority, the same agency behind earlier renewal drives, describes current commitments to urban revitalization, historic preservation, "responsible growth," and affordability, but housing supplies remain tight, prices to own and rent high, and affordable housing severely undersupplied.[106]

Industry pressures to control costs also became accentuated in the post-recession period. Students who interviewed contractors and developers in spring 2015 learned that contractors' profit margins were slimmer and more uncertain. Construction expenses increased amid the labor shortage, and smaller operators needed to keep costs down to win contracts in a competitive field. Because the industry is sensitive to boom-and-bust cycles, "when business booms, contractors overextend themselves to make up for the fallow periods."[107] One representative of a large construction firm commented, "Since the recession . . . budgets are very tight . . . fees are down . . . it has become super competitive . . . and time frames are very tight." The representative clarified, "Owners' fees . . . we used to build in, maybe a 6 to 7 percent profit fee into our bid . . . now we're lucky if we get away with 2 to 3 percent. . . . You have to do more work to make money." He then cited a postrecession effect, "After that recession . . . it's not like the recession is over, so the fees went back up. The owners are like, 'Oh no, why would I do that now?' "[108] Consumer confidence in retail construction also declined from 2008 to 2011, which decreased the amount of available investment.[109] Small contractors and subcontractors faced more difficulties competing with larger firms in a low-margin climate. As Gleeson notes, when contractors aggressively underbid one another to win contracts, "that leaves labor costs as the primary savings and profit-generation mechanism."[110]

In a state like Colorado with weak union representation and an industry that already heavily relied on subcontracting, contractors came to depend more on labor brokers and low-cost subcontractors to respond to increased market volatility.[111] When wages fall too low to attract the industry's traditional workers, employers have often turned to recruiting workers willing to work for less, like unauthorized immigrants[112] Day laborers could not leverage the labor shortage and construction boom to their advantage because small-level operators tend to seek them out precisely for their willingness to do almost any job at low cost.[113]

According to union representatives and worker advocates, labor brokerage arrangements seemed to accelerate after the recession. Brokers could operate with "little more than a cell phone and a $40 business registration from the Colorado Secretary of State."[114] Brokers may supply workers to ten to twenty different contractors at once with little scrutiny. The name painted on their truck may not even be a registered entity. Many individuals we investigated with the Direct Action Team had businesses that the Colorado Secretary of State website listed as delinquent or defunct, but they operated anyway. Or they simply rebranded, operated under different names, or opened new enterprises.

Enforcement in Colorado's construction industry was notably farcical until recently. According to attorney-scholar Matthew Fritz-Mauer, who interviewed Jeff García, executive director of Denver Labor (nested within the Denver Office of the Auditor), a lawless atmosphere of willful ignorance was all but greenlighted by the government before Timothy O'Brien became the new Denver auditor in 2015 and brought on García.[115] The prevailing wage laws hadn't been updated in over half a century, and not much was being done to enforce newer provisions. Because the office checked certified payrolls only every fourth week, García learned that employers had caught on and were out of compliance "three out of four times."[116] Fritz-Mauer told me, "It is no wonder people were getting cheated . . . there was no willingness to take a look." After modernizing systems, rewriting and updating the prevailing wage law, and boosting staffing, Denver Labor collected a whopping $701,787 in O'Brien and García's first year compared to $85,000 the year prior.[117] In addition, Colorado is not an Occupational Health and Safety Administration (OSHA)–approved plan state, which refers to states that conduct their own workplace health and safety enforcement and are generally more comprehensive, stringent, and sensitive to local needs than federal coverage alone, which complements a climate that deprioritizes workplace oversight.[118]

The structure of residential construction means that booms have rarely benefited the most vulnerable workers.[119] Day laborers suffered from the same pressures that contractors and subs faced to speed up work, keep costs down to compete for projects, and deskill work, pushed downward in the form of aggravated risk and workplace violations. Instead of being able to negotiate higher wages or more regular work, day laborers remained valuable to the most demanding and insecure jobs precisely because of their willingness to work and the heightened discrimination and anti-immigrant sentiment that accompanied the recession's economic anxieties and its aftermath.[120] Construction held the largest share of violations of the Fair Labor Standards Act (wage and hour violations) in Colorado since 2007 (as of 2014), accounting for 21.1 percent of violations.[121] It is within this context that advocates like Marco saw extensive wage theft, the subject of the next chapter, as a natural consequence of the boom.

3 DREAMING FOR FRIDAY

How Employers Steal Wages

You might work with someone for a few weeks and then they don't pay you for the next week. You might work with them for a few days and then on the last day, they just won't pay you. And what can we do? They take advantage.

—*Day laborer at Dayton and Colfax*

BERNAL WAS LOOKING FOR WORK at Centro Humanitario para los Trabajadores (Centro) when an employer came in to hire him for a job.[1] The employer drove him to Colorado Springs, nearly seventy miles away, for a construction project. Bernal worked from nine in the morning until eight at night, but when the workday was finished, his employer didn't pay him. The employer told him, "I will come back to pay you tomorrow. I didn't bring money to pay you." But as many workers fear when they are taken for long-distance work, the employer abandoned him in the parking lot without a ride home. Bernal resisted his employer's excuse. How else would he get home? He confronted his employer: "No, you will pay me now or I will take your car. One or the other. If you come tomorrow, give me the money and there won't be any problems [and I will return your car]." The employer relented and gave Bernal a check. But when Bernal tried to cash the check, it bounced. Bernal was then stuck with a bounced check fee from the bank.

Bernal called the phone number on the check to inform the employer that the check had bounced. He insisted that the employer pay him or he would call the police to investigate his business. Bernal had learned from others who had worked with this employer in the past that the employer didn't have insurance or even a contractor's license and he also owed other workers thousands of dollars. Once the employer realized that Bernal knew this information, he implored him not to contact the police and promptly deposited money into his account. The employer told Bernal that he wanted him to be the first to cash his check, referring to the many workers to whom he owed wages. Otherwise he feared that Bernal would cause him further problems.

Bernal's experience demonstrates the many ways employers attempt to cheat day laborers out of their earned wages. Employers may strand them far from home, promise to pay later, argue that they were not paid, or issue bad checks.[2] Other employers misclassify workers as independent contractors, dismiss responsibility for employing them, or even try to make workers responsible for their fellow workers, as in Nico's case in the previous chapter. Because day laborers lack written contracts, employers offer facile excuses to avoid payment; they claim the work was subpar or done incorrectly, change the nature of the job, or claim that workers did not complete all tasks. When employers hire workers off-the-books for cash, they may try to claim they never hired the worker at all. If workers complain, some employers threaten to report them to immigration or tax authorities.

Employers tend to excuse wage theft as an accident or an accounting error. However, this chapter shows that wage theft is frequently an intentional and patterned practice that becomes a way of doing business across many low-wage industries. Wage theft is conditioned by, as it also reinforces, multiple aspects of precarity that ripple through low-wage immigrant workers' social lives. I show how the myriad forms of exploitation that workers endure extend beyond wage theft to encompass other forms of harmful and humiliating employer mistreatment that may be a consequence of, prelude to, or independent of wage theft. As such, wage theft may point to but also fail to address other abusive labor practices, especially those that fail to reach any legal threshold. Despite the significant impact of wage theft on day laborers, the chapter concludes by exploring why rates may not be as high as expected.

WAGE THEFT IN DAY LABOR MARKETS

Many industries are vulnerable to wage theft, but it is especially pervasive in day labor, contingent, and low-wage markets. The National Day Labor Survey (NDLS) documented that about half of day laborers nationwide had experienced at least one pay-related violation in the week prior to being surveyed.[3] Other studies found similarly high exposure to wage theft. In a survey of 304 Latino day laborers in New Orleans, 78 percent had experienced wage theft in the prior year,[4] and about 50 percent had suffered wage theft in a study of day laborers in New York City,[5] as well as in a study conducted with day laborers in New Jersey.[6] The Workers' Defense Project highlighted that, from a sample of nearly two thousand construction workers across five large Texas cities, more than one in five workers had experienced wage theft.[7] The unregulated, competitive, and informal nature of day labor hiring, combined with the fact that the majority of day laborers are undocumented and wary to complain, provides employers with assurance that they can take advantage of workers with little accountability or record.[8]

Marco Nuñez, Centro's former director, frequently began his outreach chats to day laborers with the following statistic: "7/10 day laborers experience wage theft." His goal was to engage workers in conversations about their experiences to stimulate strategies to organize among themselves. One day when I accompanied him to the hiring site at Federal and 19th, he asked, "Has anyone been a victim of wage theft?" A few men raised their hands; one ironically smirked, "Almost all of us." Workers frequently echoed the extent of the problem. One explained, "Out of the ten of us you see waiting here, maybe three of us will not get paid today." Of 393 day laborers surveyed, 68 percent had lifetime experiences with wage theft, and 19 percent reported at least one incident in the six months prior to being surveyed. These numbers were significant, but they raised the question, given other day labor studies and day laborers' perceptions of the problem, of why rates weren't even higher over the six-month recall period.

EMPLOYER TACTICS TO STEAL WAGES

Day laborers were aware of the methods employers used to try to cheat them. The next section explores these common strategies: (1) promising to pay later or stringing workers along on subsequent projects to forestall and deny payment, (2) stranding workers and changing the nature of the work, (3) misclassifying workers as independent contractors and arranging to make workers into the employers of other workers, (4) arguing that work was poor quality, and (5) claiming to have never hired the worker. As in Bernal's case, employers' machinations frequently intertwined as they drew on multiple tactics to deprive workers of their wages and dignity.

Promising to Pay Later and Dreaming for Friday

Manuel trusted his employer because he had worked with him previously and he had always paid him for each day of work, so he agreed when his employer suggested moving to a monthly pay schedule. When his employer failed to pay, Manuel blamed himself: "I never should have allowed him to pay me monthly."[9]

Promising to pay later was a recurrent theme that highlighted how employers commit wage theft and delay workers from pursuing unpaid wages. Employers take advantage of trust to stall or withhold payment, often by making workers think they will make good on their promises. These employers may begin a work arrangement by paying every day and treating workers well, as Manuel experienced. After they cultivate some trust, the employer may change the arrangement to pay weekly or bimonthly. As in Bernal's case, some employers claim they didn't bring sufficient funds or that they themselves were not paid. They may promise to pay the following week or even on the next job. These promises string workers along as employers gradually start shortchanging them amounts, only to eventually vanish. One day laborer explained, "[Employers] say they will pay weekly or give you a little and say they will pay later, but you can't trust that. There is no trust. In a rare case if you know someone very well you [may] agree to weekly [pay], but that is rare." Another worker chimed in: "You can never trust that. . . . Otherwise [the employer] may pay you a little bit, say they will pay the rest later and you keep working with them. [Then] at the end of the week, they leave or don't show up."

Employers' excuses that they cannot pay workers because they were not paid are not only legally invalid, but also hard to verify when workers have scant information about a larger project aside from the person who hired them. It is difficult to hold higher-up contractors liable when employers attempt to pass the blame down their subcontracting chains. In the construction industry, filing a mechanic's lien, a legal document that prevents a property from being sold, refinanced, or transferred until wage disputes are resolved, can be an effective tactic to hold more actors accountable because they zoom up the subcontracting chain to incentivize all stakeholders to address the problem. However, they generally require the assistance of an experienced attorney.

Employers' promises to pay later can easily mislead precisely because they encourage workers to believe that payment is forthcoming. Such manipulations can make it difficult for workers to prove that cases of wage theft are intentional or willful. Departments of labor tend to more actively punish willful incidents, and police take them more seriously. For example, the damages under Colorado's wage laws allow workers to collect 125 percent of their unpaid wages, and this increases 50 percent for violations considered willful.[10] Workers may also delay submitting a complaint if they believe they will be paid soon.[11] Some employers pay a little at a time to dangle confidence, insisting they will make up the remainder when able. As the worker keeps working and the employer pays little by little, this arrangement generates continuous underpayment. In the most egregious cases, the employer never pays and disappears. Bernal was rightly wary when his employer promised to pay him tomorrow.

Ivan, "the jewelry man" mentioned in the Introduction, suspected such promises. He was forty-seven years old, originally from El Salvador, and had lived in the United States for twelve years. He came to Colorado in 2012 after spending time in Tennessee and Mississippi because he had heard that work there was more plentiful and wages were higher. He shared a two-bedroom apartment with six other men he had met at the Aurora corner. He had always been paid. Yet although he had never personally experienced wage theft, he was aware of the risk. He called a common mistake "dreaming for Friday," meaning that employers promise to pay at the end of the week and then disappear. He cautioned, "Some [workers] hold onto the dream for Friday," hoping that the employer will pay them for the entire week on Friday. But then when the employers fail to pay or even show up, "all is lost. There is nothing you can do."

Employers take advantage of trust, day laborers' lack of knowledge of a project's larger scope and contracting arrangements, and their desperation for work to string them along on subsequent projects. It can be difficult to evaluate whether the employer is telling the truth. For example, Rogelio had worked for his employer for three months and had always been paid well. Then on a condominium construction project, his boss failed to pay the workers for the last week of work. Rogelio believed that his boss did not pay him because his contractor had not paid him. Rogelio blamed both the contractor and his employer, stating that there "should have been a contract." After this incident, the employer kept approaching Rogelio to work with him again so he could pay him what he owed. "But, at that point," Rogelio reflected, "there was no longer trust." The employer still drove by the Aurora hiring site to look for Rogelio to entice him with more jobs.

When employers like Rogelio's claim that they cannot pay because they were not paid, this could be true. Vast subcontracting arrangements that squeeze labor down the chain not only incentivize this, but offer employers an easy excuse. It becomes difficult to know if employers are telling the truth and who to hold accountable. To make amends, employers may offer workers a job on the next project with a promise to make up the difference. The practice of employers' intentionally manipulating workers into performing more jobs in this fashion is called *kiting*. As employers string workers along on subsequent projects, they risk performing more unpaid work to the employer's advantage. Kiting can even make workers more invested in employers' promises. As Nik Theodore argues, the longer a day laborer has worked on a job, the more difficult it is for them to leave it, even as more unpaid wages accumulate.[12] A vicious cycle ensues whereby workers are more dependent on these employers because of the time and effort they have already put in when employment is scarce. If they keep working with these employers, they chance accruing more risk and unpaid wages.

Stranding Workers, Vague Arrangements, and Changing Work

The very insecurity of day labor inherently favors employers. The goal of a day laborer is not just to acquire paid work every day, but to have one job turn into additional jobs and, ideally, a longer contract or ongoing relationship. Day laborers strive to cultivate a list of repeat employers to increase the reliability of work and improve the chances that employers will request them to perform more jobs. The desire for more work motivates day laborers to curry favor with their employers, which may foster more transparent relationships and opportunities for more stability and mobility.[13] But this arrangement can also expose day laborers to exploitation through their willingness to accept suspect terms and take on additional tasks without the guarantee of commensurate compensation.[14] Day laborers may accept employers' requests to add tasks or redo work because they fear otherwise not "being paid for work they have already completed."[15] When workers are paid by the hour and given additional hours, it can be beneficial to take on extra jobs, but it can prove disastrous for workers who agreed to a daily fixed rate. For example, when Santiago was asked to repaint a house because the color reminded the homeowner of the neighbor's house, his boss never compensated him for the extra work. Workers may even be asked to perform tasks for which they lack experience or the necessary equipment, which exposes them to workplace accidents and bolsters employer excuses to avoid payment because the work was not done to satisfaction.

Although he didn't necessarily conceptualize what happened to him as wage theft, Bryan's case exemplifies how employers exploit day laborers' desire for more work by stringing them along and stranding them. In doing so, employers usurp not only day laborers' wages but also their time and dignity. Bryan and his friend were hired for a moving job and spent five hours loading a moving trailer. After they finished unloading at the storage facility, the employers asked them to follow in their own vehicle to another location to load additional boxes. They eagerly agreed to extend their workday for more hourly pay. But when Bryan and his friend attempted to follow the employers' vehicle, they quickly understood that the employers were trying to lose them: "How fast they lost us. . . . They disappeared." Bryan knew the name of the company that had hired them but had no other information: "Nothing. I can't call. I never asked for the phone number. The man just came to pick us up [for work]." It turned out that Bryan and his friend had actually been hired by a different man, who brought them to these employers and the moving site. This broker had also vanished.

Others, like Bernal, were left stranded at worksites far from home when employers refused to return them. We met day laborers who told us they originally came to Denver because an employer had brought them there from another state for a job opportunity but never took them back. They couldn't afford transportation home and stayed to find work.

Lack of contracts; vagueness about the extent, length, and nature of projects; and the subjectivity of evaluating work facilitate employers' excuses, including that the work was of poor quality or incomplete. As in Bryan's case, loose work arrangements may offer new opportunities for more work and to extend an employment relationship, but they also provide leeway for employers to rapidly change their minds, hold workers to unclear or impossible standards, and cut them loose.

Misclassification, Contracting, and Making Workers into Employers

Workers like Bryan, even for a discrete task like moving that could easily be negotiated between a homeowner and worker, often access employment through a host of intermediaries, as demonstrated in Chapter 2. Some employers attempt to offload their responsibilities informally, but others try to legally insulate themselves through a paper trail by convincing workers to sign 1099 agreements. These forms attempt to certify that workers are independent contractors who forego their rights as employees. Misclassification occurs when employers inaccurately classify their employees as independent contractors, which facilitates wage theft and obscures accountability. Because this subterfuge is extremely profitable, employers do not generally misclassify their workers inadvertently.

When employers classify workers as independent contractors instead of employees, they shirk the legal requirements demanded of employers under wage and hour laws.[16] Under these arrangements, employers are excused from paying minimum wage and overtime, as well as their contributions to workers' compensation, payroll taxes, and other insurance and benefit obligations.[17] In turn, workers classified as independent contractors forfeit their rights to these protections, including their coverage under wage and hour laws, as well as the right to form a union, antidiscrimination protections, and unemployment benefits.[18]

Misclassification in construction has become an epidemic. Just 7 percent of US workers are independent contractors, but 20 percent of independent contractors operate in the construction sector.[19] Potentially somewhere between 12.4 and 20.5 percent of construction workers are misclassified or employed under-the-table for cash.[20] Yet misclassification has spread to various industries, especially in the gig economy and service sector.[21] Misclassification harms not only workers. As a 2004 Harvard Labor and Worklife Program study found in Massachusetts, it also withheld about $152 million in income tax revenues and $35 million in unemployment insurance taxes, and it cost insurance companies $91 million in owed workers' compensation premiums.[22] Employers may accrue $6.2 to $17.3 billion from these cost-cutting practices.[23] An investigation by the Southwest Regional Council of Carpenters demonstrated how misclassification and tax fraud are pervasive and relatively unchecked in Colorado's construction industry, leading the former governor to initiate the Misclassification Task Force in 2018 to issue recommendations.

Departments of labor can investigate cases of misclassification, but guidance at the federal level has swung between different administrations,[24] enforcement is weak, and state guidance is often unclear.[25] The 2011 report of the Colorado Department of Labor and Employment (CDLE) to the Colorado legislature, combined with audits from 2009 and 2010, revealed that 14.2 percent of Colorado workers were misclassified as independent contractors, robbing the state of $167 million in income tax revenues and an additional $744,359 in unpaid unemployment premiums.[26] Construction was among the top five culprits, with "53.3% percent of employers misclassifying 20.1% of the total construction workforce."[27] Although Colorado passed the Misclassification of Employees as Independent Contractors Act in 2009, enforcement lagged. According to Jim, a representative from the Southwest Regional Council of Carpenters, the CDLE is supposed to issue a report on misclassification to the legislature every year. As of 2018, there had been zero prosecutions and no fines levied.

Such 1099 independent contractor forms rarely hold up to legal scrutiny because departments of labor tend to analyze the economic realities of control in an employment situation rather than merely accept what employers state on the forms. Yet workers rarely understand these forms or are aware that they have been misclassified. Even when these violations are enforced, penalties for misclassification are rarely sufficient to counteract the labor cost savings from continuing the practice.[28] For employers, misclassification continues to be relatively low risk and high reward.

It is challenging to identify and enforce misclassification because many abusive contracting practices occur entirely off-the-books when subs and brokers hire temporary workers for cash.[29] In these cases, creative 1099 paperwork is unnecessary. Jim explained, "But most of these guys [that labor brokers recruit] don't sign anything. If you're undocumented, what will you complain about? There is no record of you existing in the country anyway." Lack of worksite enforcement and underdocumented work arrangements lead misclassification, payroll and other kinds of related fraud, and wage theft to proceed in tandem.

Exploitation inheres among lower-tiered subcontractors, where there is fluidity between subs and labor brokers: both increasingly act as labor suppliers to contractors. Increasing tiers of suppliers, many of whom are unlicensed and technically have no employees, make them difficult to monitor and assess who is liable. Jim explained how such worksites operate: "You could have 100 people working under you, cash pay, and no one goes to the job site [to manage or oversee it]. The employer says I'm a two-person shop with subs, I don't have anyone who works for me and there is no one [with whom] to follow up." The chain stretches so far down that many subs have no books at all to verify and subs may classify the fifteen people working for them as independent limited liability companies (LLCs). This complicated structure makes it unlikely that any of these actors are traceable through a contractor or were ever documented at all. For subs who do not technically have any employees, and hence also evade payroll taxes and insurance premiums, labor become 100 percent profit. For these actors, it's not a big leap to not pay their nonexistent workers at all and assume the profits of their labor. Some employers may even have one roster of employees working on the books to maintain legitimacy while employing others informally.[30] When such unscrupulous practices become rampant in industries like residential construction, they alter the competitive field by making it possible to offer artificially low job bids.

One employer's written response to a CDLE wage claim submitted by an individual I call Damián exemplifies how employers use contracting arrangements to evade payment:

> It was not my business. I was also an employee. I also never got paid. I was a supervisor. . . . Mr. Damián has his facts wrong. Mr. Carlos Hernández was also my boss . . . owner of Construction Ltd. One of my

texts w/Damián states, "I do not have checks. They will bring them to my office around 7 . . . or I will pick them up. I will let you know." Why would I pick up checks if I am the one paying? Mr. Damian states I am going to drop off my W-9 on another text. I was not even working or supervising that property on [street name redacted]. I referred him to the supervisor Juan García and gave him his number. I just made the 2 parties work together. I never hired nobody because it was not my company. I referred him to Carlos and Pamela [Carlos's wife]. They did not pay me either nor Juan García and many other people.

She further typed after her handwritten response:

Here is my response even though I am NOT the employer. Also, I have other people that would like to make a statement in regards to Construction Ltd. They were doing the same kind of work like myself, we were working as supervisors for Construction Ltd.

Damián send [*sic*] me all his hours and I told him he was NOT in my crew to contact Juan García and gave him his number. I referred Damián to work with Carlos and Pamela not for my company but for Construction Ltd. Damián has been my friend for many years and I would not go out with him and he became very angry at me. He knew nobody got paid at that job. . . . I keep telling him to leave me alone because he would send me inappropriate messages. This is a personal matter he has against me. I am looking to get the texts from an old phone that I have so I can prove he is lying and prove that he is only showing part of the conversation he has deleted some messages where I explain that I am not his supervisor nor his employer. We all had our crew and they reported to each supervisor with hours and questions about pay. . . .

Pamela refused to pay Damián because he was working with no supervision. Damián would go and work at night time when the house was empty. He hired his nephew, Pamela told him would give him $25 for each person he brought to work with him but had to be experienced in carpentry and he brought his nephew that I did not know anything about until Pamela told me he was a kid and he was not going to pay Damián to do what he pleased. His nephew knew nothing about con-

> struction and Pamela was upset. That's all I know because he was not working in my crew and did not supervise him. I just referred him to Pamela because he was looking for work.
>
> If you need anything else from me please let me know. I will get statements from people to say it was NOT my company and we worked with Construction Ltd.

The response reveals the malleability of the term *employer*, which becomes subject to interpretation and contestation. When excuses extend all the way down and across fissured workplaces, avoiding blame is easy. Although employers frequently provide incentives for workers to recruit other workers, they use vague directives to defend not paying them.

Instead of complex contracting and legal maneuvers, employers who hire day laborers tend to use informal tactics to deny accountability (Figure 7). Ronaldo explained how employers attempt to transfer their responsibilities to other workers. He was hired by an individual whom workers at Federal and 19th called the "burrito man" because he frequently drove by the corner

FIGURE 7: Day laborers negotiating with an employer at the Federal and 19th hiring site. Photo by author.

selling burritos out of his van. The burrito man had approached Ronaldo a few days prior with another worker. Ronaldo expected to see him come to recruit more workers because his daughter was remodeling her home. Ronaldo, however, would not take the job: "I don't like the way he works; he doesn't work well." He had already worked for the burrito man on his daughter's home. He had promised Ronaldo $600 for work on one bathroom and $1,000 to remodel the other. At first, Ronaldo assumed that tools would be provided, but because the tools were not appropriate for the work, he brought his own the next day. But as the project progressed, the burrito man claimed there wasn't enough money to pay the workers. The man blamed his boss—in this case, the homeowner. He said that the homeowner no longer needed any work. Ronaldo knew the burrito man was lying because "the boss [homeowner] is his daughter." They still owed Ronaldo $30, and his tools were still at the worksite because he assumed he would be returning.

Larger problems soon surfaced for Ronaldo. When another man at Federal and 19th asked him if there was work on the project, Ronaldo agreed. He calculated bringing him along based on the work and wages he was promised. Because Ronaldo was undercut, he then owed the other worker $150 because he was supposed to pay him out of his portion. Worse, the burrito man passed the blame to Ronaldo. Ronaldo knew why the burrito man did not pay the workers directly: "They want to keep their hands clean." He noted that employers never seemed to mind if they brought more people to work and they often even requested it, but they never wanted the responsibility. We learned that Ronaldo had come to the corner only that day in hope of running into the burrito man to recover his money and his tools.

Denying Payment by Claiming Work Was Poor

Misclassification facilitates other tactics to commit wage theft, especially when employers offer excuses that they will not pay because the quality of work was poor. Employers rationalize that they had to use their own time, money, and additional supplies to fix mistakes or hire replacement crews. The classification of the worker matters in these instances because the quality of work is not a legally valid excuse to deny wages to an employee, although it may lead the employer to dismiss the worker. However, depending on the terms of the contract, this argument can hold more water for independent contractors. Alonso's case is instructive.

A contractor hired Alonso to paint some apartments at an hourly rate, but the contractor was actually an intermediary to a larger contractor's company. Alonso was working on just a few units of the apartment complex while a multitude of contracting arrangements like his likely existed across many aspects of the larger project. Alonso and his wife owned a small painting business, which they opened after years of experience so they could negotiate higher rates and gain more autonomy in the industry. The contractor liked Alonso's work, so he asked him to paint a remaining unit because other workers were running behind. Alonso agreed, but negotiated a higher amount to work as an independent contractor (instead of the hourly rate) because of his skill, experience, and sole responsibility for this unit. The employer concurred, but nothing was written down. It was a verbal agreement.

After completing the work, the employer agreed to pay Alonso only at the lower hourly rate. The contractor's excuse, a common one, was that the work quality was poor and he had to pay others to fix Alonso's mistakes. Nevertheless, he had hired Alonso for additional side jobs. So, why, Alonso asked, "did he keep asking me back for other jobs [if he did not like my work]?" For the subsequent jobs, the contractor refused to pay him anything. Alonso feared issuing a wage complaint because of his undocumented status and the flimsy record of the work arrangement. He had only a mix of promised hours, notes of the hours he worked, and a verbal agreement.

Contractors may coax workers into choosing to be independent contractors by offering a choice between a higher contracted wage and a lower employee hourly rate even when the actual work is the same.[31] Some individuals like Alonso favor these arrangements to earn more money and independence. While the higher payment for a contract can be tempting, employers realize substantial cost savings when they recategorize employees as independent contractors, cutting as much as 30 percent of their labor expenses.[32] The classification as an independent contractor also limits avenues for redress when employers fail to pay. Colorado wage and hour laws allow "employees" to collect additional damages on top of their unpaid wages when employers commit wage theft, but this process applies only to those designated as employees. This specification means that independent contractors are not covered under the wage laws, which means that even if they take their employer to court to recover unpaid contracts, they are deprived of the Wage Act's penalties. Without penalties, even if workers win, they merely get what they were owed in the first place—often many months later. Marco called this "an interest-free loan," which does little to deter employers from violating the law.

Meanwhile, unwritten contracts and power discrepancies make it easy for employers to change their terms and withhold payment by subjectively claiming that the quality of work was subpar. As one worker told student Kendra Allen, "The boss will say good job, good work the whole day and then at the end of the day complain that it wasn't done well enough and not pay the entire amount [promised]." In Alonso's case, his undocumented status provided his employer with extra insurance that he was unlikely to complain.

Denying Payment by Erasing the Worker

In some cases, employers claim to have never hired the worker at all. In Colorado, employers are legally required to maintain payroll records for at least three years. In fact, the legal burden rests on employers to prove that they *paid* the worker once a worker files a claim. However, many lower-tier subs and brokers keep no such records, have no license to operate, and are difficult to find in employment registries. Moreover, when individuals like Alonso are undocumented and hired off-the-books, there is no formal record of their employment. It is likely that neither the employer nor the worker leaves a clear paper trail, which enables employers to exploit nebulous arrangements to deny payment.

When workers, especially those who are undocumented, fear retaliation, some employers attempt to erase them altogether. Dominica, who worked cleaning houses, came to the Direct Action Team (DAT) for assistance with a wage case. She had worked for her employer for three years, cleaning homes every day except weekends, when she cared for her son. She often worked late shifts that required her to pay someone to watch her son after school. She usually cleaned three homes a day, each taking five to six hours and received only $30 or $40 per house. She suspected that she was being paid below Colorado's minimum wage and might even be owed overtime. However, because her employer always paid, she never complained.

One day Dominica's son came home from school with a note advising that there would be no school the next day. Unable to find child care, Dominica called her employer to request the day off. The employer told her that there was no work for her and proceeded to inform Dominica that she no longer worked for her. Her employer even tried to assert that Dominica had *never* worked for her. Dominica struggled to demonstrate that she had ever worked for her employer. She had only had an ongoing verbal arrangement, with no formal contract or record of her employment. Dominica was always paid in cash so she had no pay stubs or checks, so it was her word against her employer's. When Dominica tried to request more Supplemental Nutrition Assistance Program (SNAP) benefits for her US citizen child after she lost her job, her employer denied that she had ever employed Dominica, and her child's benefits were cut off entirely. Only after she recovered text messages from her employer did the Colorado Department of Human Services partially reinstate her assistance.

Despite the fact that the Immigration Reform and Control Act (IRCA) requires employers to verify employment eligibility prior to hiring, employers intimidate workers by requesting immigration paperwork (I-9 for employees or W-9 for third parties or independent contractors) or Social Security numbers after they have already performed the work. Legally, if employers do not verify this information prior to hiring, they are still required to pay for the finished work.[33] However, employers manipulate these legal requisites and unauthorized immigrant workers' fears to discourage complaints.[34] Because many unauthorized workers are employed off-the-books, it is all the more difficult to make themselves legible to labor agencies when employers fail to pay.[35] There is nothing to complain about.

In many instances, when workers asked their employers for payment after completing a job, their employers told them they would pay as soon as they furnished their authorization paperwork. But these employer requests are backward and not how the law is intended to work. Rather than an innocent error, employers use these requests to absolve themselves of their legal responsibility to verify employment eligibility prior to hiring. In doing so, they leverage immigrant workers' fear to deter complaints and cloak their own illegal actions by redirecting the legal risks at workers.[36] Some employers issue more direct threats to report workers who complain to immigration authorities. These forms of retaliation are illegal and could even invite felony charges, but such threats are rarely investigated or enforced. In this fashion, workers are compelled to play along as they are dragged further into employer delaying tactics in the hope that they may produce payment. For example, when employers make these requests of workers who are legally eligible to fill out employment authorization paperwork, DAT volunteers usually encourage them to comply because the goal is to "get the worker paid," although they recognize that employers are manipulating the legal requirements. Even if workers eventually receive payment, it is often much less than they were owed. On the other hand, workers who lack legal authorization and are unable to fill out these forms experience such belated requests as defeating or even threatening. The employer's responsibility to verify employment eligibility prior to hiring is thus deflected onto aggravated risk for the worker after they have already done the work. Workers' acquiescence to these manipulations then perpetuates employers' abilities to weaponize undocumented status to withhold payment and deny their own complicity.

In another case, in September 2018, Armando and Jacinta sought the DAT's assistance after they were not paid for painting work on a hotel alongside six other people. Armando was owed $7,300 and Jacinta $3,244. Although they sent a demand letter for their wages to their employer, Julio, he claimed the letter wasn't legal. Julio even called Armando before the court date. He threatened that he had hired a lawyer who was "really racist" and that ICE would be present. Armando still showed up, but Jacinta was afraid. The other six workers were also too fearful to attend court. They knew that Áxel, an associate of Julio, was recently deported. When they went to court, Julio did not actually have a lawyer. However, the judge gave the workers the runaround. The judge admonished them that they should have pursued Julio as an individual in court instead of his company, so the workers proceeded to serve Julio. Julio retorted that the workers could do as they wanted: he could just declare bankruptcy. Julio then pivoted to complain that his concern with paying the workers had to do with taxes. He worried that paying "illegal" workers would constitute tax evasion.

To get the workers paid, DAT volunteers proceeded to negotiate with Julio. They proposed to settle for a lower amount to avoid court, assuage Julio's tax concerns, and get the workers paid. However, Julio kept changing his story. He claimed that Áxel was responsible for paying Armando and Jacinta and that Áxel was actually a subcontractor, not his business partner. To avoid court, Julio finally agreed to settle but offered one rate if the workers produced work authorization papers and a lower rate if they did not. If they complained, he threatened to report them to the IRS for tax fraud. Armando and Jacinta made a counterproposal for an amount they were willing to accept that was lower than their owed wages but higher than Julio's paltry offer. Julio argued that if they went to court, he could probably still delay paying them for months. To further discourage them, he told them he had only $100 in his account and might declare bankruptcy. In January 2019, after months of negotiations and threats, Armando and Jacinta finally got paid $2,000 and $1,000 respectively, a fraction of what they were owed.

The intention of including unauthorized workers into US wage and hour protections, as well as IRCA's stipulations to verify work eligibility, is to deter employers like Julio from accruing a competitive advantage by exploiting immigration status to depress wages, deny payment, and suppress complaints. Instead, because of selective enforcement, workers' fears of deportation, and informal contracting arrangements, employers like Julio receive a perverse incentive to hold legal status and laws like IRCA over workers to silence their complaints and get away with wage theft.[37] He knew it was unlikely he would be held accountable.

Other Harms and Humiliations

Only a fraction of harmful employer actions are actually illegal. Wage theft is a symptom of the wider degradation of work, whereby low-wage workers are also subject to poor working conditions, low wages, enhanced disciplinary tactics, the entrenchment of insecure work, evaporating benefits and protections, and increasingly lopsided power relations between employers and workers.[38]

Many of the humiliations to which workers are subject have no legal remedy but are interconnected with their vulnerability to wage theft. Some individuals complained that their employers harassed them, hurried them, discriminated and berated them with racist remarks, and shoved them. Others mentioned employers who denied them time to rest or access to food and drink. Rafael, who was looking for work at Federal and 19th, explained that some employers mistreated workers by reprimanding them during the job to work differently, do more work, work faster, or even work more slowly, depending on if they were paying by the hour, day, or job.[39]

Rafael explained, "They yell something very ugly at you even though you are working . . . and working well . . . they want you to work in a different way. Because we don't speak English, many [workers stay] silent and don't really respond back."

Misclassification constitutes one of the most egregious forms of wage theft that laws often fail to capture fully. Attorney David Seligman explained that misclassification doesn't always result in wage theft in the ways we narrowly define it: when workers are not paid what they are entitled. A constricted lens can cloak wider harm and industry impacts, including altering the competitive playing field, evading tax and insurance obligations, and even antidiscrimination coverage and workplace safety requirements under OSHA. Most people are still technically employees, but what constitutes an independent contractor has become increasingly warped beyond its intentions and more challenging to monitor.

When DAT volunteers explored Dominica's case further, they grasped how the suffering she experienced did not fall neatly into wage theft. Yet once they accounted for her work and wages, volunteers realized that she was being paid minimum wage. Though her pay was low, her hours long, late, and unpredictable, and her employer's treatment callous, none of these actions constituted wage theft, and none were actually illegal. Her sudden dismissal was unfair, but it was hard to prove that firing her constituted illegal retaliation for lodging a labor complaint, which she had yet to officially make. There was nothing to be legally done about her unjust termination under at-will employment arrangements, whose assumptions allow employers to terminate workers for nearly any cause aside from a small subset of illegal discriminatory reasons.[40]

In the end, volunteers were uncertain if Dominica came to the DAT to recover wages, to contest her termination or her employer's harsh behavior, or because she hoped for anything that could help her and her son. How could she differentiate what was legal or illegal in the context of her unjust treatment—for which the legal system offered no solution and erased her in ways that enacted violent effects? This was the first time anyone had listened.[41]

Jesus, a paralegal at Towards Justice, mentioned that he unfortunately had to repeatedly let down clients because "it is not illegal to be mean to your workers." Dominica and many other immigrant workers "overestimate the laws covering them as at-will employees" in a legal system that recognizes only a narrow subset of the routine forms of exploitation that low-wage immigrant workers endure.[42] Meanwhile, lack of legal status subjects unauthorized immigrants to varying forms of exploitation, many of which are legal, accepted, and routine in low-wage industries.[43]

WAGE THEFT AND ITS IMPACTS

Wage theft exerts wider impacts that ripple inward and outward. It affects workers in the short, medium, and long terms when they are unable to pay rent, buy necessities, or send money home to family members. It also inflicts a broader assault on workers' dignity and sense of self beyond the dollar amounts lost. One man lamented not being able to send his daughter a birthday cake because he had not been paid. Others were rendered homeless when they couldn't pay roommates for rent portions month after month. For many individuals, wage theft spiraled to reinforce precarity in other aspects of their lives, creating a vicious cycle between underpaid and nonpaid work, housing insecurity, depression, poor health, susceptibility to injury, and substance abuse.[44] These compounding precarities impaired workers' abilities to regroup and find respectable work that offered decent wages and working conditions.

Wage theft is enabled by, but fails to fully capture, what day laborers in Ordóñez's study in the San Francisco Bay Area called "*la situación*"—the inextricable yet compounding impacts of precarious work and life. Day laborers in Denver referred to finding work on the street and risking wage theft as an ongoing struggle. One man reflected how this ongoing struggle led to his friend's descent into mental illness: "Logically . . . it was from so much suffering." He added, "I too have suffered all these years here. . . . It is pure struggle and struggle. We have to fight for everything."

Day laborers often attributed their vulnerability to a mixture of racial discrimination, unauthorized status, poor English abilities, and employers' power over them. Our survey attempted to assess if individual human capital, including English skills, experience in the United States, legal status, or education helped some day laborers improve their plight or whether the rugged contingency of day labor employment flattened the associated hazards. None of these distinctions mattered for income; only never being homeless, having a smartphone, and having spent less time in the United States were positively associated with higher earnings.

Time and experience in the United States can ostensibly help immigrant workers develop market knowledge and employer connections, learn to eschew risky employment, and negotiate for higher wages and better working conditions.[45] This reality was more complicated for contingent workers. Immigrant day laborers with longer tenure in the United States since first arrival (coded as twenty or more years) had lower exposure to wage theft in the past six months. Just 13 percent of day laborers who had been in the United States for twenty years or more reported wage theft in the past six months versus 34 percent of more recent arrivals (coded as zero to nine years since first arrival). However, despite the lower risk of wage theft, longer-duration immigrant day laborers had significantly lower overall earnings after controlling for work effort. Although these workers actually commanded a higher average hourly wage—perhaps because of accumulated street savvy—than more recent arrivals ($16.27 per hour versus $14.74), any benefit was cancelled out and reversed by their lack of work hours (see Table 1 in Appendix B).

Duration in the United States, in addition to providing immigrant day laborers with more experience to avoid bad employers and dubious work arrangements, was double-edged. It was unclear whether more recent arrivals worked more because they were more industrious and would perhaps successfully transition out of day labor, or perhaps employers saw them as willing to work for less. It is possible that longer-duration immigrant day laborers had been negatively selected to remain in day labor, which stymied opportunities for occupational mobility. Perhaps they had been particularly unsuccessful at garnering the kinds of social capital that proved valuable to leaving contingent work behind. Alternatively, the kinds of social capital they had at their disposal, resulting from work and daily lives beset by discrimination, neglected and racially surveilled neighborhoods, immigration enforcement, exclusion from basic services, and precarious work, might compound negative incorporation experiences and disadvantage over time.[46] More time in the United States could provide workers with more street smarts, but also posed potential liabilities if it meant becoming entrenched in and increasingly exposed to the indignities and insecurities associated with contingent work.

CONCLUSION

Before exploring the strategies day laborers draw on to prevent and seek redress for wage theft, it is necessary to consider why wage theft incidents were not higher given the extent of the problem in other national studies. Day laborers also perceived wage theft as a pernicious occupational hazard. Understanding workers' actual exposure to wage theft must be contextualized within an overall atmosphere of work scarcity and the trade-off between risky work and the desire for any work.[47] As depicted in the previous chapter, despite a construction boom, day laborers had low employment prospects. On average, owing largely to lack of work, the average day laborer earned an average of only $1,060 in a twenty-five-day work month. First, one has to work in order to have one's wages stolen. Day laborers in the Denver area may have had less exposure to wage theft because they were so unlikely to work at all.[48] Therefore, lower wage theft incidence was an insufficient indicator of vulnerability and economic insecurity.[49]

Wage theft is certainly indicative of labor precarity, but it fails to capture its full extent when insufficient work and income to subsist may be more pressing. It is the very nature of precarious work, which does not provide enough to withstand periods of uncertainty, that thrusts workers into a bind between needing to accept a good enough job and a potentially perilous situation, whether it be the risk of injury, wage theft, or both.[50] Mazen Labban argues that in low-wage industries, "workers are already cheated by earning wages below the value of their labor-power" that prevent them from subsisting and reproducing themselves before wage theft even occurs.[51] Given this context, the next chapter details how the opportunity cost of avoiding suspect employers and pursuing lost wages is further tilted by the potentially costlier decision to forego work.

4 A DAY WORKED IS A DAY PAID

Preventing and Confronting Wage Theft

Among individuals, as among nations, respect for the rights of others is peace.

—*Day laborer at Federal and 19th quoting President Benito Juárez of Mexico*

TO AVOID WHAT HAPPENED TO Bernal when his employer promised to pay "tomorrow," day laborers insist on being paid for each day of work in cash. A common dictum at the corner states that "a day worked is a day paid." The men grasp the risks of what Ivan called "dreaming for Friday": waiting for employers who promise to pay at the end of the week. They warn against accepting checks, knowing that a bounced check will place them on the hook for a corresponding bank fee. Day laborers have accumulated a tool kit of strategies to prevent wage theft largely as a result of their own experiences, conversations with other workers, and workshops led by Centro and other worker advocacy organizations.

Students met Juan, a nineteen-year-old man from Honduras, at the Federal and 19th hiring site.[1] He had been in the United States for three years when we met him in 2015 and he began to share his experience with wage theft and what he had learned. Eight months earlier, he had completed a ten-hour workday for an employer in Highlands Ranch, a Denver suburb. When they were returning to Denver, Juan told the employer he needed to pay his phone bill. The employer stopped outside a store so he could pay, but when Juan returned to the car, the employer, and Juan's payment for the workday, were gone. Juan recalled, "I didn't get his license plate, I didn't [even] know his name. . . . I had just gone to work with him." There was no way to pursue his money. He attributed his exploitation to his undocumented status, but he also saw the value of gaining experience.

Since this incident, Juan had learned strategies to avoid wage theft, including how to recognize when methods of payment appeared dubious: "And if they pay me badly, and it doesn't seem like a way of payment, well, I'm not going. . . . I will look for another job." He would no longer take any job with unknown conditions. Juan summarized what he learned: "When I first moved here, I'd go with [any employer]. . . . Not anymore. Now I have experience."

Juan learned how to prevent wage theft from experience and from fellow workers. Day laborers advised each other to request clear terms up front, insist on payment in cash at the end of each workday, work for known or repeat employers, get the employer's phone number, and take pictures of completed work. They warned each other about employers with bad reputations when they drove by the hiring site. However, none of these strategies offered assurance against exploitation when, by definition, day laborers are considered interchangeable as they compete in an unregulated, competitive market.[2]

This chapter traces the tactics that day laborers use to protect themselves, assesses their legal knowledge, and details challenges to outreach and organizing. It focuses on the difference between what day laborers know about preventing wage theft and their actual behavior when faced with troubling trade-offs. Workers weigh risky work propositions with the recognition that lack of work may be a bigger gamble. They make decisions among a variety of options including no action or tolerating the abuse, efforts to try to avoid future harm, and legal and nonlegal strategies to pursue unpaid wages.[3] Still, even when workers know their rights and are aware of protection strategies, they realize that they offer few guarantees in day labor markets. They are therefore circumspect about their ability to prevent wage theft and hesitant to organize with one another, entrust legal agencies, and confront employers for unpaid wages.[4]

HOW TO PREVENT WAGE THEFT

Pablo, originally from El Salvador, began to rely on day labor at the Dayton and Colfax corner in Aurora after the Great Recession. He used to work as a busboy in a restaurant near the affluent Washington Park Denver neighborhood, but he was let go during the crisis. He kept coming back to the corner because, he said, "I have become accustomed to it here." Pablo went on to tell us a story he had heard from four workers earlier that morning. These workers shared their story at the hiring site to warn others about their employer. They had spent two hours cleaning an apartment site and were promised $50 each. After work, the boss took them to the Wells Fargo bank on nearby Colfax Street so that he could cash a check to withdraw funds to pay them. He instructed the workers to go to the bathroom to wash up, but when they returned, the boss had vanished. Some of the men returned to the worksite to look for him, but according to Pablo, they couldn't do much: "The boss had left. . . . They couldn't find him when they looked for him." When I asked Pablo how workers could avoid wage theft, he responded like many others: "Take the employer's name and phone number . . . get paid for every day [of work] is a way to avoid it. Some say they will pay the end of the week or after a job . . . but that is dangerous. . . . You don't know so it's better to be paid *todos los días* [every day]."

Day laborers in the Denver area are relatively well versed in street corner strategies to avoid wage theft. The survey results echoed Pablo's list: get paid every day in cash and collect information on the employer. Figure 20 in Appendix B details how workers responded to the open-ended question that allowed for multiple responses: "What can you do to make sure an employer pays you?" Sixty-six individuals responded that they would only accept daily payment in cash, and eighty-seven mentioned gathering employer information, including a combination of the employer's contact information, information on the job site, or evidence of the work completed. Forty-eight respondents mentioned the need to get a written or verbal agreement to clarify the terms of work, and eighty-seven said it was important to assess the employer's reputation or to work only for known or repeat employers. For example, when the four workers told the other day laborers what happened to them, no one at the site would entertain offers from this employer. He had acquired a bad reputation. When day laborers attempt to blacklist employers, whether by yelling "don't go" or remaining tactically silent when they pass by, they simultaneously try to protect themselves and signal to employers that they cannot get away with exploiting workers. One worker at the Stout site put it this way: "So if cars stop here, we already know who pays and who doesn't. And so we'll yell, 'that guy doesn't pay!' . . . and so we run them out of here!" As we were talking, a man in a purple taxi drove by. Pablo mentioned that he came by a lot and was a contractor, but that no one would work with him because he had mistreated others in the past.

Judith, a former Centro employee, trained my graduate students on labor rights outreach. They began to assist Centro by conducting know-your-rights workshops at street corners to help workers prevent wage theft. Amy Czulada, a lead research assistant who also briefly worked for Centro after graduation, trained other students to conduct workshops using Judith's guide. The sessions were designed to prompt interactive discussions so workers could learn from and help one another.

Two to three mornings per week, we stopped by a coffee shop, calling ahead to ensure they had our carafe to fill with fresh donated coffee. Depending on day-old bagel donations for the week, we could have over 150 bagels or just a handful. Whether it was a day to spend time with workers and conduct qualitative interviews, survey workers, or provide know-your-rights trainings, upon arrival we gathered workers to introduce ourselves and explain our presence. Workers came to fill coffee cups and grab bagels, albeit repeatedly asking us why we did not bring doughnuts instead.

When they arrived to conduct trainings, volunteers gathered workers and began by asking, "What is wage theft [*robo de salario*]?" Before providing a definition, they waited for workers to give examples and then continued, "Raise your hand if it has happened to you," to encourage workers to see how many were affected, and they followed up with, "As you see, this is a big problem but you have rights! We also have information that can help you."

Volunteers then asked, "What can you do to prevent wage theft?" to stimulate workers to share strategies. We designed a small double-sided booklet that folded like an accordion and specified workers' wage and hour rights, minimum wage information, guidance on information to collect from employers, a list of resources to call if they were not paid, and a weekly grid to track hours and wages (Figure 8).[5] The bottom had a space for work-

KNOW YOUR RIGHTS; A JUST WAGE

HAVE YOU BEEN A VICTIM OF WAGE THEFT?

- Were you paid for the work done? Or are they only paying part of what you're owed?
- Did you make less than $9.30 an hour (as of Jan 1, 2017)? Or did you not receive payment for extra hours when you believe you should have?

What is wage theft?

Wage theft occurs when an employer does not pay the worker what the law requires. Examples of wage theft include payment for only part of what was agreed upon, payment for less than the minimum wage, non-payment of overtime, not providing lunch or breaks, and more. Wage theft is a crime!

Know your rights!

YOUR IMMIGRATION STATUS DOESNT MATTER, YOU HAVE LABOR RIGHTS IF YOU ARE EMPLOYED. ***The following may not apply in certain industries:***

- Minimum wage in Colorado is $9.30 per hour as of January 1, 2017
- Minimum wage for workers who work for tips is $6.28 per hour
- 10 minute breaks
- 30 min lunch break (without pay) after 5 consecutive hours of work
- After 40 hours of work in a week (or 12 consecutive hours in a day) you have the right to "time and a half"

Resources if you have not been paid or other problems in the work force:

ORGANIZATION	CONTACT	DESCRIPTION
Towards Justice	1535 High St, Suite 300 Denver, CO 80218 720-441-2236	**Legal services** organization that helps with wage theft. **Free or low-cost services**
Workplace Rights Projects	PO Box 372299 Denver,CO 80237 720-808-1231	If you need a lawyer for a wage theft case, discrimination, retribution in the work force, **were** laid off, or unemployment case.
Colorado Department of Labor and Employment Department of Labor Workers compensation	633 17th St. Suite 200 Denver,CO 80202 303-318-8441 633 17th St. Suite 400 Denver,CO 80202 303-318-8700	They have a claims process related to the Law of Minimum Wage, including overtime. Process workers claims, when the employer does not want to respond.
Centro Humanitario Para Los Trabajadores	2260 California St Denver,CO 80205 303-292-4115	They have an employment **program**, workshops on cleaning and other areas. Organizes the day labor community and domestic workers to exercise their rights.

KNOW YOUR RIGHTS; A JUST WAGE

HAVE YOU BEEN A VICTIM OF WAGE THEFT?

- Were you paid for the work done? Or are they only paying part of what you're owed?
- Did you make less than $9.30 an hour (as of Jan. 1, 2017)? Or did you not receive payment for extra hours when you believe you should have?

What is wage theft?

Wage theft occurs when an employer does not pay the worker what the law requires. Examples of wage theft include payment for only part of what was agreed upon, payment for less than the minimum wage, non-payment of overtime, not providing lunch or breaks, and more. Wage theft is a crime!

Know your rights!

YOUR IMMIGRATION STATUS DOESN'T MATTER, YOU HAVE LABOR RIGHTS IF YOU ARE EMPLOYED. ***The following may not apply in certain industries:***

- Minimum wage in Colorado is $9.30 per hour as of January 1, 2017
- Minimum wage for workers who work for tips is $6.28 per hour
- 10 minute breaks
- 30 min lunch break (without pay) after 5 consecutive hours of work
- After 40 hours of work in a week (or 12 consecutive hours in a day) you have the right to "time and a half"

Resources if you have not been paid or other problems in the work force:

ORGANIZATION	CONTACT	DESCRIPTION
Towards Justice	1535 High St, Suite 300 Denver, CO 80218 720-441-2236	**Legal services** organization that helps with wage theft. **Free or low-cost services**
Workplace Rights Projects	PO Box 372299 Denver,CO 80237 720-808-1231	If you need a lawyer for a wage theft case, discrimination, retribution in the work force, **were** laid off, or unemployment case.
Colorado Department of Labor and Employment Department of Labor Workers compensation	633 17th St. Suite 200 Denver,CO 80202 303-318-8441 633 17th St. Suite 400 Denver,CO 80202 303-318-8700	They have a claims process related to the Law of Minimum Wage, including overtime. Process workers claims, when the employer does not want to respond.
Centro Humanitario Para Los Trabajadores	2260 California St Denver,CO 80205 303-292-4115	They have an employment **program**, workshops on cleaning and other areas. Organizes the day labor community and domestic workers to exercise their rights.

FIGURE 8: Know-your-rights booklet. Version produced by Yessenia Prodero in coordination with the author and Centro Humanitario para los Trabajadores.

When you arrive at the work place, make sure to:

a. Ask in detail the work that you need to do.
b. Write down the address of the place you are working, the number, name and address of the company and/or the employer who hired you.
c. Evaluate the situation; you have the right to reject a job if you are not provided with the appropriate equipment or your health is in danger.

Its always better to be prepared

Date	Monday	Tuesday	Wednesday	Thursday	Friday	Saturday
Start time	8:00 am					
End time	5:00 pm					
Lunch	12-1 pm					
Total hours worked	8 total					

Employer information

Employer name: ______________________

Employer phone: ______________________

Company name: ______________________

Company number: ______________________

Address of the employer and/or the company:

____

Address where the work was done:

____

Wage agreed upon: ______________________

Always ask who is going to pay you.
Don't give employers credit.
A day worked is a day paid!
It **is** recommended to accept payment weekly or biweekly only if the work is permanent in a company where you filled out an employment application.

When you arrive at the work place, make sure to:

a. Ask in detail the work that you need to do.
b. Write down the address of the place you are working, the number, name and address of the company and/or the employer who hired you.
c. Evaluate the situation; you have the right to reject a job if you are not provided with the appropriate equipment or your health is in danger.

Its always better to be prepared

Date	Monday	Tuesday	Wednesday	Thursday	Friday	Saturday
Start time	8:00 am					
End time	5:00 pm					
Lunch	12-1 pm					
Total hours worked	8 total					

Employer information

Employer name: ______________________

Employer phone: ______________________

Company name: ______________________

Company number: ______________________

Address of the employer and/or the company:

____

Address where the work was done:

____

Wage agreed upon: ______________________

Always ask who is going to pay you.
Don't give employers credit.
A day worked is a day paid!
It **is** recommended to accept payment weekly or biweekly only if the work is permanent in a company where you filled out an employment application.

ers to write down employer contact information. Volunteers stressed that it was important to document everything and cautioned them to "not trust anybody." Discussions encouraged workers to ask who was going to pay—the homeowner, subcontractor, or contractor—and the mode of payment to prevent the pass-the-blame problem. The booklet warned, "Do not accept work from bosses with bad reputations" and "Do not trust an employer unless you know he is honest." As Juan learned, workers should not agree to just any job with unknown conditions.

When they do not have prior experience with a particular employer or verification from other day laborers, workers try to assess an employer's character from their initial interactions. However, because of the rapid and competitive nature of street corner hiring negotiations at the *liebres*, it is difficult for workers to ascertain an employer's true character. Although initial conversations are brief and ripe with linguistic challenges, employers' demeanor can signal how they may treat them on the job. One late April morning at the Dayton and Colfax *liebre*, a truck drove by and the driver yelled out that he needed workers—$80 for the day. Daily pay rates can be risky because they can lead employers to give workers more and more tasks and hours without additional pay. Elías noted after hearing the $80 offer, "I always ask, well, how many hours? [Maybe] if it is for eight hours, but for eleven or twelve? You always need to establish an agreement before you get in because if you don't get on well here, imagine what can happen when you go to work for them." Intuiting the employer's character can be bolstered by clarifying the terms of employment or establishing a verbal agreement. However, written contracts are largely unheard of in day labor markets.

Volunteers probed for examples of what makes a good employer, stressed the labor rights afforded to workers regardless of immigration status, and ended by discussing what could be done if an employer did not pay. They concluded:

> Wage theft is an epidemic that greatly impacts the day labor community. Because of this we must prevent and prepare ourselves the best we can. Also, although the process to recover wages is long, do not desist! Unite with your *compañeros* and look for help from organizations in the community. Don't forget, *compañeros*, that you have human and labor rights! All deserve respect, justice, and dignity.

Still, only 3 of 393 day laborers surveyed mentioned "know your rights" as a strategy to ensure payment. Others expressed doubt about trusting past or repeat employers. They feared that once an employer knew them, the person could figure out how better to exploit them. Only 3 workers mentioned using Centro for employment opportunities to prevent wage theft. A much larger portion of responses—65—responded that they helped ensure payment by working hard or doing a good job, which outreach materials also encouraged. However, working hard may expose workers to more exploitation as they take on more tasks and strive to please employers who continue to wield the power to subjectively assess, or change their minds about, work.

The largest number of responses, 113, expressed doubt that anything could be done. They claimed that they did not know how to ensure payment, nothing could be done, or they just had to have faith (see Chapter 6). Nine workers argued that taking matters into their own hands was most effective, like how Bernal threatened to take his employer's car. The next section discusses why street corner strategies and rights-based trainings frequently collapse when workers face insufficient work in a competitive market.

PREVENTION OBSTACLES

Gabriel knew the rules of the street, but proceeded to explain an incident when an employer shortchanged him $50. He accepted the amount without complaint because he needed the money. It was not worth fighting over a small amount. However, Gabriel surprisingly went back to work for the same employer again although he knew he was taking a risk. When student interviewers inquired why, Gabriel responded matter-of-factly, "Out of necessity. . . . If someone is offering you money, you do the job. There is no [alternative]. . . . I am not going to fight over $100." For Gabriel, it was more rational to search for the next job than to fight over $50. He knew that returning to work for this employer was risky, but not working was a graver gamble he was unwilling to take.

Some workers may reluctantly accept underpayment out of fear of not being paid at all.[6] Rafael, who discussed how employers mistreat workers in Chapter 3, had left a job even though the employer was willing to pay for extra hours because he treated workers harshly. Most of the other workers, though, remained on the job because, as Rafael explained, "They don't leave because of the fear . . . because they have families to support. They fear not earning [money]."

Victor weighed the need for work with accumulated street smarts.[7] He was born in Mexico but had lived in the United States since he was a toddler. Unlike most other workers at the corner, he had legal authorization and previously had held full-time jobs. However, after an unfortunate turn of events, he was homeless and looking for work on the street. He believed he could assess honest employers based on previous experience, but also asserted that he protected himself by speaking English with employers. He explained, "I mean, I got my papers and everything, but some people . . . they see you talking Spanish or something and they . . . don't want to pay you because you're an immigrant. So they take advantage of you." Victor said employers frequently use Latino appearance and language to assume "illegality" and discriminate against and exploit Latino day laborers regardless of status.[8] Victor insisted on speaking English to avoid discrimination and assumptions of being unauthorized. Workers who did not speak English found it more difficult to assess employers and advocate for themselves. One man, for example, explained that if you could not speak English, "there is no way to defend yourself if you have a problem."[9]

As the interview with Victor was ending, a truck pulled up offering work, but no one would take it, a telltale sign of an employer who had exploited workers in the past. The driver yelled, "Do any of you actually want to fucking work?" after which Victor got into the truck. He was willing to test his luck as unstable housing and insecure work viciously reinforced each other. Neither his English abilities nor legal status were sufficiently protective. Victor knew the risks, especially to work for an employer whom others had blacklisted, but he had little choice.

Assessing employers isn't clear-cut in day labor markets. Toño, for example, wasn't sure if he should avoid his former employer or return to work for him. His employer had promised to pay him every two weeks, but the first payment was late. The employer promised the check was on its way, but Toño grew wary and stopped working for him because he had lost trust. It was difficult work, Toño lamented, "sun up to sun down . . . Monday through Saturday." Toño had even begun to research the legal process to reclaim his money, but then the employer paid in full. Yet the employer was still calling Toño to work and even recommended him to others. "I'm a good worker," Toño noted, "but I probably won't go back . . . too risky." He struggled whether to reject the employer's offer. If he declined, would he be eschewing an opportunity for potentially decent work? Because of scarce and unpredictable work, day laborers are often willing to take a chance in exchange for decent wages.[10]

Ethnographers frequently focus on the differences between what people know and say versus what they actually do because context and contingency shape social interactions and behaviors. Even when day laborers like Gabriel and Victor knew what they should do, they frequently acted in ways that undermined this knowledge because the necessities of work and life restricted their options. Lack of transparency in day labor markets led workers like Toño to second-guess their better judgment if it might cost them work.

Although day laborers acknowledged that it was important to collect information on their employers, only 41 percent did so, and this was frequently basic information like their name and cell phone number. The percentage declined to 21 percent when we adjusted for relevant information. For example, many day laborers collect photos of license plates, but this information does not help because the Department of Motor Vehicles does not release it. Still, even when workers knew strategies to protect themselves, they grasped their limits. In response to the survey question asking workers how they could ensure payment, we coded multiple answers because it was not uncommon for respondents to mention practical strategies like insisting on daily payment in cash while also saying that nothing could be done.

Ultimately, scarcity of work means that there are more day laborers looking for work than jobs available.[11] Victor's employer assumed he would eventually find someone desperate enough to take his offer.[12] Insufficient work positions workers' strategies to protect themselves as potentially counterproductive to getting work entirely.

SOLIDARITY AND ITS LIMITS

The individualized, competitive, and unregulated structure of day labor markets and day laborers' legal precarity and economic desperation also cut against their attempts to organize to support one another.[13] Michelle Camou conducted her research around the time Centro opened, and she observed that organizers and day laborers held different ideas regarding what a worker center should mean and do.[14] Organizers stressed ideals of collective action and solidarity, but workers were more concerned with day-to-day material necessities, "whether jobs, other income opportunities, or the successful resolution of grievances."[15] It is difficult to inspire collective action among workers to achieve a longer-term vision of justice when there are pressing insecurities in the present.[16]

Day laborers cultivated a sense of solidarity at the corners by helping others avoid bad employers and harmful workplaces and bringing others along on jobs; some even shared rental expenses during tough times. Casimiro explained, "We help each other, we lend each other a hand. . . . If [others] arrive at the home of your *compañeros*, they give them lodging, they help each other like that. Sometimes they give you . . . the two dollars, the five, or they give you a meal. And you keep moving forward, moving forward."[17] He continued, "When that person . . . has already recovered, sometimes he works to pay [back], catch up. That's how it is here at the corner of the day laborers at Federal and 19th."[18]

Some individuals embraced a desire to organize and welcomed Marco and volunteers' efforts. Workers jokingly referred to one man at the Federal and 19th site, who prided himself on organizing others as *el Presidente*. Others purposefully distanced themselves from him: they had little interest in our outreach presentations or even our presence, snidely remarking that we could offer little. Some, especially workers who congregated at Stout Street, deliberately avoided Centro due to disputes with staff or other workers, dislike of the lottery employment system, or their resentment of Centro's application fee and rules. Still others joined Centro for reasons beyond the employment program and trainings—for a warm and friendly place to cook a meal, store belongings, and pass the time with *compañeros* even when work was not forthcoming. One man described Centro as a good place to pass the time with computers, WiFi, and books; it helped "keep the mind occupied because otherwise you just worry."[19] Others thought there was more work available at the *liebres* and chided the communal benefits offered at Centro. One man elaborated, "[Centro] is like a second home, where [people] go to watch TV, use the kitchen, and not work. Members can be very territorial, having special tables that are 'theirs' and . . . unfriendly." Because he believed they were less serious about working, he preferred the *liebre*.[20] He reasoned that more employers frequented sites known for workers who were "serious" about working, which would improve his own prospects.

Efforts toward solidarity were thus palpably strained by precarity, transience, and competition for work. Fellow workers might provide them with job opportunities, but as Nico and Ronaldo's cases revealed in previous chapters, the employer might not offer sufficient payment or undercut them, pitting them against one another. The sting of nonpayment seemed greater when workers were exploited by friends or family members. Even when workers agreed to a set minimum wage at the corner, they knew that there would always be someone like Victor who out of necessity—whether homeless, recently arrived, or in particularly dire straits—would swallow his pride and undermine collective efforts by taking low offers or jobs from an employer with a bad reputation. Strained solidarity also manifested within individuals like Toño, Gabriel, and Victor as the desire to uphold street corner norms that could uplift their fellow workers weighed against their own doubts and necessities to land a job.[21] One man realized that they "had to look out for themselves." Another man at Stout explained the friction between solidarity and self-reliance: "We are united, but there is a cancer in the heart," which he explained meant that there was also selfishness and competition.[22]

Scholars have found day laborers more difficult to organize than other Latino immigrants because of their extreme material deprivation.[23] The atomistic and competitive nature of day labor markets may make day laborers "less solidaristic" and more focused on "self-reliance."[24] Camou argues that the obstacles to organize day laborers may be even more pronounced in Denver compared to other cities because of higher incidences of homelessness, economic deprivation, paucity of work, and weak migratory social networks.[25] However, her study was largely confined to the area around Centro in its early days, which may not be representative of the diversification of day labor sites and workers. In contrast, studies that are more optimistic have tended to focus more on those engaged with worker centers, who may be more inclined to organize or have had more exposure to its benefits.[26] Our survey demonstrated similar struggles that workers continued to face across the metro area, but the most extreme indicators of precarity were concentrated around Stout Street and Centro. Nevertheless, forms of strained solidarity varied as cautious trust and friendship coexisted with competition and suspicion across hiring sites.

RIGHTS DON'T PAY: LEGAL KNOWLEDGE

I was curious whether the know-your-rights outreach was having an impact. What did workers know about their labor rights, and did it matter? Student volunteers continued workshops during the survey period, and some surveyors were also trained to assist. I arranged outreach sessions to occur on days that surveys were not being conducted to prevent interference. In turn, a survey question asked workers if they had attended these sessions, received one of the know-your-rights booklets, or had attended other workplace rights trainings. Upon completion of the survey, surveyors offered a know-your-rights booklet to workers with a brief explanation.

Day laborers were generally receptive, took the booklets, and engaged in conversations. When individuals who had listened to outreach presentations came into Centro's Direct Action Team (DAT), or even to legal intakes with Towards Justice (also advertised on the cards), they began bringing more thorough documentation of their cases, including pictures of work performed, strings of saved text messages, and even the booklets we provided. Others grew frustrated from hearing presentations with little change in their plight. One individual's response to Amy Czulada during an outreach session stuck with us: "I already know my rights but still don't have my money." Another morning at the Aurora site, a few men yelled at two student outreach volunteers to stop sending rich white students. This particularly struck one international student from South America, who began to more deeply explore how the intersections of her racial, class, and gendered identities shifted from Uruguay to the University of Denver's predominantly white campus, to her interactions with Latino and African American male workers at the Aurora corner.

Some workers wanted different information and were tired of hearing only about labor rights. They told us they preferred to receive information on immigration instead. They asked us how they could protect themselves from a raid, adjust their immigration status, or pay their taxes. For example, one man at Federal and 19th asked if he could be granted a U visa for discrimination "for [employers] calling us *mojados* . . . they treat us badly, don't want to pay you."[27] Immigration-related anxieties became even more urgent after Donald Trump was elected in November 2016, but these questions had circulated widely before. We began to collaborate with local immigrant rights organizations to receive training and disseminate their information at the corners alongside the labor rights booklets. However, we worried that we were just adding to workers' piles of cards, which they frequently shoved into creased, overstuffed wallets or even into folders in their backpacks. Workers sifted through their wallets to show us their Centro membership cards—sometimes expired, cards from attorneys their friends had passed to them, cards for medical discounts at Denver Health, the Mexican consulate, and even old copies of paperwork they had submitted to courts or attorneys.

Scholars have discussed impediments that low-wage immigrant workers face asserting their labor rights, mainly that lack of legal status and economic precarity present high opportunity costs with low chances of reward.[28] Yet other studies found that when day laborers knew their rights, they were more inclined to organize, which resonates well with first-line advocacy responses: worker education and trainings.[29] Other scholars demonstrate that worker centers can upgrade day laborers' working conditions and wages and mitigate risks of wage theft and injury.[30] While this information is certainly useful, rights-based outreach approaches, devoid of a more concerted organizing strategy, can risk exaggerating individual agency and eliding sociostructural inequality by shifting the responsibility to the most vulnerable to modify their own behavior and know their rights.[31] Trainings are not sufficient unless they are embedded within a strategy to build worker power to question and change their circumstances.[32] Centro strives to do just that, but has had more difficulty extending its efforts to nonmembers at street corners.

Despite well-honed street strategies, day laborers' knowledge of laws and protective strategies to prevent wage theft was low. We captured this knowledge with the survey using an eight-point index that scored up to two points each for knowing about three laws—the Fair Labor Standards Act (FLSA), the Colorado Wage Act, and the Colorado minimum wage—and one point each for recording employer contact information and recording days and hours worked.[33] The mean protection score was just 2.4 out of 8, with workers reporting more informal strategies, such as collecting contact information and noting days and hours worked, than legal avenues. Nineteen percent of workers were familiar with Towards Justice, and 22 percent accurately reported the Colorado minimum wage within 10 percent of the actual value, 14 percent knew about the FLSA, and 10 percent about the Colorado Wage Act.

Even so, day laborers had a strong general understanding of wage theft and knew that being denied payment for work was illegal. In interviews, they frequently articulated sentiments such as, "I don't know how the laws work," but in reality, this did not necessarily reflect a lack of knowledge; instead, it was a conviction that the laws did not serve them. One man elaborated, "I don't think the laws function," especially for day laborers. Although most day laborers knew that immigrants possessed labor rights regardless of legal status, they believed the law didn't take them into account and was more likely to punitively target them.

The gap was not in day laborers' legal knowledge, but in their ability to exercise the limited rights they are afforded and the inability of these rights to hold employers accountable and prevent future harm.[34] Day laborers who mentioned that their rights had been violated would frequently, in the same conversation, say that there was no way to prevent what happened or seek recourse, or that it was pointless to do so because the opportunity costs were high and the likelihood of wage recovery was low.[35] For day laborers, a legalistic rights-based approach individualizes what remains a structural predicament—informal and contingent work arrangements, discrimination against Latinos, lack of English skills, weak labor standards enforcement, and precarious immigration status—that continues to subject them to workplace exploitation with relative impunity. A basic knowledge of labor rights is necessary but not enough. However, all too often, the responsibility is thrust onto workers to become educated and organize and to put aside short-term concerns for a collective future that may not materialize.

There were significant differences in protective knowledge among day laborers. Factors significantly associated with higher protective and prevention knowledge included authorized immigrant status, English fluency, membership in Centro, and never being homeless.[36] Legal status and Centro membership had particularly strong associations, although the differences in both cases were quite small. However, having more protective knowledge wasn't necessarily protective. In contrast to other studies, although Centro members possessed more protective knowledge, membership conferred no wage advantage.[37] Moreover, none of these factors, aside from never being homeless, had any significant impact on shielding workers from actual wage theft exposure.[38] It is therefore understandable why many workers stated that nothing could be done to prevent wage theft and why they hesitated to organize or why perhaps only 28 percent of the day laborers surveyed were members of Centro.

Camou argues that worker "centers have the potential to transform local day labor markets and expand day laborers' rights commensurately *if* they are able to eliminate localized day labor corners and gain 'monopoly control' over the supply of day labor."[39] However, Centro has been unable to exert sufficient control over the day labor supply and offer enough jobs to displace the street corner frenzy. Employers will shift to using centers when day laborers do, which has too often required workers to collectively mobilize with their feet in ways that undermine their shorter-term prospects of getting work.[40] This is why many worker centers, including Centro, have begun actively recruiting employers to Centro and educating them to treat workers with respect and offer a fair wage.

Even when workers knew how to hypothetically prevent wage theft, their vulnerable sociolegal position, desperation for work, power discrepancies with their employers, and the nature of contingent work weakened prevention and mitigation strategies. The same factors that made workers vulnerable to wage theft not only made many protection tactics untenable and suggestions to do so potentially insulting, but possibly counterproductive to securing work.

ALTERNATIVE TACTICS: WORK FOR THE GRINGOS

Given that many of the prevention strategies supported by advocates unravel in the face of precarious work, day laborers devise other mechanisms to protect themselves while ensuring a market niche. In the qualitative interviews, day laborers responded to the question, "How do you avoid wage theft?" with similar answers to the survey, but many offered that they would "only work for the gringos, Americans or whites," often glossed as one and the same because they conflated Americanness with whiteness.[41] Ivan stated, "I mostly like to work for the Americans. . . . The majority are good, pay well, and are responsible." As demonstrated in Chapter 2, workers leverage racial tropes and legal status to justify, as well as climb up, the contracting hierarchy while pushing risk and blame down the chain.

To prevent wage theft, day laborers draw on US racial stereotypes to evaluate employers. In doing so, they reproduce the US racial hierarchy and their own subordinate position while doing little to alter their own risk.[42] Day laborers repeated US racial stereotypes by claiming that Asian employers, racially glossed as "Chinos," paid but pushed workers too hard. One man complained that "they work you to the bone . . . to death" and castigated Black employers as racist toward Latinos. Ivan concurred that Asian employers were accustomed "to cheap labor in their countries and want to do that here." Workers were especially wary of Mexican employers who, as Claudio noted in Chapter 2, were most likely to take advantage of them, largely as a function of the racial and legal stratification of contracting chains and their acute knowledge of the vulnerabilities facing undocumented Latinos and their own desire to distance themselves.[43] One worker warned that Mexican employers and their fellow Latinos "know most how to exploit us."[44] Yet through this banter, day laborers also commiserate with one another about the role of discrimination that they simultaneously suffer and perpetuate.

Day laborers also invoked racial stereotypes to avoid certain hiring sites and self-segregate at particular corners.[45] They believed this tactic would improve their access to good jobs and employers as they strove to distance themselves from workers they thought did not "work hard" or were prone to vices, which frequently carried racial undertones.[46] At the Aurora site, non-indigenous Latinos (mostly from Mexico but also some from Guatemala,

FIGURE 9: "1511 Dayton St., Aurora, Colorado." Watercolor and photo by Diego Bleifuss Prados.

Honduras, and El Salvador) separated themselves from African American workers they depicted as "lazy" (Figure 9). Nonindigenous Latinos stood on one side of the street, African Americans on another, and a few months later, we noticed a smaller contingent of mostly indigenous Guatemalan workers congregating down the street. Some Mexican workers suggested that the newer Guatemalan arrivals, who were mostly indigenous or more likely to be from rural parts of the country, worked for less, while the Guatemalan men associated the main corner of drug and alcohol abuse and rowdiness. Meanwhile, workers at the Federal site claimed it attracted day laborers "serious" about working in contrast to vices they associated with the downtown sites, where the day labor and homeless population often intertwined.

By drawing on racial stereotypes, Latino day laborers identified as hard workers, which boosted their own sense of camaraderie and pride but also played into employers' stereotypes that they would take any job out of desperation. Nevertheless, many Latino day laborers advocated for this more favorable identity against alternative tropes that criminalize Latino men.[47] Yet by substituting logics of race to explain labor exploitation, day laborers reaffirm the very racial hierarchy that depends on, and justifies, their subordinate inclusion in the United States as disposable labor that can be underpaid or cast aside when no longer amenable.[48] Angela Stuesse describes this racial pecking order in Mississippi poultry plants that rely heavily on Latino immigrant labor: "This racialized system incentivizes people of diverse backgrounds to invest in the workings of white supremacy in hopes of reaping its benefits at the expense of those identified as Black."[49] The US racial hierarchy, which elevates but erases whiteness, depends not only on dominating minority groups but also on fomenting division among them, such that the essentialization of racial and gender differences becomes a tool for labor stratification and discipline.[50]

The stratification of workplaces by race, status, and gender pits individuals against one another in ways that discipline the workforce, distract workers from recognizing common forms of oppression, and detract attention from how management strategies, corporate deregulation, and weak labor protections erode working conditions more broadly.[51] Day laborers' racialized evaluations of their employers generated some solidarity among workers as they shared their experiences in a field otherwise marked by competition.[52] But these discourses also promoted racialized suspicion and segregation at the sites and did little to deter wage theft.

Day laborers organize not only to blacklist employers with bad reputations but also to insist on a $12 per hour minimum wage, which has recently risen to at least $15. However, one July morning at the Stout Street corner, I overheard workers laughing as a small white car pulled up requesting workers. One man commented incredulously, "They want to pay $8 [per hour]!" No one got in the car for this rate. But then another worker yelled after the driver, "Go with the *morenos* [meaning dark-skinned and here used to refer to Black Americans in an offensive manner], they will work for $8." These scripts perpetuate the racial hierarchy that contributes to day laborers' exploitability and undermines the kinds of solidaristic organizing that could upgrade working conditions. Moreover, racist discourses about vice and laziness feed further into periodic attempts by neighboring businesses, police, and residents to pass antiloitering ordinances and police day laborers' very presence.

RECOURSE FOR WAGE THEFT

Just as day laborers' knowledge of prevention strategies contrasted with their actual behavior, they exhibited similar differences once they experienced wage theft. What day laborers said they would do in the future if they experienced wage theft diverged from what they actually did when forced to balance pursuing unpaid wages with the exigencies of daily life. As in Gabriel's case, it wasn't worth chasing down $50 when he needed more work. Of 253 workers who had ever experienced wage theft, about half reported taking any action at all, which encompassed calling the police, seeking an attorney, or even confronting their employer. Just one-third took the explicit step of requesting any form of outside assistance.

When all day laborers surveyed were asked what they would do or who they would call if they experienced wage theft in the future, there appeared to be willingness to seek assistance, at least hypothetically. Sixty-three mentioned they would call Centro, 87 would contact Towards Justice or other attorneys, and 107 mentioned the police. The results of the question, "What would you do or who would you call if an employer did not pay you what he/she legally owed you?" are depicted in Figure 21 in Appendix B. In juxtaposition, of 253 workers who had ever experienced wage theft, 90 requested assistance from the entities shown in Figure 22. Of these, over a third sought help from Centro. Still, just 48 workers who sought assistance reported actually receiving help, but they did fare relatively well with Centro, which accounted for 23 responses, as shown in Figure 23.

The tables with responses demonstrate that many day laborers had relatively decent awareness of the available options, and some were more likely to bear fruit than others—notably Centro and Towards Justice or other attorneys. However, their knowledge was often incomplete. For example, when surveyors asked respondents if they would call the Colorado Department of Labor if they experienced wage theft, 70 percent responded affirmatively. However, in the open-ended question that asked who they would call for assistance (see Figure 21), only 26 mentioned the "Department of Labor" in a more generic sense. Most did not know the difference between federal or state branches or how to access these agencies, and frequently they mislabeled them the Labor Commission, which is not an official entity in Colorado.

Most workers did not pursue outside assistance. The legal process, as well as other nonlegal alternative mechanisms[53] to pursue redress such as seeking out friends, Centro, or even the lead contractor, frequently took too much time to be worth the effort, leading to differences between what workers said they would do versus what they did when they experienced wage theft. Few workers mentioned actually contacting the Colorado Department of Labor and Employment (CDLE) for a wage case, and just one reported receiving assistance. Others were discouraged because of prior experiences. One worker interviewed at Centro in 2015 lamented that he was underpaid for two weeks of work and submitted a claim to the CDLE, but "nothing happened." The CDLE's failure to pursue his case or update him in a timely manner could be due to a number of factors. However, in this worker's mind, he believed it was because he was not a priority and that they prioritized larger cases. Another individual who managed to recover money through the CDLE was upset that he could recover only half, which he felt did not fairly compensate him for his time, effort, or suffering. Workers who knew the legal process or had gone to court complained that it was too many steps or took too long to produce too little, too late for workers who need to, as one day laborer put it, "keep trying to earn money" every day. Even workers who had called Towards Justice for an intake, which works relatively quickly compared to the CDLE, could not afford to wait the two or three weeks they were told to get a response.

Despite the obstacles, many workers expressed enthusiasm about seeking help from Centro regardless of survey site, which is supported by the survey responses. One worker mentioned, "I don't know why people don't try [Centro]. They come here helping people out" and repeated that they spoke Spanish. He added an example of when Centro called an employer and got him to pay the worker. While lawyers and "no one" accounted for a larger share of responses of what workers would do in future hypothetical wage theft cases, Centro was the actor from which wage theft victims most often sought support. When one worker learned that the DAT provided wage claims assistance at Centro on Tuesday nights, spoke Spanish, and helped pressure employers to pay workers, he told his friend who had not been paid. He noted enthusiastically that Centro put pressure on the employer who then "paid voluntarily!"[54] Others, however, became disillusioned with advocates and attorneys, who, they claimed, did not help or, worse, expressed favoritism.[55] The limited resources of worker centers and other nonprofits and state agencies, coupled with the fact that advocates also face difficulties holding recalcitrant employers accountable, can lead workers to presume more dubious motives.

Claudio, for example, said he lost faith in Centro because he had called them after his injury for assistance, but no one returned his call. His friend had given him another card of a woman who could help, which he showed me after rifling through his wallet. He thought she might work for a missionary organization, but when he called, the message was only in English so he didn't leave one. He thought his friend could help him and took out another card, which said something before the word *justice* scrawled on the back, but I couldn't make out the first word and neither could he. He let his Centro membership lapse and added his expired ID to his wallet full of cards.

Interactions with attorneys were similarly complicated. Although eighty-seven workers mentioned they would call a lawyer or Towards Justice if they experienced wage theft, many complained that attorneys rarely helped or returned their calls. Like Claudio, they had pockets and file folders stuffed with business cards. Perhaps their cases were too confusing, the phone number provided was no longer functioning, or their cases did not fall within the attorney's expertise. Their case may have been too small with insufficient evidence for an attorney to take, but workers interpreted this lack of response to mean that they were unimportant. Because attorneys work on a fee-for-service basis and for these cases on a contingency fee basis for a percentage of the award, many wage theft cases are simply uneconomical.[56] Towards Justice cannot represent small cases, but after conducting a free intake, it will guide workers through submitting a claim to the CDLE, send them to Centro's DAT for assistance, or refer to a growing network of collaborating pro bono attorneys. Still, there are insufficient attorneys to make private representation a scalable, economical, or practical solution, especially for the most vulnerable who experience the additional indignation that their cases are considered economically insignificant.

Many of the attorneys workers do find are through word of mouth, business cards, television and radio ads, or even billboards, and are not free. Some are not even attorneys, but entrepreneurs who have developed a niche taking advantage of immigrants' limited legal knowledge and vulnerability. One individual reported that he had spoken to lawyers three times about his case but could not remember their names and had lost their information. As another noted, "Sometimes we don't have a phone number, we don't have money to pay a lawyer . . . it is difficult and it takes time. I don't want to waste time."

Even when workers held out hopes for a legal remedy, they were frequently discouraged by their immigration status. One day laborer knew that he could go to court regardless of his legal status, but he admitted that "there is about a 50/50 chance" when pursuing a wage claim: "If you do not have papers and you are being paid under the table, you will inevitably lose." He added that "the laws are beautiful," but he was convinced that they were not intended for day laborers. Another man explained, "Because I am undocumented, I do not like to ask for help."

Many day laborers interpreted such interactions with attorneys and legal agencies as "they refused to help me," "they never called me back," or "they did nothing," which only provided evidence of their lack of concern. These experiences show that the problem is less that day laborers do not know the laws and their rights, but that they have little utility when legal agencies are not proactive, workers' claims are not taken seriously, and they are unlikely to receive their money. Still, many recognized that the advocates, attorneys, and agency staff who attempted to help also encountered obstacles.

Workers surveyed demonstrated a surprising willingness to call police for wage theft incidents, but the qualitative interviews revealed more hesitation.[57] In one instance, a day laborer called the police when his employers refused to pay. When the officers arrived, they declined to get involved and referred to the dispute as a civil disagreement not warranting police intervention. But once the officers saw the employers laughing about this interchange, they interceded to insist that the employers pay. In one dramatic incident, a worker drove his employer's car to the police station after he refused to pay him. We were uncertain what the worker expected to materialize, but to him, it symbolized his conviction that the police ought to do something. Some held more idealized visions of the police, which they compared to stories of corrupt police in their home countries. Yet they also recounted abuses at the hands of migration officials and law enforcement on both sides of the US-Mexico border when they migrated. Interestingly, some workers who had previous problems with US law enforcement seemed more willing to engage the police for wage disputes. Perhaps they realized they had little left to lose or were more familiar with how the police operated.

Other day laborers were nervous that if they reported wage theft, the blame would be cast on them in a climate of heightened racialized surveillance of Latino immigrants. Francisco, who was originally from Honduras, was assaulted and robbed, but he resisted: "I fought back, I defended myself," he stated. However, when the police arrived, they took both men into the station. Francisco spent five days in jail that he could have spent working. He was eventually released, but his attacker was released first. According to Francisco, "He [his attacker] knew how to talk to the police." Francisco explicitly mentioned that his attacker was US-born, but of Mexican descent versus his own identity as an undocumented Honduran. He was convinced that this man was well aware of his vulnerabilities, including that Francisco was likely to be carrying cash and unlikely to report a crime.[58]

Rather than subjects of concern, day laborers worried who the police would believe when street corner hiring sites are often treated with racialized suspicion. Day laborers are easy targets because they have to remain somewhat visible and stationary to attract employers.[59] Workers complained that prior to intervention from Centro, police used to hurl racial slurs at them while they waited at street corners for work. Street corner hiring sites in the Denver area are now relatively tolerated, largely owing to advocacy from Centro and its allies. However, their existence is still tenuous and negotiated with neighbors, local businesses, and city authorities.

Day laborers frequently feared employer retaliation, whether being fired, reported to immigration, or blacklisted in the industry, or that their social connections who still worked for an employer might suffer repercussions. For example, Armando and Jacinta (in Chapter 3) feared immigration agents showing up to small claims court when their employer threatened them. Although ICE had never shown up at small claims court in Denver, its agents were more present in and around courthouses during the Trump administration, sometimes in plain clothes and unmarked vehicles. This presence makes immigrant workers hesitant to report various kinds of crimes or collaborate with law enforcement.

Lack of options led others to resort to desperate measures or to take matters into their own hands. One man confided, "The law exists so we can talk to the police . . . [but] if not I take the law into my own hands." Another man at Centro recalled a violent incident when a group of workers beat up two employers who refused to pay: "They beat them in their garage because they wouldn't pay. . . . Sometimes it gives you the nerve [when they don't pay] and [you] can't call the police. You have to fight for them to help you. Police tell you to go to court [but] that takes a lot of time." Such stories reverberate at the *liebres*.

Some day laborers have threatened to steal, or have actually stolen, a tool, especially when equipment may be valued close to the wages owed. Juan once took a roofing tool from his employer when he refused to pay. "Then pay me with this," he threatened. Normally reserved and hesitant to confront employers, he mustered the courage. His employer became agitated but paid him. Day laborers rely on such insurgent tactics to pressure employers to pay, and in Juan's case, it worked. However, these tactics can backfire. One morning when I accompanied attorney Raja to the Lakewood hiring site, we met a woman who had grown exasperated by her husband's employer and his refusal to pay. Out of desperation, the husband stole a laptop from the employer's home. Raja had to inform him that his own actions now carried more serious criminal consequences than his employer's original offense. Such crimes of desperation culminate from mounting experiences of injustice and for some constitute a refusal of a legal system that pays little heed to their exploitation. Yet, they are also frequently weaponized to justify further criminalization of Latino immigrants instead of the employers who cheat them.

Still, 98 workers (the largest proportion of responses after the police) surveyed mentioned that they did not know who they could call or said they would do nothing if they experienced wage theft. Prevention seemed futile. Despite the large portion of these responses, they do not reflect the same lack of knowledge documented in other studies. For example, Nik Theodore's Houston survey found that 92 percent of day laborers could "not name any organization or entity that could provide assistance with wage recovery."[60] In Denver, many day laborers knew they had options to reclaim unpaid wages, and some had already pursued them. Responses that looked like ignorance or resignation did not necessarily mean that workers did not know what to do or where to go. Instead, they pointed to an acute awareness that these avenues were unlikely to be worth their time and effort. When day laborers pursued and even received help, few actually recouped their money, let alone additional penalties. Moreover, these measures often did little to prevent future exposure. Tolerating lost wages and continuing to look for more work instead becomes quite reasonable.

When workers did not hear back from attorneys, nonprofits, the police, or the CDLE, silence supported their conviction that they were not valued. It is this same devaluation and relative powerlessness that led employers to take advantage in the first place. To workers, the CDLE, attorneys, and sometimes even volunteers are symbolic of a larger system that exploits immigrant workers and disregards their concerns.[61]

CONCLUSION

For many workers, the costs of coming forward are too steep. They fear retaliation from employers, wasting precious time and resources, and the opportunity cost of days that could otherwise be spent working. Many decided to come forward only once wage theft had occurred multiple times, the amounts were particularly large, or they summoned the courage to prevent their employers from exploiting others. Alonso, the painter in Chapter 3 who had experienced wage theft, sought assistance for the first time. But his family had lost $20,000 over the years from similar incidents. At this point, it was no longer just about the money. He wanted to prevent his employer from doing the same thing to others.

Gabriel's desire to move on to the next job, or even to chance returning to the same employer, is more common than workers like Alonso who came forward. The amounts of money that day laborers lose from individual wage theft incidences tend to be small, especially because they work temporary jobs for low pay. Most brush off small losses in the hope of acquiring more work the next day. It is not worth it to go around "fighting" or "struggling," as workers described pursuing unpaid wages, when they needed more work to survive. Although nonaction, or tolerating the abuse, may be the most reasonable course of action in the short run, it reinforces the power discrepancy and employer impunity that facilitate wage theft. When wage theft is left unchecked and becomes pervasive in particular industries, it hurts all workers and honest employers who struggle to compete in an atmosphere where rules do not apply. The amounts lost and associated indignities add up over time to lower workers' incomes and deprive them of their dignity and livelihoods.

The average amount owed to day laborers surveyed who experienced wage theft in the past six months (19 percent of workers surveyed) was $348, which could amount to about one-third of one month's pay for the average worker.[62] For some, this meant the difference between having enough money for rent or sleeping on the street. Immigrant day laborers who had been in the United States for longer periods of time were 40 percent less likely to have experienced wage theft in the past six months than more recent arrivals (see Table 1 in Appendix B). On average, they lost $10 less per month to wage theft than more recent arrivals did. We were uncertain whether longer-duration immigrants avoided wage theft more than recent arrivals because they had cultivated the experience to avoid bad employers, as Juan had learned, or maybe they were working less, which would give them less exposure to wage theft.

However, it is also important to recall that longer-duration immigrant day laborers earned much less than counterparts who were more recent arrivals because they worked less. In fact, they earned $350 a month less. Their income deficit from lack of work was more significant than the slight monetary advantage of lower exposure to wage theft.[63] Although day laborers aren't performing these precise calculations, the opportunity costs are clear. Wages lost to wage theft certainty mattered, but for many, avoiding work incurred greater financial risk.

In a low-work environment, where all work is potentially risky, day laborers face a troubling trade-off between the risks associated with working (i.e., wage theft and injury) and the peril of not working.[64] Organizing can be hazardous if collective action interferes with the ability to compete for work. Some day laborers valued individual self-reliance over solidarity because it offered one way to exert some control when life and work are otherwise unpredictable.[65] In an informal competitive market, workers can't trust that other workers or employers will uphold street norms or their promises. Employers understand this calculus: they assume day laborers will be easy to exploit and accept work even under dubious conditions. They know that the odds of getting caught are slim or at least not very costly.

Meanwhile, the structural factors that make day laborers valuable to contingent markets and vulnerable to wage theft—desperation for work, precarious immigration status, low English proficiency, and racial discrimination—aggravate the costs they bear to prevent exploitation and pursue redress. These factors make trying to exercise the few rights immigrant day laborers are afforded uneconomical and potentially risky.

5 FAILURE TO PURSUE

The Legal Maze

The legal system is inaccessible also because it's its own culture . . . like stepping onto another planet.

—*Tammy Kuennen, professor of law, supervisor of the Sturm Civil Litigation Clinic, and DAT volunteer*

ONE CRISP MORNING IN FEBRUARY 2015, I arrived at Federal and 19th to meet up with Marco, then director of Centro, and attorney Raja. We hoped to find Andrés, an undocumented worker from Honduras in his early twenties, to proceed with his workers' compensation case. Andrés broke three ribs when a tree fell on him during a trimming job. He even took his employer to court when he refused to cover his expenses. Andrés received a judgment entitling him to medical expenses, unpaid wages, and penalties because the employer was not carrying the requisite workers' compensation insurance. When we added up the total, Andrés was owed nearly $70,000. After hearing about his predicament, Raja took his case. However, none of us could locate the employer.

By the fall, Andrés had still not received any money and grew desperate. His family was evicted from their apartment and living day-to-day in a motel, depending on if he got work. He even removed a chest brace that he wore because of his injury to make himself more attractive to employers. One morning, graduate student Kendra Allen and I ran across the street to the Dollar Store to purchase diapers for his toddlers, and Marco gave him a list of organizations that could possibly assist, but there was little else we could do. Andrés continued to be shortchanged by employers who saw he was injured and took advantage. He risked aggravating his injury by attempting to hide and work through it.

Raja then contacted an investigator to locate the employer, but the investigator thought he might have moved to Texas. Raja lamented, "It's a dead end." Tracking down employers is one of the biggest challenges for day laborers and advocates. Amy Czulada, a former DU student who also previously coordinated the Direct Action Team (DAT), noted that it is like "chasing a ghost." Even if employers are found, they may be bankrupt or still refuse to pay. In the following months, we stopped seeing Andrés at the corner. We could no longer reach him by phone, which he often had trouble paying to keep in service. He was gone.

This chapter examines how workers maneuver the legal claims process with a focus on the Colorado Department of Labor and Employment's (CDLE's) new administrative process. Despite good intentions, during its first few years, chasing wages through the CDLE's administrative claims process easily evolved into an exercise in bureaucratic absurdity. Even when workers learned how to translate systemic humiliations into claims and win—like Andrés—they rarely received the paltry means of restitution the system coughs up in exchange for ongoing exploitation. Pursuing claims required what paralegal Jesus calls a "herculean effort" as society's most precarious workers attempted to navigate a process that resembles a labyrinth with no exit. Still, if given more proactive enforcement capacities, the CDLE has the potential to be one player that can help shift the power dynamics around wage compliance. These are exactly the kinds of changes the division began to pursue in 2019.

By tracing how workers and advocates traverse the legal maze, it becomes clear why day laborers are wary of the law's ability to provide justice. Even if workers eventually recoup some money, I argue that the legal claims pursuit further embeds them into the banalities of bureaucratic power in ways that reproduce the subordinated inclusion of low-wage immigrant workers. A substantial portion of the CDLE's closed claims fall into the category of "failure to pursue," which refers to workers who fail to pursue cases. This chapter inverts this framing to demonstrate how the legal claims system routinely fails workers.

FROM SMALL CLAIMS TO THE CDLE'S DIVISION

In recognition of the obstacles that low-wage workers face mobilizing their rights and weakening labor standards enforcement resources and oversight at the federal level, in the mid- to late 2000s various states and localities began to devise or improve their own wage protection laws.[1] One Denver city employee phrased his office's efforts to strengthen wage protections during the Trump administration in this way: "When they [the federal government] go low, we go local." Expanding public enforcement and administrative processes at the state and local levels addresses the fact that many workers who labor for small employers are not covered by the federal Department of Labor's focus on larger enterprises. Low-wage workers' claims are usually too small to be of interest to attorneys, especially when they cannot be aggregated to bring a class action suit. In response, between 2005 and 2018, 141 laws or regulations were instituted to address wage theft across US localities.[2] Some of the most effective laws ratchet up penalties to allow individuals to collect liquidated damages to deter violators and compensate workers for the time and effort chasing wages that should have been paid.[3]

In 2014, Colorado passed an amendment to its Wage Protection Act after a stronger version of the legislation had failed the previous year. The amendment went into effect on January 1, 2015, and gave the Division of Labor Standards and Statistics of the CDLE the authority to investigate and adjudicate wage claims of $7,500 and below, order wages, levy fines, and assess penalties that allow workers to collect 125 percent of their owed wages and potentially more for willful violations. Previously it could only mediate wage disputes. Workers can also recover the fines and penalties set out in the statute and reasonable attorneys' fees if they pursue their wage theft cases in court outside of the division's administrative process.

The division's amplified capacity was intended to assist some of the state's most vulnerable workers. Jonathan Singer, former Colorado state representative (2012–2021) and one of the bill's sponsors, articulated the obstacles facing low-wage workers:

> One of the women who came to visit me when I was working on the bill was Lucy. She had just left an abusive relationship and was working at a daycare. She told her boss that she thought the worker to child ratio was dangerous and in violation of state law, and she was fired. She was never paid under the threat of getting arrested, while she was trying to get her family on their feet. . . . Prior to the passing of the bill, you could go to the CDLE, but all they could do was send angry letters. The employer wrote her a check, but it bounced, the fees of which Lucy had to pay. Lucy was in a position where she did not have time to pursue the case, she had to keep that roof over her family's head. They [undocumented workers] are afraid of being referred to ICE which is illegal too, but that doesn't mean the fear isn't real.[4]

The bill catered to some of the assumptions implied by the legal mobilization and access to justice literature—workers lack access to the law and the time, resources, security, and knowledge to pursue claims.[5] It further addressed how the majority of disputes are dropped before the claim phase, largely owing to workers' fears of retaliation, as well as anxieties about navigating the legal system and "lack of personal power and faith in the government."[6] However, by tracking the wage claim process, it becomes apparent that the process still failed to adequately serve low-wage and immigrant workers.

Public enforcement entities can be one player to help take the burden off workers, but they need to leverage their power to hold employers accountable.[7] Instead, a reactive and individualized approach to wage theft that largely focuses on facilitating access to the legal claims process after violations have already occurred leaves its sociostructural causes intact. Specifically, contingent work and fear of removal continue to expose unauthorized immigrants to workplace violations and concentrate them in the most underprotected sectors of the economy.

Prior to the amendment to its Wage Act, Colorado workers could pursue wage theft cases in small claims court on their own. These courts are designed to deal with smaller dollar amounts and are intended to be accessible. In practice, however, they frequently disadvantage low-wage and foreign-born workers.[8] Forms are available only in English, each filing carries a fee and fee waivers can be hard to find, and interpreters must be scheduled in advance. Claimants need to serve their employers or pay a sheriff to do so.

Small claims forms are generic to cover a variety of monetary disputes, which means that they provide no information on state or federal wage laws or guidance on the distinction between being an employee or a contractor. These differences are important because employees are covered under the Wage Act, which entitles them to the additional penalties that recognize the power discrepancies that facilitate wage theft, whereas independent contractors are not. Legally, contractors can pursue unpaid or violated contracts in court, but they are treated on more equal footing with those from whom they are trying to collect. Claimants, as well as small claims court judges, are frequently unfamiliar with wage and hour statutes.[9] Judges therefore often treat wage theft cases like a breach of contract, which means that they do not award the liquidated damages or consider the power disparities that drive wage theft.[10]

The new CDLE Division administrative process was designed with some of these obstacles of access to justice in mind. By training investigators with knowledge of wage and hour laws, the division attempts to recalibrate the opportunity costs that prevent workers from mobilizing their rights. Its forms explicitly address wage and hour laws, and its staff are well versed in identifying and investigating wage and hour violations. Forms are available in Spanish and English, and the division made conscious efforts to hire more bilingual investigators. Workers still need to come forward to submit and pursue claims, but then the knowledge burden shifts to the division to investigate and adjudicate. Because the division sends notices to the employer, it tried to assuage workers' fears of directly confronting their employers.

Although the division's administrative pathway is a vast improvement, it was largely individualized and reactive, at least until 2019. Most people never make a legal claim, especially those who work in the industries most prone to violations.[11] The 2008 Unregulated Work Survey of over four thousand low-wage workers found that 33 percent perceived that their rights were violated, and of these, 57 percent made a claim.[12] However, only 4 percent of these claims were made formally through a civil or administrative justice system, meaning that just over 2 percent of workers who perceived that their rights had been violated issued a formal complaint.[13]

The cases that individuals file with the CDLE barely poke at the scale of wage theft. In 2018, the division received only 2,673 claims, sent notices of violations in 727 cases, and 818 workers received payment for a total of just over $1 million.[14] Spanish-language claims represented just 4.8 percent of total claims received that year, although foreign-born Latinos are six times more likely to experience wage theft than US-born whites.[15] CDLE claims are a minuscule selection of wage theft incidents and may elude those most at risk.

The division may waive or significantly reduce penalties to encourage violators to pay within fourteen days of a determination. While this practice can incentivize payment, some advocates worry that stripping down penalties impedes their deterrent impact.[16] If employers can get away with merely paying what they owed in the first place, why should they change their behavior?[17] Some scholars therefore question the effectiveness of penalties, especially because enforcement tends to be inconsistent.[18] Absent proactive investigations and a culture of enforcement, penalties alone do not alter behavior if employers assume they will never be caught.[19]

The division's enhanced mandate also went into effect prior to the sufficient allocation of funds to hire and train investigators. The bill expanded the CDLE's charge, but according to one attorney, it was given "a very basic amount of money for the budget." The agency was stuck because it could not start hiring with the funding structure dictated in the fiscal note until January 1, the same day the legislation was to go into effect.[20] Insufficient investment remains plagued by Colorado's revenue restrictions under its Taxpayer's Bill of Rights (TABOR), which, as former Colorado state senator Jessie Ulibarri (2013–2017), another of the bill's sponsors, explained, "limit[s] the ability for us to fully invest in public structures and make them robust and meaningful."[21] Colorado's Wage Act was modeled on the one in Washington State, which has about the same number of annual wage claims. However, whereas Washington funded thirty-three investigators, Colorado's bill provided for only eight employees to conduct investigations for 50 percent of their time.[22] Ulibarri lamented how underfunding can gut well-intentioned measures, leaving the legislature to "play with incredibly small pots of money with the hope of big results."[23] The CDLE's lack of resources combined with a widened mandate generated a long backlog. Cases were taking nearly a year to go through the claims process, nowhere close to the ninety days (after a notice of complaint is sent to the employer) stipulated by the statute.

Colorado workers experienced additional gaps as a result of compromises reached in order to pass the legislation. A criminalization measure, which would have attached potential criminal penalties to wage violations that met a certain threshold, was considered to be a nonstarter and was ripped from the bill's first attempt in 2013. Although some advocates debate the effectiveness and ethics of criminalization when it may intensify the policing of marginalized populations, others contend that civil penalties are an insufficient deterrent.[24] Wage theft is a crime of power that thrives in the imbalance between employers and workers.[25] For proponents, bringing the tools of criminal law to bear on unscrupulous employers can help "correct [this] power imbalance," send a message that violators will be punished, and provide monetary restitution.[26] Criminalization measures can incentivize district attorneys, law enforcement, and other public enforcement agencies to take wage theft and other forms of workplace abuse more seriously.[27] Individual liability provisions were also omitted from the bill, which made it challenging to hold individuals accountable when they attempted to hide beyond defunct or bankrupt entities. The legislation included damages to permit workers to recover penalties, but the stipulated 125 percent of owed wages fell below the treble damages required in other states. Treble damages, which allow workers to collect 300 percent of their wages, have proven to be one of the most effective deterrents because they demonstrate that violating the law will be sufficiently costly—but only if they are enforced.[28]

In the past few years, the division has restructured to increase staffing capacity and hired more Spanish-speaking compliance investigators. However, cases were still taking over six months, often languishing most when they are waiting to be assigned.[29] As of November 2020, the average number of days from receipt of claim to assignment was 177 days, whereas the time from assignment to determination was 62 days.[30]

Given the lengthy time line, some advocates began to hesitate to recommend the CDLE's process to low-wage workers. At first, the DAT encouraged workers to file with the CDLE as they worked informally on their cases, and Towards Justice trained over fifty volunteer navigators across the state between 2014 and 2016 to help workers fill out CDLE claims forms.[31] However, as cases languished, the DAT began to stop suggesting that workers file with the CDLE.[32] Towards Justice hosts legal nights to assist workers with CDLE forms but shifted to focus more on its collaborating attorney network to refer workers for representation.

BUREAUCRATIC ACROBATICS

To file with the division, individuals must first ensure that they and their violation are covered under the Colorado Wage Act. They must fit the designation of an "employee," work in the state of Colorado, and work for an employer who meets the definitions under the act. Violations must fall within the jurisdiction of the corresponding agency or court and be identifiable as such within corresponding wage and hour statutes. The division's website clarifies that it cannot assist claimants with "independent contractor pay disputes," harassment, sick and severance pay, wrongful termination, discrimination, retaliation, "pay disputes where an employer has filed bankruptcy," along with other workplace issues for which it lacks authority. Workers must chase these violations elsewhere, although these problems often overlap with, or follow, a wage claim.

The division's procedures are structured to handle violations that are individual, objective, and discrete, but low-wage immigrant workers' experiences with unfair labor practices are often overlapping, messy, and compounding.[33] Andrés experienced multiple injustices in conjunction with wage theft. He struggled to collect workers' compensation for his injury and to pay his hospital bills, suffered unpaid wages from the same and subsequent employers, and was trying to pursue an employer that was likely bankrupt. Andrés was also on the precipice of homelessness. Each of his problems directed him to a different agency, but much of his suffering had no legal remedy. Other workers struggled not only to shoehorn workplace indignities into discrete violations accessible to investigators, but as Santiago's case illustrates, even to meet the basic qualification as an "employee" covered under the Wage Act.[34]

Santiago's case exemplifies how the law's confusions around employee coverage and strictures for documenting work may preclude claims before they are filed. Santiago worked for an employer in August 2020 on two painting jobs. A month later, he remembered well the date that the employer had stopped responding to him, and he had proof in his text messages. But when DAT volunteers asked when he performed the work, his recollection was shakier—for two or three weeks. Volunteers struggled to help Santiago add up the amounts he was owed. The accounting was confusing due to a variety of factors: the employer paid Santiago some money to encourage him to complete a subsequent job; Santiago paid a portion to an assistant; Santiago incurred materials expenses on one job, but the employer provided materials on the other; and additional costs emerged during the job. Specifically, Santiago had to repaint the home when the homeowner changed her mind and requested a different color. The homeowner also asked him to perform additional tasks, like power-washing the house prior to painting, which weren't originally accounted for. Santiago didn't have an invoice or a contract. He also didn't track his hours. The employer was paying him for the job, not hourly .

From prior experience, Santiago knew what each of these steps should cost, but he had only verbally arranged the amount with his employer. He trusted that his employer would pay him fairly when accounts were settled, especially because his sister and the employer's wife were friends. When the employer failed to pay and stopped responding to his calls, Santiago struggled to make his case legible to a labor agency or court. The forms required exact amounts and dates. Because Santiago was technically subcontracted by a contractor who had been hired by a homeowner, it was unclear whether he would be covered under the Wage Act as an "employee." If he were an independent contractor, he could pursue his case as a breach of contract in court, but without any access to penalties or the assistance of division investigators.

As volunteers broke down and priced out each aspect of his work, they debated if they should recalibrate the amount into hours and wages to make it more intelligible to the division or small claims court. If all that Santiago had was a verbally contracted amount and he couldn't explain his work arrangement in more detail, would a judge throw his case out? At the same time, as we tried to squeeze his case inside the legal claim's boxes, we worried that this process winnowed away much of what actually happened to him. As Kim Bobo cautions, "Way too much time gets wasted on figuring out whether or not workers are covered by the Fair Labor Standards Act (FLSA) rather than helping workers recover their wages."[35]

Wage and hour laws remain based on relatively traditional relationships between employees and employers even as the nature of work has changed. The labor enforcement regime largely demands documentation of work in a grid-like fashion, with clear relationships between employers and their employees.[36] These outdated classifications neglect how immigrant and low-wage workers tend to be concentrated in forms of contingent or contract work that lack employee status[37] and that employers increasingly mold jobs this way to their benefit. Most of these workers should still be legally treated as employees, but the complexity and informality of their work make translating their arrangements difficult. It is even easier to deny coverage when workers are undocumented and indirectly hired through vast contracting chains and paid in cash. By tying employee status to labor protections, the proliferation of contingent work arrangements entrenches workers more deeply into underprotected and precarious work.[38]

UNFILLABLE FORMS

The division's website issues guidelines to help claimants provide sufficient information up front to facilitate a timely investigation. Claimants must sign the complaint form and provide information on themselves and their employer, information regarding the declared violation, and the amount owed. The process appears straightforward, but this formalized understanding of work poses obstacles for those laboring under nonstandard arrangements. Even when workers know they have been cheated, they often significantly underestimate what they are owed.

Despite recent revisions to the division's forms to make them more user friendly, low-wage immigrant workers often lack much of the basic information requested. Santiago did not recall the exact days he worked or track his hours. Andrés had insufficient information on his employer, just his extremely common first and last name. Whereas 41 percent of 393 day laborers surveyed collected some type of employer contact information, only 13 percent noted the employer's address. More often, workers had only a first name and a cell phone, which employers easily dodged or disconnected. Without the employer's address, workers and attorneys cannot send demand letters to initiate a legal case, and the division cannot send a notice to begin an investigation. Some workers are fearful to ask for or provide information on themselves and their employers given weak retaliation protections.[39] Even in jurisdictions with stronger retaliation protections, they rarely provide a "meaningful remedy . . . and [put undocumented workers] at risk of further and potentially irrevocable harm, including detention and deportation."[40] For example, Luciano and his wife, Victoria, came to the DAT for assistance for their unpaid wages. They kept good records and arrived for their intake with text messages from the employer, emails, and bank documentation of bounced checks. However, as undocumented workers, they were wary about going to court because they had a friend who was threatened by his employer: "[The employer has our address], that is what worries us."[41] In response, the DAT often uses Centro's letterhead and address when sending demand letters to prevent the employer from knowing where the worker lives.

Due to transience and high incidences of housing insecurity, many day laborers do not have stable addresses or reliable phones for when the division needs to request more information. About 40 percent of day laborers we surveyed had experienced homelessness in the past year, 64 percent had smartphones, and just 30 percent were fluent or proficient in English.[42]

The division's forms have a grid to fill in wages and hours that resembles a timesheet. Yet the division understands that many low-wage workers do not have time sheets or pay stubs. They therefore do not require any official documentation aside from the complaint form and will accept photos of work, text messages, and even hours jotted down on a napkin. Still, just 64 percent of day laborers surveyed tracked their hours and wages.[43] When surveyors asked them to recall their five-day retrospective work histories, the process often resulted in guesstimates as surveyors scribbled out the grid and tried again. Many individuals worked for hourly and contracted pay by the job simultaneously, and even for the same employer like Santiago. Or they might have a more general estimate of what they are owed. Advocates help workers retrofit a complicated work history into a grid for work that usually occurred months prior while the worker likely held other jobs. DAT volunteers continued to debate whether they should cross out Santiago's list of jobs and estimated payments and provide an alternate version with hours and wages.

The DAT volunteers took great care to clarify Santiago's information to make sure the amounts were correct, but experienced attorneys usually push for more. Attorneys are more likely to recognize when employers are committing other violations. For example, employers may have also denied breaks or overtime, misclassified workers as independent contractors, or issued checks with insufficient funds. Workers can add in three times the amount of a bounced check on a claim form to remedy this injustice, but they are often unaware this is possible. Many judges in small claims court also fail to award these additional amounts for bounced checks, let alone the Wage Act's penalties. In a claims-driven enforcement system, volunteers, judges, and even division investigators may miss such nuances that deprive workers of their due justice.

Classificatory carve-outs in the state's wage and hour protections also made it difficult for workers and advocates to determine if workers were being denied overtime. The lack of standardized and clear federal and state labor codes prevents workers from clearly knowing their rights and obstructs their ability to receive their fair pay.[44] When DAT volunteers were assisting one individual in filing a division claim, they realized that he was not only owed a few days of unpaid wages, but that his employer was also intentionally avoiding paying him overtime. The employer paid him through two separate checks to avoid triggering extra pay.[45] The man stated on the claim why he came forward: "I think that this is an injustice and want his company to be investigated not just for me, but also for others who work there and who have experienced maltreatment." The division eventually awarded the man his wages and overtime, but it is unclear whether the employer was investigated beyond this individual instance when it is likely he may have been doing the same to others.

According to the Colorado Wage Protection Act Rules,[46] "an employee must provide an explanation for the basis for the complaint that is clear, specific, and shows the worker is entitled to relief." Once a claim is submitted, the "burden . . . shifts to the employer to prove [the case to the contrary], by a preponderance of the evidence."[47] A division investigator explained that there is a low bar to prove what workers are owed: "Just a complete form is needed."[48] But this explanation obscures the laborious process by which low-wage immigrant workers and their advocates must construct themselves into "employees" and claimants.[49]

Forms and the claims-making process often "take on a life of [their] own" in ways that reshape the very nature of the employment relationship into established bureaucratic fields and make individuals into legal claimants.[50] As such, the legal system selectively recognized violations that fit the bureaucratic parameters while silencing and effectively allowing others.[51] Justice becomes narrowed to a confined subset of employees and kinds of harmful employer behavior that qualify. The very process of making a claim ends up erasing the underdocumented work arrangements that continue to make immigrant workers structurally vulnerable to wage theft and underprotected by labor laws. In this fashion, wage theft is narrowed to its individual manifestations rather than its pervasive and systemic ones.[52] The acrobatics the process demands of workers detract attention and resources that could be placed on pressuring labor agencies to pursue more proactive and targeted investigations of repeat violators and prone industries that may be exploiting many workers at once.[53] Because the claims process relies so heavily on the aggrieved, legal expertise is unevenly distributed, and enforcement is weak, workers frequently receive less than they should even when they come forward and prevail.

ABSURDITIES OF THE CHASE

To even begin to hold employers accountable, workers need to find them, whether to serve them a demand letter for owed wages to take them to court or to provide an address for the division's form. As Daniel's case demonstrates, this can be exceedingly challenging. Daniel worked for ten days in March 2018 for Emiliano and Ricardo painting trim and molding on a house. He had known Emiliano, who had recruited him for the job, for years. When Daniel finished the job and asked Emiliano for payment, he claimed there were items missing from the house and that the homeowner didn't like his work. Daniel returned to fix some of the work, but Emiliano still refused to pay. After Daniel and his wife kept calling, Emiliano deflected to Ricardo. He claimed Ricardo was responsible for payment. Both Emiliano and Ricardo soon stopped answering his calls. Daniel and his wife were afraid to proceed further because both were undocumented.

Daniel sought assistance from the DAT in late April, and volunteers reached out to Ricardo on his behalf. Ricardo complained that Daniel never sent an invoice and performed the work incorrectly. He then diverted attention from his own refusal to pay by demeaning Daniel and patronizingly imploring him to be "patient." And then he threatened to sue him. Despite

Ricardo's complaints, both he and Emiliano admitted that they owed Daniel money and would pay but never provided any specifics. A larger problem soon emerged: no one could find a reliable address for Ricardo or Emiliano. Without this information, they could not send a demand letter to initiate a case, let alone confront them.

The DAT proceeded to send flurries of demand letters and to drive by multiple addresses for both men that kept emerging through creative detective work. Ricardo finally called Daniel. He was irritated and intimated that if Daniel kept knocking on doors, he might get arrested or even deported. The DAT was unsure how to proceed, especially given the not-so-subtle deportation threat. After two months of waiting, Daniel decided to go to court. Emiliano then called back asking if he was being sued. He agreed to a payment plan to avoid court but stopped answering calls shortly after and never followed through with payment.

The team was running out of options and transferred the case to the Sturm Civil Litigation Clinic, which has represented cases pro bono when DAT negotiations stall and workers fear representing themselves. The letter, this time on the clinic's letterhead, sternly warned Ricardo to desist from making threats toward Daniel, especially related to his immigration status. The clinic filed the case in county court on August 28 for a September 26 hearing date. However, they could not locate Ricardo to serve him the court paperwork.

It was time to escalate pressure. The DAT planned a protest outside Ricardo's home. They found yet another address in Parker, a far-flung suburb, which belonged to Ricardo's in-laws. It looked as if Ricardo was using it as his business address. However, the team was still unable to locate Ricardo. Because they were unable to serve Ricardo, the clinic had to keep resetting the court date. Daniel's case finally went to court in January 2019, but Ricardo never showed up. In February, the court dismissed Daniel's case without prejudice because Ricardo could not be found. Cases like Daniel's do not inspire confidence in a legal process that largely abstains as it compels individuals to expend more time and resources chasing employers who failed to pay them.

FAILURE TO PURSUE

According to one compliance investigator, "failure to pursue is a huge challenge" for the division. The division applies the designation of "failure to pursue" to cases when workers fail to respond or follow up, which prompts it to close the case. Investigators were aware why some workers fail to pursue cases: worker transience, no real address to send communication, and possible lost letters. In addition to long wait times, in some cases, initial claims were incomplete and the division was unable to reach workers to furnish missing information, which causes delays.

Between 2016 and 2018, the division received an average of 3,476 claims each year and closed an average of 3,745 per year accounting for its backlog. The division places closed claims into three categories: Complaint (no violation), Dismissed Claims, Total Closed with Violation, and Responded to Inquiry (Mediation and Inquiries). Three-quarters of all closed claims were categorized as dismissed. The division may dismiss claims for various reasons, which it subdivides into failure to state a claim, employee withdrawal of the claim, no authority or jurisdiction, and failure to pursue. In contrast, only 16.7 percent of closed claims were closed with a violation of the Wage Act. The division also sent only an average of 768 determinations to employers per year. Of these determinations, 167 (average per year) found no violation (employer in compliance) and 601 (average per year) were found to be in violation of the Wage Act, resulting in a citation and notice of assessment to the employer. Within the dismissed claims category, failure to pursue alone accounted for roughly half of all closed claims between 2016 and 2018 for a total of 5,635 claims. In contrast, just 1,927 cases resulted in payment from the division.

If the worker returns to pursue the claim, it can be reopened, but as an investigator noted, "Claimants have to be active participants in the . . . process."[54] Yet workers' failure to pursue is not due just to transience, lost communications, or even a lack of worker agency. Instead, the category obscures the obstacles inherent in an individualized reactive enforcement system and how the demands of bureaucratic rationality clash with the exigencies of workers' lives.[55] The designation of failure to pursue does not account for the reality that in many cases, there is nothing or no one to pursue. Instead, aggrieved individuals like Andrés and Daniel shoulder the additional labor of chasing their employers, court dates, and judgments into dead ends. The collections process demonstrates that even when workers successfully pursue their cases, the system routinely fails them owing to lack of enforcement capabilities.

COLLECTING WAGES

If the division issues a determination that there was a violation of the Wage Act, it sends the claimant and the employer a citation and notice of assessment. The employer has fourteen days to pay the full amount owed to be eligible for reduced fines and penalties. Both parties have thirty-five days to appeal the decision. If the appeal is exhausted and the worker fails to receive payment by day thirty-six, the worker can file the determination in the appropriate court of jurisdiction to begin the collections process. While this appears somewhat straightforward, the collections process viscerally shows how the legal system is not designed for low-wage immigrant workers.

The CDLE can issue a determination and order fines and penalties but can't compel employers to actually pay. Nor can the CDLE enforce its determinations beyond coaxing employers to comply by reducing fines and penalties.[56] My follow-up information request to the CDLE showed that the division applied 1,961 fines for failure to pay wages since 2016, but waived 1,085.[57] The data demonstrated further shortcomings in the collections process. Between January 2016 and April 2021, an average of 37 percent of violations were resolved, which meant that the worker received the full wages and penalties ordered by the division. Collection rates are abysmally low across many jurisdictions. In California, for example, only 17 percent of workers who received a judgment from the California Division of Labor Standards Enforcement between 2008 and 2011 recovered any money.[58]

When employers ignore or refuse to honor determinations, claimants can file them in court to begin the collections process. Until recently, however, the state provided no specific guidance. Courts treated CDLE determinations as foreign judgments, as if they were issued by out-of-state jurisdictions entirely. It was often unclear which court to file these determinations in: Where the work was performed? Where the business was located? Or where the employer lived? The associated filing fees that courts requested were inconsistent, leading Zachary Mountin, who advises the

University of Colorado Boulder student wage clinic, to label this "clerk-made law." According to Mountin, "It depends on what jurisdiction or even who the clerk is on a particular day." Some courthouses charged $201 to convert the CDLE determinations, others less, and some charged nothing at all. He had heard about cases in rural counties where claimants were giving up because they could not pay the $201 conversion fee after they had already waited months for their positive determinations.

Noel's experience navigating Towards Justice, the CDLE, DAT, and small claims court reveals how the collections process can embed low-wage immigrant workers into forms of bureaucratic banality that inflict further indignities on top of their unpaid wages.

COLLECTIONS: THE WILD GOOSE CHASE

Noel was the first CDLE case brought to the attention of the DAT in April 2017. He had completed a free legal intake with Towards Justice, which referred him to its Just Wages Navigator program to receive help from a navigator to fill out his CDLE form.

Noel had completed two weeks of work for his employer, Mr. Abebe, at a community center in July and August 2016. He was paid only $300 of the $2,400 he was owed. Noel eventually quit because he was not being paid and began contacting Mr. Abebe for his owed wages. Mr. Abebe complained that Noel was harassing him and threatened to call the police. Noel filed his CDLE claim shortly after, with the help of a Just Wages navigator trained by Towards Justice. However, in April 2017, Noel was still checking on his case. That spring, I was supervising a group of graduate students who were conducting research on wage theft while volunteering with the DAT. Students Arianne Williams and Aaron Nilson were put on Noel's case to help contact the employer. They began to call Mr. Abebe.

Mr. Abebe curtly responded to the students that he had not hired and did not know Noel. Then, however, he pivoted. He asserted that Noel was lying. Noel had worked for someone else, not him. Mr. Abebe argued that the DAT was after him, threatened to take them to court if necessary, and abruptly hung up. A few weeks later, the students accompanied Noel to the community center where he worked to gather more information. They met the center's technical manager, who concurred that Mr. Abebe was dishonest, which can be helpful in supporting a worker's claim. He provided the volunteers with copies of documents demonstrating that Mr. Abebe was indeed in charge of the work.

Although the CDLE notified Noel that his claim was received, he had been waiting for eight months. The lack of timely response prompted him to sign papers to initiate the small claims court process to see which would yield faster results. Individuals generally cannot pursue small claims court and the CDLE simultaneously because they are considered to be duplicative, but given the lack of progress, Noel wanted to diversify his options. Once a case is decided in either venue, the claim should be dropped in the other.

Volunteers worried that Noel might have reservations about going to court because he was undocumented and Mr. Abebe was aggressive, but Noel assured volunteers that he was more concerned about recovering his money. Volunteers submitted his paperwork to small claims court, and Noel received a mediation date for the middle of June—nearly a year after his unpaid work. He also had to pay a $30 fee for mediation. If mediation was unsuccessful, his case would be heard in court the following day.

The next step was to serve Mr. Abebe for court. At this stage, Noel grew nervous. Alluding to his lack of immigration status, he asked volunteers if he could face any repercussions. The DAT had never seen ICE at small claims court, which would constitute illegal retaliation. However, it was the spring following Donald Trump's presidential election and ICE agents had become increasingly emboldened, including stationing themselves in and around other courthouses in the metro area. Volunteers admitted they could not make any promises.

Noel began to rethink things: maybe he would accept less, $1,800, to be done with Mr. Abebe, but the team encouraged him to wait to see what the judge would decide. A judge could award him 125 percent of what he was owed according to the Colorado Wage Act. These extra penalties could provide some additional justice as time continued to mount from his unpaid work. Or maybe the penalties would deter Mr. Abebe from doing this again to someone else.

The next day, before they could serve Mr. Abebe, the team received an email from the volunteer navigator who assisted Noel (and who took the additional step to become an authorized representative) that the CDLE had finally decided in his favor. The determination even entitled Noel to an additional $2,000 in damages on top of his unpaid wages if Mr. Abebe failed to pay within fourteen days. If Mr. Abebe did not pay or appeal after thirty-five days, Noel could file the determination in court to begin the collections process. The team returned to Noel to discuss his options: wait for Mr. Abebe to comply with the CDLE determination or continue with small claims court. It depended on how much more time Noel was willing to continue waiting. Inspired by the CDLE decision, he withdrew his small claims paperwork to await day thirty-six.

Day thirty-six came and went, and so did the summer and a new crop of DAT volunteers. Five months later, in November 2017, Noel's case was still open. Mr. Abebe never complied, and the CDLE's hands were tied. The next step was to file interrogatories in court to locate and garnish Mr. Abebe's assets. The DAT leveraged the tools of direct action to coordinate a protest outside Mr. Abebe's home to compel payment. However, by February 2018, Noel had yet to receive any money. He even approached the DAT with other friends and family who had been cheated by Mr. Abebe. He wondered if they should try small claims court again since others had taken him to court.

Noel became increasingly frustrated and tired of chasing Mr. Abebe. He began to debate a more aggressive approach with Mr. Abebe that made volunteers wary. Volunteers asked Noel if he wanted to file a contempt of citation from the court and issue a bench warrant to get Mr. Abebe arrested if he should otherwise encounter law enforcement. A bench warrant, however, does not accomplish much. Such individuals can be arrested only if they have another encounter with law enforcement that triggers an inquiry into outstanding warrants. It also does little to get workers paid. Yet a bench warrant was the next legal step after Mr. Abebe's failure to comply with interrogatories.

Each of these legal steps requires more legal knowledge, time, court filings and fees, and serving an employer who has already proved difficult to locate, recalcitrant, and sometimes overtly hostile. When workers file interrogatories, it frequently prompts employers to close accounts and move assets, if there were any to begin with. It's a game of chase with the worker a step behind. Some attorneys suggest skipping interrogatories if workers know where their employer banks—perhaps from coworkers or prior issued checks. With this information, a worker can directly file a writ of garnishment, for a fee of $45, to take to the bank before the employer can move assets. The bank then pays the worker directly from the employer's account and the worker circumvents more interaction with the employer. Garnishing wages without first filing interrogatories, however, requires time, creative detective work, legal savvy, and a lot of foresight. You need to assume that the employer will not pay and is likely to abscond, and precollect information accordingly. And this is all after a worker has already gone through the court process, paid corresponding fees, and won their case.

Noel asked sarcastically if filing a contempt of citation would take another two years. He expressed a hesitant willingness to try this next step, but he was also ready to take matters into his own hands. The last we heard, Noel had returned to Mexico. Meanwhile, the DAT received three more cases against Mr. Abebe on which they were also unable to collect.

Unlike the collections industry that aggressively pursues the poor when they fail to pay their debts, there is no bounty hunter for wage thieves. Nor would doing so absolve the sociostructural problems of workplace fissuring; the vulnerable social, economic, and legal position of unauthorized immigrants; and pressurized labor contracting arrangements that make such "thieves" likely to be insolvent, also cheated down the chain, or already policed and living on the brink.

WHOSE FAILURE?

Despite improvements, the CDLE division's administrative claims process remains out of reach for many low-wage and immigrant workers. If sufficiently enforced, a more proactive and targeted enforcement approach could help the agency bring justice to and work on behalf of workers and shift the climate to deter violators.[59] Attorney-scholar Matthew Fritz-Mauer told students Brianna Klipp and Kat Englert that "the problem with strategic enforcement is that it requires government actors to care" and envision themselves not as neutral dispute resolution bodies but as entities that can use their power to proactively locate and investigate violations.[60] Advocates became optimistic once Scott Moss, who truly understood the issues, took over as the CDLE's director in 2019 and began to pursue a more ambitious targeted enforcement approach.

The landscape started to improve largely because of advocates' efforts to push for new, and enforce existing, policies and tools to enhance workers' rights in Colorado. In 2017, Colorado passed the Wage Theft Transparency Act, which made it possible to publicly release information on offending employers. Previously the information was repressed under an antiquated trade secret provision. Without this information, proactive enforcement to target prone industries and past violators is even more difficult.

Colorado recently pursued steps to recognize wage theft as a crime beyond a civil infraction. In 2019, Colorado revised its Felony Theft Statute, which opened avenues for criminalizing wage theft and, perhaps more important, broadened definitions of individuals who qualified as employees under state wage laws and provided avenues for individual liability—all provisions that were stripped from the 2014 legislation. In 2020, the CDLE opened a rule-making process that resulted in extending overtime protections to more Colorado workers. Prior to the revision, Colorado construction workers were excluded.

Denver's 2019 minimum wage ordinance gave Denver Labor, a division of the Denver Auditor's Office, a mandate to enforce minimum, overtime, and prevailing wage protections in the City of Denver. The office made impressive strides in just a few years, especially with cases involving public sector or city-funded work.[61] Denver passed its own wage theft ordinance in 2021 that authorized a Wage Theft Unit within the city attorney's office to criminally prosecute wage theft cases up to $2,000 and pursue associated remedies for individuals without the need of an attorney. Yet attorney Matthew Fritz-Mauer shared data through a Colorado Open Records Act (CORA) request to the city attorney's office that showed that within six months of the ordinance, the city had prosecuted no employers and recovered no money for workers.

Towards Justice, Colorado Jobs with Justice, the DAT, Centro, other collaborating attorneys, and unions like the Southwest Regional Council of Carpenters, have advocated for stronger liability provisions within the city of Denver. At first, advocates proposed a wage bond for the construction industry, which would require employers to pay into an insurance pool with a certain amount of liability coverage so that workers can recover money even when employers are bankrupt or disappear.[62] A bolder proposal, which they plan to introduce shortly, would provide for up-the-chain liability to address workplace fissuring, address accountability from the top, and allow workers to collect from a solvent entity without having to prove that these higher-up actors were their employer.[63] For example, New York State passed a bill in 2021 to make general contractors liable for wage theft on their projects, which can incentivize them to monitor, rather than offload responsibility to, their subcontractors.[64] Colorado stakeholders also proposed statewide legislation to increase the investigative authority and power of the CDLE, including to help enforce collections and grant the Attorney General's office more authority to enforce wage determinations, which passed in the 2022 legislative session.[65] The CU Boulder Clinic has taken on challenging wage collection cases, which helped spur judicial change to facilitate the conversion of CDLE determinations in court and remove the haphazard fees. These approaches all attempt to shift the responsibility away from individual claims and workers toward more proactive enforcement that recognizes wage theft as a systemic and structural problem abetted by dynamics of power.

The sociolegal mobilization literature, alongside attorneys, advocates, and division employees, often attributes low-wage immigrant workers' failure to pursue claims to their interlocking vulnerabilities and steep opportunity costs including lack of time and money, fear of retaliation and deportation consequences, low English-language abilities, transience, and economic desperation.[66] However, the structure and culture of the labor rights enforcement system also overdetermine the result. Its dependence on reactive, claims-driven enforcement and outdated "employee" designations inhibits legal mobilization beyond the problems noted in the literature that center around naming, blaming, and claiming—or the process by which experiences are perceived to be harmful, turned into a grievance, and finally transformed into a dispute or claim—and access to justice.[67] An individualized reactive approach obscures the factors that precipitate wage theft and expose low-wage immigrant workers to unjust working conditions. Instead, it leaves these power dynamics intact by expecting some of least powerful to take initiative and exhaust valuable time, energy, and additional filing fees to garner wages that should have been paid in the first place. The very pursuit of unpaid wages constitutes an additional theft, when as Chris Newman at NDLON notes, "for every hour of time . . . you're doing uncompensated work that depresses the value on your work to begin with. Every hour you spend means you earn less per hour even if you do get the money."

A lengthy legal process with uncertain outcomes that largely leaves society's most vulnerable to solve their own problems means that most cases are unlikely to be discovered, let alone remedied. Stronger wage statutes and policy reforms lose their purpose when they are underenforced or simply do not work for those they intend to serve.[68] Rather than workers who fail to pursue, day laborers complain that attorneys, the division, advocates, and the legal and court systems have more routinely failed them. Even when the labor rights bureaucracy offers new tools, it continues to frame the problem as one of access and individual harms.[69] In doing so, it risks reinforcing the power imbalances that facilitate systemic exploitation or, worse, blaming workers when they fail to take initiative.

Individuals like Andrés and Noel vigorously pursued their cases and even won, but their efforts dragged them further through the entrails of intricate court systems and bureaucracies in ways that appeared designed to strand them and their claims. They never saw their money. The very process of chasing wages makes low-wage immigrant workers more keenly aware that their limited rights are not actionable.[70] The pursuit can also risk stressing social and kinship networks on which workers depend because they often find work through, or for, these very connections. Workers want their money, but not necessarily at the expense of being blacklisted in their industries or among their social networks if they keep chasing their employers.

CONCLUSION

For low-wage workers, the legal process to reclaim unpaid wages is simultaneously transparent and opaque, simple and impossible. Legal definitions and requirements, indeterminate waiting times, and back-and-forth communications position the labor rights bureaucracy as a "gatekeeper, with control over the flow of information and resources" in ways that exert legal, economic, and symbolic forms of violence over immigrant workers.[71] The labor required to rationalize a wage claim neatly packages economic and legal violence. By making structural and legal violence bureaucratically digestible, the claims process restricts recognition to a limited set of violations and employees while leaving the broader exclusion of, and harm inflicted on, workers intact.[72] Violations become the work of a few bad actors or individual aberrations rather than structurally and systemically driven.

Staff at the CDLE, as well as many judges, have workers' best interests in mind. Some investigators go to great lengths to investigate and creatively reconstruct cases with scant records, but others may summarily dismiss cases when they fail to fall within specified parameters even if there could still be a violation. Educating workers, compliance investigators, and judges, as well as removing barriers to make claims forms and systems easier to use and more accessible, are important steps. However, absent more proactive strides and sufficient political will and resources, legal education falls short of addressing how state bureaucracies are embedded in, and reproductive of, the larger sociolegal system that remains silent on the rise of precarious employment and excludes undocumented workers from legal protections while enacting more proactive punitive governance over their daily lives. The supposedly objective and technical legal work of courts and legal agencies operates to preserve the marginal structural position of low-wage immigrant workers, which concentrates them in precarious work that is prone to labor violations and underprotected by labor laws.[73]

Even if workers recover their money, there is no guarantee that their employer will not do the same to others or that they will not suffer again.[74] Day laborers grasp the limits of laws that have rarely protected low-wage, immigrant, and racialized workers but have instead policed them.[75] Yet they are guided to seek recourse from a legal system that through its other manifestations otherwise surveils and threatens to remove them.[76] Until 2016, the CDLE was also tasked with enforcing the Colorado Employment Verification Law, which doubled up on federal efforts by requiring employers to "complete an affirmation of legal work status."[77] The limited ways the law offers to help immigrant workers by encouraging them to help themselves and the humiliating requirements it requests in order to do so reveal how legal violence inflicts systemic forms of suffering.[78]

As the CDLE moves toward a more proactive approach, its outreach efforts and strong relationships with nonprofits, unions, and worker centers that workers trust will be key to investigating violators, coenforcing the law, and convincing workers that government agencies care or at least are trying to help within their limitations.[79] Yet well-intentioned advocates and enforcement agencies should also consider the limits of legal and regulatory fixes to contend with the sociostructural problems that continue to incentivize legal and illegal types of workplace exploitation: the proliferation of nonstandard work arrangements, escalating inequality, and the pervasiveness of immigration fear that continue to leave more workers underprotected and wary.[80]

These challenges do not mean that workers do nothing to contest wage theft, but they do put in perspective the dynamics of the next chapter: why some workers may place more faith in God or alternative forms of justice than the magic required to believe that the legal system will somehow summon vanished wages.

6 GOD'S JUSTICE

Resignation and Reckoning

Life is difficult, but work is sacred.

—Day laborer at Dayton and Colfax

ONE MAY MORNING IN 2015, graduate student Kendra Allen and I arrived at Centro to conduct interviews. Kendra had designed a participatory workshop to stimulate group analysis of the social factors that contribute to workers' vulnerabilities. Kendra had recently returned from the Peace Corps in Panama and was eager to try a problem-posing approach she had learned from her training.[1] Such participatory discussions can help workers build collective knowledge to analyze the problems they face and develop strategies to take action as they develop leadership skills.[2]

The group began with eight men, some participating and others listening nearby who occasionally interjected. Kendra asked the workers why they thought employers committed wage theft. Grabbing dry erase markers, she jotted quickly on the board:

—"They don't want to pay . . . because of racism."

—"Who knows?"

—"They want to abuse, [they] want free work. They say they have money, but don't."

—"They . . . take advantage, like work slaves."

—"Maybe since workers do not speak English, they haven't studied, they don't understand, they don't have anywhere to go . . . like a lawyer. They don't have resources to contest it. There is no protection."

—". . . [Workers] don't have money to pay a lawyer, there are no funds, they [employers] don't care about people."

—". . . If you are from another country [they take advantage]."

—"Or the boss will say the work isn't good."

—"The boss won't recognize you . . . they lose track of you and how much they owe you. Or they make it seem like they don't recognize you. I've had this happen . . . I'll pay you tomorrow, I have no money."

—"To become richer themselves, they don't pay you."

—"They are greedy."

One man commented, "Some people won't stand up for themselves. The bosses don't pay and they [workers] say, 'I can't do anything so I won't speak up.'"

As Kendra encouraged the men to systematically rank the challenges to preventing wage theft, some lost interest and trickled off to other conversations in the room. One man, originally from Texas, attempted to disentangle and rank the obstacles, stating, "I think being poor is worse than being undocumented if we don't have the money to follow up." However, given his US citizenship status, another man interrupted, "If an employer robs you, you can go to the police. But if you don't have papers, I think this is more important." Another ranked lack of English skills higher: "If you don't speak up, ultimately there is nothing one can do." "Fear is important no matter what [language] you speak," the man from Texas responded. One of the men turned to ask Kendra, "What do you think? If you have money, [then] there is no racism for you, but if you don't, both reasons [poverty and racism] matter."

Day laborers' difficulties with ranking the structural roots of their oppression reflected how lack of legal status, poor English skills, poverty, and racism combine to inflict a larger cumulative effect.[3] Workers understood this compounding effect well. One man at Stout Street, Matías, explained and repeatedly checked in to make sure student Laurel Hayden understood:

> We have suffered a lot from wage theft because we are without any social security number or ID. So when they [employers] abuse us, it is difficult for us to defend ourselves for the reason that they threaten us. You understand me? We feel threatened. For us, arguing with a person means calling the police for any reason and we don't have any form of ID or identification card. You understand me? That's why we have that abuse. Most of the people who work at the *liebre*, day laborers, suffer from this abuse because they take advantage. No . . . there are many good people, there are a few bad ones but yes that causes damage. Yes, they do damage.[4]

However, as conversations developed during that morning workshop at Centro, the men diverted from discussing these sociostructural vulnerabilities because they were less relevant to how they understood what happened to them and why. Nor were they necessarily conducive to inspiring the types of collective consciousness raising or action we anticipated. Instead, when talking about wage theft, workers kept emphasizing the character of unscrupulous employers. Employers who cheated them were "bad" or "amoral" people, "thieves" and "crooks" who did not care about others. One man explained, "Some people take advantage . . . they are bad people." To him, such employers were skilled at picking out vulnerable people to take advantage of. By isolating exploitation to the machinations of "bad people," such framings obscure structural workings of power, as well as the more systemic and structural nature of wage theft experienced by low-wage immigrant workers. Even Matías, who spoke with Laurel, ended their conversation by attempting to distinguish the mostly good people from the few bad ones.

Wage theft is not just an economic crime. It is a fundamental assault on dignity, which workers often admitted to with a tinge of shame that they had been duped or devalued. Centro's former director, Marco Nuñez, explained:

> When we talk about [wage theft] it often becomes minimized to just dollars and cents, but that isn't the case. One of the biggest crimes is the

> psychological effect of the stresses that come from not being paid for months on end, the self-doubt, how did you become a victim in the first place? Or a desperate spouse who says to you, "How could you let this happen and put our family in this predicament?"

As an affront to dignity, wage theft may trigger stress, rage against the employer, self-doubt, powerlessness, and sometimes internalization of the blame.[5]

When workers cast blame on an employer's character, this justification can easily lead workers to feel that little or nothing can be done. Instead, they must be more wary in whom they place trust. When we surveyed day laborers, we asked, "What can you do to make sure an employer pays you?"(Figure 20 in Appendix B). Many responded with strategies that were informed by a combination of street smarts, experience, and outreach, as documented in Chapter 4. However, a much larger portion of responses centered on a combination of "nothing," "don't know," or you just need to have "faith" or "trust" (113). Eighty-seven responses mentioned that working for known employers or assessing their reputation was important, while sixty-five responses placed the responsibility, as well as potential blame, on workers themselves, responding "work hard" or "do a good job." This chapter focuses on these responses to unpack how day laborers understand their predicament and act and plan accordingly.

Day laborers sorted employers into good and bad people. Some assessed potential employers by their heart, how they treated and talked to them, or what one worker pinpointed as a "gut feeling." Good employers paid; equally important, they treated workers with respect, including offering breaks, food, and drinks.[6] One day laborer explained how he attempted to evaluate employers: "I just look at the guy's face, see if they're real. You know, you can tell when somebody's being honest, or if they're just . . . you know."[7] These assessments, of course, are inherently unpredictable.

Nevertheless, given that day laborers are vulnerable to exploitation and have few avenues for restitution, resorting to faith, trust, or moralistic evaluations of "bad employers" and "hard workers" should not be discounted as workers' misperceiving the locus of their oppression. Day laborers struggle to make sense of these risks, maintain pride, and make plans for the future when each day is uncertain.[8] The best-laid plans or protection tactics can easily collapse in the face of precarious work. Even workers who had never experienced wage theft knew it was a possibility. When one man was asked how he assessed which employers were likely to pay, he responded, "You have to have faith."[9] When day laborers invoke discourses of morality, faith, karma, and exhortations to work hard, they may appear to resign themselves to, as well as reproduce, the conditions of their exploitation. However, this chapter demonstrates how these values also articulate a politics of justice as immigrant day laborers insist on their right to dignity.

Alana Lee Glaser's research with domestic workers in New York documents how domestic workers engage in collective complaints about their female employers' parental values instead of airing formal workplace claims.[10] She argues that collective complaint can foster collective consciousness when labor laws fail to address the structural conditions that continue to make domestic workers vulnerable to exploitation.[11] For day laborers, individualized rights-based labor laws, and even knowing their rights, are insufficient to prevent the labor violations that abound in unregulated day labor markets.[12] Day laborers blame employers' moral characters when they steal their wages. In turn, they stress their own faith or a belief in an eventual reckoning to uplift their marginal position in the world as they navigate daily lives and bureaucratic systems that are unjust and unlikely to prevent future harm. In doing so, they upend dialectics of oppression and resistance, of agency and acquiescence, that have less resonance with the exigencies of their lives. These seemingly mundane reflections can be considered as what Asef Bayat calls "encroachments"[13] into, and challenges of, the status quo to reimagine the social and moral order. As such, they can constitute a form of building collective consciousness and tentative solidarity, whether at Centro or at street corners. In the meantime, however, day laborers' predicaments remain unchanged.

THE RIGHTEOUS PAY FOR THE SINNERS

Leonardo, a man in his mid-fifties originally from Yucatán, Mexico, began a side conversation with me as Kendra and the workers drifted from the exercise. "What you are describing," he said as he pointed to the whiteboard of structural vulnerabilities, "does not work for me." He continued, "I think these are people that are accustomed to stealing money. They are thieves.

They don't care about the lives of others. . . . Then they make sure they are not caught."

Leonardo recounted an incident that had occurred two years earlier. He had decided to open a mechanics workshop and asked Fredy to be his business partner. Fredy's mother-in-law and her daughter were Leonardo's neighbors and he trusted them: "I thought he was a good person." Leonardo and Fredy both agreed to put some of their own money toward the business. Fredy didn't have the money so Leonardo loaned him $5,000, and then another $2,500 to build a car lift. However, Fredy never did any work and never repaid the loan. Frustrated, Leonardo hired a lawyer to take Fredy to court. "It has been two years," he lamented. "The lawyer [took the case] to court, but Fredy never showed up. I paid $800 to the lawyer and still nothing." Leonardo told me about this incident to show me, as he insisted, that "the laws do not work." The judge ruled in Leonardo's favor and issued a bench warrant for Fredy when he still failed to honor the judgment. But, Leonardo noted, "He was being very careful [to avoid police] . . . like a professional thief."

Leonardo believed that people who cheated workers frequently changed residences to avoid accountability. "It was not just me, but he has robbed other people." Leonardo had US citizenship, but thought that people like Fredy, who were born in the United States, perceived people like him, born in other countries like Mexico, as "stupid. . . . They seek a good person without problems, who works, respects people . . . [They] take advantage to rob [good people] because they are crooks." Leonardo continued with a glimmer of justice, "[Fredy] thought I couldn't do anything, until the final consequences." Leonardo learned from his neighbors that Fredy had died alone in his home.

Leonardo felt a small sense of vindication after Fredy's death, but he still didn't have his money. He was just as angry with the attorney, who he felt had taken his money without following up, as he was with the ghost of Fredy. To avoid wage theft, Leonardo advised, "Don't believe in anyone. . . . I fought a lot for the money for [over] a year. . . . I almost don't want to believe anymore. The righteous sometimes pay for the sinners."

Leonardo grasped that immigrant workers were vulnerable to exploitation and intimidation, as well as the fact that the laws did "not work" for them. However, these explanations failed to fully account for his *own* misfortune, which he attributed to Fredy's character. To Leonardo, Fredy was a thief and a sinner who took advantage of his own righteousness. The sociostructural causes marked on the whiteboard could explain how and why wage theft generally occurred, and even why Fredy exploited Leonardo. However, it was less helpful for individuals like Leonardo to grapple with why they personally suffered. Why could they do everything right, win in court, and still never see their money?

Day laborers often spoke of faith, the wrath of karma, or God's justice for unscrupulous employers when they received little material justice for their suffering. Appeals to morality, faith, and karma may resemble resignation, but they also constitute a moral refusal of a political economy that devalues day laborers' work, time, and dignity. Employers frequently try to avoid paying workers by claiming that they did a poor job. These excuses not only deprive workers of their hard-earned money but are personally demeaning. Luis Carlos, a worker from Cuba, admitted, "I will do what [work] there is, but I need them to respect me. The important thing is for employers to respect a worker's experience and [be] honest about the work."[14] Day laborers valued respect, character, and sincerity when evaluating a sense of justice and good employers beyond the legal system's narrow consideration of compliance with wage and hour laws.

When workers maintain hope for an eventual reckoning based on a deeper sense of morality, this is not just magical thinking. Instead, their faith operates on the same continuum of actions available to low-wage immigrant workers as navigating the labor rights bureaucracy, whose forms of bureaucratic power are equally shrouded in mystique. Juan, whose wage theft incident was described in Chapter 4, preferred to leave his theft claim to God because "only God speaks justice for people who do not have papers and are here undocumented." By sharing their moral evaluations of their employers, workers speak back against a legal system that attempts to individualize and legalize what is otherwise systemic exploitation endemic to precarious work.

GOD'S WILL, FAITH, KARMA, AND WITCHCRAFT

Kim Bobo introduced her path-breaking book *Wage Theft in America* with a quote from Exodus: "Thou shalt not steal."[15] Throughout her book, she inscribes wage theft within historical and theological Christian, Hebrew, and Jewish concerns with theft as an affront to "justice-seeking traditions."[16]

As such, religious groundings have often inspired broader expectations for justice, hope, peace, and reconciliation.[17]

Many Latino day laborers had Catholic upbringings, which informed their general ideas about faith, God's will, and justice.[18] Their expectations for justice for offending employers often mixed vaguer Christian-informed views of faith and God's justice with an everyday folk understanding of karma. Although they did not necessarily understand Buddhist beliefs, the idea that "personal destiny is seen as inherited as a consequence of the ethical quality of one's actions" that may play out over time and even lifetimes is appealing.[19]

When day laborers mention faith, God's will, or karma, they are not drawing from their theological origins. Instead, they invoke their own experiential understandings of these ethics to articulate how they believe the world should operate and make sense of their place within it. These beliefs ground a hope for justice that is not necessarily forthcoming in this life or through law and rational action. Instead, workers envision eventual justice meted out by God or justice that accumulates and bears consequences in a near or distant other future.

Day laborers' use of terms like *karma*, *faith*, and *God's justice* also echo anthropological debates around witchcraft accusations. Over four decades ago, anthropologist Evans-Pritchard's (1976) ethnography of the Azande in southern Sudan argued that witchcraft accusations offered a culturally specific understanding of misfortune and suffering.[20] Rather than a mystical explanation of how harm occurred, witchcraft accusations provided insight into the particular and the *why*—to this person, here, and on this day.[21] Most day laborers grasp the mechanics of wage theft and the roots of their vulnerability, but these explanations cannot account for why them, why now, and how or if amoral behavior will be righted. These convictions further reflect and inform a habitus,[22] or way of being and acting in the world, required to navigate daily lives shaped by uncertainty.

FAITH AND GOD'S WILL AMID SOCIAL ISOLATION

Graduate students Laurel Hayden and Elayna McCall arrived at the corner of Dayton and Colfax an early April morning in 2015. They watched a few trucks drive by, but no workers approached them, so they began to strike up a conversation with Edgar, originally from Guatemala. Edgar had never experienced wage theft but was aware of employers who did not pay. He complained that not paying was against the law in the United States but also stressed that "the law of God is that they have to pay." However, the law did not necessarily take day laborers into account. Edgar explained that if he went into a store and stole something, the police would come and make him pay or arrest him. In contrast, police paid little heed to "the thieves who do not pay [their workers]." The only justice in which Edgar held faith was that of God: "Therefore they say God punishes those who do not pay."

Another individual, Timo, told graduate student Camden Bowman about his experience with wage theft. He had worked for a particular employer before and he had always paid, but this time, the work was for the employer's son. Timo recalled:

> I went with the father and the work was good. But then they didn't want to pay me because they had not been paid. I said, "I don't care, I just want to be paid for my work." . . . I thought about filing a report . . . but I had to fill out the paperwork. At the end I didn't want to. I left it like that. It's not worth so much time fighting for so little. I left it so that God could punish them.

Timo never pursued his claim but did not necessarily acquiesce to exploitation either. He believed that God would eventually exact justice and was wary of the time and effort required to pursue a legal claim that might go nowhere. Héctor, another worker who had been cheated by his employer, believed that employers would eventually be punished. He contrasted God's wrath with the small advantage employers accrued from stealing from the poor; "If that makes him [the employer] happy, that's fine. The one who loses is him [from] living that life of . . . evildoing. . . . The money he owes me is not going to make him rich." He agreed with Timo, "Like the truth, everything has its time. Things will get paid . . . according to the will of God. I am not the owner of anyone's life or judge anyone, but God does. And I believe in God. I say, God makes justice. I do what is [God's] will."[23]

For individuals like Edgar, Timo, and Héctor, their general convictions around faith and God's will had little to do with whether they considered themselves religious or attended church. One man explained to graduate students Natalie Southwick and Sarah Johnson at Centro, "God is in everyone, no matter what church we go to." For them, faith provided a sense of belonging in a country where they suffered from legal insecurity, insufficient work and low wages, and isolation from family and friends.[24] To some immigrant workers, only God cared about them. One remarked, "God takes care of foreigners, but they have to have faith." By offering a sense of support and social engagement, faith helped mitigate the stress and anxiety of precarious work. Boyas, Valera, and Ruiz's study of Latino day laborers' subjective well-being in Texas found that religiosity and strong social connections to family and friends improved day laborers' perceptions of their well-being.[25] Nevertheless, religiosity did little to change their plight.

Many day laborers in the Denver area were older men (mean age of 45.5) who had lived in the United States for a long time (mean of 22.5 years). Many suffered from isolation and disconnection.[26] Older men warmed to students, who they said reminded them of their grown children back in Mexico they had not seen in decades. Some had wives and children in the Denver area, but most had left partners, parents, and children back home. Others had separated from partners, who now lived with their children in other US states. One man remarked that his ex-wife kept his son in Iowa, but he couldn't live in the small town; he was "bored" and there was no work. But he video-chatted with his son and sent money when he could. Others, like Umberto, felt ashamed to burden their adult children with their own lives; they relished their children's accomplishments but hid their own struggles.[27] Umberto originally migrated to the United States with his wife and two children. In the United States, they had two more children and settled into a home in Aurora. But he and his wife had since separated, and when I met him, he was living at a shelter. After experiencing an injury and wage theft, he was searching for another apartment.

Many immigrant day laborers initially relied on social networks to migrate to the United States and sometimes to find a first job or place to stay. New immigrants often expect more established members of their networks to assist them, but as Cecilia Menjívar documents, such supports may fail to materialize or dissipate quickly after arrival.[28] The legal and economic insecurity of even more settled members of the immigrant network may strain their already limited resources.[29] Because many day laborers came to Colorado from other states rather than directly through migratory networks, some of their networks were already weaker or nonexistent compared to other immigrants or even immigrant day laborers entering via more established gateways.[30] Some who moved to Colorado from other states initially followed friends, family connections, or rumors of work, but these ties often faded. Efraín's case was not uncommon. He came to Denver from Tennessee. He complained that it rained a lot in Tennessee and they "pay very little, very cheap." His sister lived in Denver and told him there was more work so he came. However, shortly after he arrived, he found out that his sister had moved to Los Angeles to marry a man who lived there. He was currently renting a room in another family's home in suburban Lakewood. Because most day laborers in the Denver area had been living in the United States for a long time and 76 percent had lived in at least one other state, many no longer relied on immigrant social networks.[31]

Some of the men experienced fractured kinship networks in both the United States and at home, especially as they remained in the United States and moved around. Ivan, the jewelry man mentioned in earlier chapters, still sent money to his children in El Salvador to help with their schooling, but he had not seen them since he left in 2003. He spoke with them via video or phone. His wife, he said, "could no longer put up with the cold," meaning that she left him for another man. Students conducting research with Centro's members in spring 2014 learned that many day laborers relied on Centro precisely because they did not have other social connections to help them land jobs.[32] Homelessness was prevalent among day laborers (see Chapter 5) and especially among workers who frequented the Stout Street site across from Centro.[33]

As they precariously remained in the United States with unstable work, insecure income, and the stigma imposed by racial discrimination—and, for many, their status—day laborers wrestled with depression, stress, poor physical and mental health, homelessness, and drug and alcohol addiction.[34] Some debated whether their migratory sacrifices were worthwhile. Day laborers stressed that they worked hard, largely to support their families in the United States and in their countries of origin. Lack of work and income were intensified by the costs of wage theft and injury, which strained familial relationships and expectations to provide for family members in the United States and send remittances home.[35] Manuel, who spoke about his wage theft incident in Chapter 3, tearfully shared the implications: "My [children] wanted a Merry Christmas, but I wasn't paid."[36] Other workers sacrificed their own well-being to send money home to preserve the fragile threads of their relationships.

Amid social isolation and fractured familial connections, some workers felt a sense of helplessness. Cristóbal, who was originally from Honduras, commented, "Here I am alone in this country." He fully dedicated himself to his work and struggled to get by. He had never experienced wage theft but had little trust in employers. Without papers or a driver's license, he felt he could do little to prevent wage theft but was animated by a feeling that "one has to do what the heart tells them." In response to what he would do if an employer did not pay him, he responded that it would be "God's business. God is responsible for bringing people to justice." However, even when workers were aware of their options, they realized their limited control. Ivan attributed his avoidance of wage theft to luck because he knew it could easily happen. He said, "I am lucky they have always paid me. . . . But I don't say it could never happen to me." He knew the risks but retained hope for a future in the United States and buying a home, stating, "We are in the land of dreams and dreams cost nothing."

Felipe, originally from Durango, Mexico, also knew how wage theft occurred and some strategies to protect himself. He complained about how employers demeaned workers. He spoke about employers who dropped workers off at 5:00 p.m. after completing the work, but would not return to pay them until 8:00 or 9:00 at night. As workers anxiously waited to get paid, they sacrificed time that could be spent resting or with their families. After he suffered an ankle injury, Felipe struggled to acquire work. He lived with his wife and children in Denver but was contemplating returning to Mexico after his previous trip home. His brother had passed away shortly after his visit. Felipe reiterated that "work is indispensable," but insecure work, injury, and his conflicting family obligations across borders exacerbated his anxiety. "One gets tired," he shared. "I need to work every day." He approached employers who pulled up offering a job, but upon seeing his ankle, the employers selected other workers. He anxiously debated how long to wait. He knew his chances of getting work dwindled as the hours wore on. If he got a job too late in the day, he would have to decide between working and his doctor's appointment that afternoon, which he had cancelled the previous week. Felipe summed up his conflicting emotions, "Life has good and bad moments. There are things that happen in life. . . . In life, you have to have faith."

For Edgar, Timo, Héctor, Cristóbal, and Felipe, a belief in faith or God's justice offered a sense of social support and comfort that improves subjective well-being amid precarious life and work.[37] Their convictions, rather than their religious underpinnings, animated a politics of hope, dignity, and survival when everyday life was uncertain, employers were disrespectful, and they faced social and familial alienation while struggling to live up to their migratory aspirations.

KARMA

Julian, a Latino man in his fifties originally from San Diego, had been coming to the street corner at Federal and 19th to search for work on and off for nearly twenty years. He said that he never experienced wage theft, but then went into an example where an employer tried to shortchange him. After completing a landscaping job, the homeowner gave his boss an $80 tip and specified that it should be split with Julian. His boss claimed that he had already given Julian what he owed him, but by refusing to give him his half of the tip, "he screwed me out of $40," Julian complained. I asked Julian what he did: "Nothing; you can't do anything." However, when Julian was finishing up and undoing the employer's trailer, he must have unrolled it incorrectly and it broke. He smirked, "I think it was karma. . . . He [his boss] was angry. Oh well, that's karma. Now you have your $40 [that you didn't pay me] to fix it." Julian's sense of vindication from this chance mishap, whether explained by karma, accident, or his own error, is shared among other day laborers who may feel they can do "nothing" in the immediate term to contest exploitation or confront employers. Instead, the accumulation of moral rights and wrongs will eventually recalibrate on the side of justice. Another worker reasoned, "Bad employers will get what is coming to them. . . . Something will get them. Karma or whatever."

One August morning in 2015, graduate student Morgan Brokob accompanied me to Stout Street. The scent of marijuana wafted through the morning breeze before the heat settled in. We met Orlando, who was not well positioned to get work that day. A large bandage covered his right wrist and forearm as a result of a workplace injury. His employer covered his expenses through workers' compensation insurance, but Orlando had been unable to work. We inquired why he was there if he could not work: "It is like a family [here]," he laughed. Some workers accordingly nicknamed Stout Street "the Mexican office." It was where they sought work, hung out, and some even slept. Others divided their time between Stout Street and nearby shelters. Unlike Felipe, who lived with his wife and children, others had nowhere else to go.

Orlando told us in a mix of Spanish and English about a wage theft incident that occurred the week before. An employer hired him with a few other workers to move boxes. They were told that they would be paid $12 an hour and the job would last all day. However, they ended up working only three hours, after which they had to wait around another six hours for the employer to pay them only $30 each. "I didn't say anything at first," he commented, "because who would I have complained to?" Although they accomplished the work in just three hours, it was heavy and grueling, leading Orlando to feel cheated and devalued.

Since the incident was recent, we encouraged Orlando to consider making a legal claim, but he hesitated. He was convinced a court would stigmatize him because he was Mexican. He felt there was a lack of sympathy for day laborers; no one wanted to help them. Life and work were unpredictable. "There are good and bad employers and that is part of being a day laborer," he said. Like Julian, he expressed hope that amoral individuals would eventually get what was coming to them: "There is payback for employers who do not keep their promises."

As the conversation with Orlando was ending, a shiny white crossover pulled up to the corner. Sure enough, it was the same employer who had cheated Orlando and his coworkers. Another worker joined the conversation: "He cheated you. Anyone that goes with him [to work] comes back sad." The car stalled for several minutes. The silent hesitation at the corner was palpable in the thickening morning air because the other workers were aware of what had happened to Orlando. Finally, three younger men got into the vehicle. I asked why the men got into the truck despite the others' warnings. One worker reasoned that the young men needed the money to purchase drugs and implied that they were addicts. Yet given the scarcity of work, this judgment discounted how unscrupulous employers are likely to eventually find workers willing to have faith that this time would be different. They might think they possess the smarts, skills, or luck to avoid the same fate. Or they just needed any job at all.

Like Orlando, many day laborers were disillusioned with the legal system. Félix recounted an experience with an employer who paid him for the first day of work but then kept telling the workers he would pay tomorrow. He never paid and Félix was owed $170. When student Max Spiro asked Félix if he tried to recover his wages, he laughed: "It wasn't worth it. I just wanted it to be over." He had little confidence when employers, as he phrased it, "hold the power." He juxtaposed different realms of justice for the powerful and individuals like himself: "There are different laws on Earth, that of God and of man, and the discrepancy between them. . . . Religious law is the greater law." Max was unsure how to pinpoint Félix's sense of justice, reflecting in his field notes, "He believed in karma, for lack of a better description, where bad things happen to bad people."

Gerardo also commented on this power imbalance. He had experienced wage theft multiple times, which curtailed his ability to send money to his parents in Mexico. He found a lawyer once, but the employer was bankrupt so there was nothing left to do. Gerardo debated pursuing the case further to send the employer to jail, but how would this help him get his money? He continued to tell student Camden Bowman about additional workplace indignities. In one incident, after Gerardo's hand got caught in a motor at work and he broke his finger, he was unable to work for four months. When he approached his employer for assistance with the hospital bill because the accident occurred at work and he could not afford the expenses, his employer simply retorted, "Neither do I [have the money]." Gerardo wanted to keep pushing the case, but feared being reported to immigration authorities: "They [employers] have all the power. . . . The courage disappears because day laborers without papers are always going to lose out in the end." However, Gerardo continued, "sometimes curious things happen." He heard that soon after this incident that the employer had fallen at work, injured his head, and was hospitalized. Gerardo sarcastically wondered aloud if the same employer who could not afford to help him had sufficient money to cover his own medical expenses.

In another example, Nelson knew he could pursue his claim with the Department of Labor, but instead, he said,

> We leave it [wage theft claims] like that. In other words, we say, with God they will pay. [Because] they are not doing good things, something bad will happen to them because everything is like karma, it goes back and forth. Sooner or later and it's common sense. You cannot do wrong and reap well. It is impossible. For a moment yes, but then there comes a time when something happens to you and you ask, why? But then you remember and you say, "Oh, because I did something wrong and now it is catching up to me." Sooner or later, it's true, isn't it?[38]

When day laborers talk about karma, they frame it as a logic of common sense for workers who are cheated and have few means to achieve justice. Karma informs a moral orientation whereby something good will eventually materialize from suffering.

Mauricio captured an ethos that guided his approach to life and work: "Bad things happen, but sometimes good things come out of it." His daughter had suffered facial injuries in a car accident when another car ran a red light. When she returned to school, a company was donating chairs to the school, and after they saw her, they ran her story on the nightly news. A wealthy individual saw the story and sympathized because his own daughter had died in a car accident. He promised to pay for Mauricio's daughter's college after she completed high school. This incident convinced Mauricio to have faith in people, although he knew that not everyone was a good person. He applied this sensibility to his work. When an employer underpaid him, he claimed it was not worth pursuing the money. It was better to move on. He reasoned, "If a small door closes, a larger one will open." He even returned to work for this employer because he needed the money. For Mauricio, his faith surprisingly worked out when the employer actually made up the previous amount on this next job.

WORK HARD AND DO A GOOD JOB

Many immigrant day laborers originally migrated to the United States to fulfill patriarchal obligations to their families at home. Once in the United States, the stresses, indignities, and risks of street corner employment affronted their sense of masculine pride.[39] Some strove to recoup a sense of dignity and endure the demeaning aspects of street corner employment by performing a hypermasculine identity that reproduced cultural stereotypes of the hard-working "man of honor" dedicated to the welfare of family and country.[40] They upheld their identities as hard workers to counter negative stereotypes that frame Latino immigrants as lazy, prone to abuse drugs and alcohol, or likely to abandon their families.[41] A day laborer, one worker insisted, "is a very hard-working person."

To improve their own position, some workers contrasted their work ethos with those they believed either deserved their fate or interfered with their own employability. One man at the Aurora corner commented, "The men downtown [at Stout and Centro] are homeless and maybe do not even want to work . . . they just depend on the shelters." Another explained, "A lot of people [here] aren't used to working . . . they don't want to work." He claimed they spent their money on drugs and alcohol, from which he previously suffered. He stressed that he was now clean. Day laborers frequently pointed to their skills and experience to counter their devaluation as unskilled workers while they also had to be ready to take any job offered. Some attributed the hardships of others to their own failings or substance abuse to insulate their own risk.

Others distanced themselves from day laborers, replicating the stigma associated with street corner employment. Although they were on the street when we met them, they would claim it was an exception. One man asserted, "I almost never come here; it's rare that I come here." Two men in particular distinguished themselves by telling us they had never been to the corner before. They spoke about day laborers: "There are a lot of people who don't work well and don't do a good job," insinuating that this was why they were relegated to day labor.

In contrast, others took pride in the flexibility[42] day labor offered not just to fill days left vacant by insecure employment, but as a preferable option to the indignities they experienced at what Max Spiro described in his field notes as "regular-ish" jobs including demanding but also unpredictable hours, low pay, excessive discipline, and disputes with bosses.[43] Although many lamented they could not find jobs outside of day labor because they were unauthorized and had weak social and employment networks, for some (especially immigrant workers with legal status and the US-born), day labor provided autonomy. They could choose when to seek work, request a pay rate in cash, choose who to work for and for how long, and decide when to attend to other needs in their lives instead.

Despite its insecurity, day labor allowed workers to pivot to other life tasks during the week or seek additional work on weekends. If a job was not forthcoming, they could run errands, take family members to medical appointments, pick up children from school, or relax. One example was Osmar, who had been in the United States since the late 1950s. He used to work for a company but no longer preferred this: "You need to go to their office, they paid very little like $8/hour . . . they want to take out for taxes and pay very little . . . [but] here [at the corner] you can get $15." Osmar described himself as *ya viejo* (already old). He was tired of working all day in companies and having to arrive at a specific hour each day. At the corner, he came and went as he pleased and took home cash.

Men who distanced themselves from day labor or attempted to upgrade it as an intentional choice, sought to uplift their own work ethic to avoid popular stereotypes of day laborers as lazy, illegal, homeless, or drug addicts. These are the same assumptions employers use to assume they can exploit day laborers. Still, workers who preferred day labor were the exception. Most preferred regular employment or at least a repeat list of employers to ensure reliable work. They had no other options and did not, as one worker noted, come to the corner *por gusto* (for pleasure).

By cultivating a reputation as hard workers, Mexican immigrants secure a niche in the labor market.[44] However, this same ethic leads employers to exploit their "willingness to work" and may motivate workers to take on risks that aggravate the potential for injury.[45] The latency of the negative stereotype allows employers to blame workers as "lazy" and cast them aside when they are no longer able to submit to these demands, claim their work is subpar, or even accuse them of criminal behavior.[46] Gerardo grasped this dilemma: "[Employers] yell at you if you work too hard or if you don't work enough." The dialectic of the hard-working versus lazy/criminal Latino immigrant also exacerbated judgment from family back home, who often suspected alcoholism or adultery when men failed to send them money.[47] These evaluations therefore obscured, and reinforced, how immigrant day laborers' marginal structural position subjected them to insecure work, low pay, and injury.

Day laborers also used impressions of "hard work" to justify exposure to wage theft. One worker explained why he thought others experienced wage theft: "There are people that go to a job and do not work. You need to respect the boss. If I go [on a job] and do not work well, you will pay me less or maybe not pay me at all. You have to work." Still, these men were aware they faced similar perils, and many went on to tell their own wage theft stories. Emilio said, "Here [at the corner] it is *suave* to look for work because there is money . . . for those who like to work," again blaming scarcity of work on individuals who did not want to work. However, he continued:

> But [there are also] many many [employers] that rob people. . . . Sometimes they [employers] steal our work. . . . In other words, it's a robbery, but as we don't have work . . . it makes it easy for them and difficult for us. . . . You shouldn't have to go around fighting—[asking] when are you going to pay me.[48]

An ethic of hard work nevertheless provided a rationale to uphold their own dignity and exert agency in a high-risk market where they had little control.[49]

Some workers also internalized their sociostructural vulnerability by blaming themselves for not working hard enough, for not exercising good judgment, or for trusting employers.[50] As Manuel explained in Chapter 3, he blamed himself for "allowing" his employer to pay him monthly. Another worker told Max Spiro, "I never should have gone [with that employer]." When workers experienced wage theft, feelings of shame and guilt—what one advocate labeled *vergüenza*—may inhibit them from confronting employers.[51]

Hard work and doing a good job were rarely sufficient. Cultivating a reputation for hard work could even motivate workers to take on more risk.[52] Nelson, who preferred to leave his wage claim to "God" to avoid "going around fighting," blamed himself for his workplace accident. He sliced open his finger while cutting tile, but was afraid to report it as a workplace accident because he had used the wrong tool, "Because you can't [cut] with something meant for tile when you are going to cut wood. . . . But it is my fault. . . . I should not have done it. . . . It's my fault . . . I didn't get paid that day."

Employers also attempted to transfer the blame to workers for unsafe working conditions and their own failure to provide proper safety equipment and training. After installing washing machines, David, originally from Guatemala, suffered a hernia.[53] When he asked his employer for assistance with medical bills, the employer told him that his hernia did not result from his job. It was from something else. After multiple hospitals refused to treat him, he finally found one that would, but they told him to sign a document stating he would never return. David's injury likely resulted from installing the washing machines, but it also resulted from something else.[54] The accumulated suffering of unauthorized migration, low-wage work, and fear of deportation made David structurally vulnerable to dangerous back-breaking work, hesitant to report violations, and cajoled into signing forms he did not understand.[55] It further conspired to encourage him to interpret structural violence as his own carelessness.

Wage theft and injury sometimes mutually aggravated one another, as in Andrés's experience in Chapter 5. Workers who experienced wage theft might take on more dangerous jobs that offered more money, like roofing, to compensate for lost wages. Injured workers might do the same,[56] or employers saw them as easier to take advantage of. Injured and older workers often were relegated to lower-paying jobs, cheated on the job, and suffered wage theft when employers saw them as no longer able to "work hard" and unlikely to complain.

Workplace injuries and wage theft not only stressed day laborers' finances and bodies; they aggravated long-standing forms of structural, physical, and symbolic violence that manifested in everyday assaults on dignity.[57] When I met Jorge, originally from Honduras, one morning at the Aurora corner in summer 2015, I saw a cast on his hand. When I inquired what happened, his response surprised me: "I had an accident in 2000. And now I broke my hand," he said. I struggled to decipher the time line. Why did he mention an accident that occurred over fifteen years ago? Did this contribute to his current hand injury, which I learned resulted from falling from a roof on a recent job?

Jorge continued to explain how he nearly asphyxiated after he was trapped inside a train on the migrant journey crossing into Mexico from Guatemala in 2000. I asked why he reattempted the journey in 2008. He responded, "I believe in God. I had faith I would be okay." This same faith, and lack of alternatives, brought Jorge to the corner that day, although his injury made it unlikely he would get work. If he worked, he risked stressing his injury. For Jorge, the violence of the migrant journey bled into the everyday suffering of day labor. The hand injury scraped against the scar of his harrowing train experience.

The forms of structural, economic, and political violence that exposed Jorge to the migrant train—poverty, legacies of US intervention in Central America, discrimination and criminalization against immigrants, and the lack of legal migration channels—are the same that rendered him vulnerable to wage theft and injury in Denver.[58] These forms of violence accumulated as day laborers remained and aged in the United States, and their value as "cheap labor" evaporated when they could no longer "work hard."[59] No longer just deportable, they sensed impending disposability as older workers debated returning home. Another man, originally from Honduras but who had lived in Colorado for thirteen years, considered his return: "When the time comes, you have to go, because being here once you get to a certain age, when you're older, you don't work, you know? . . . The US is no place for old men."[60]

Moreover, employers manipulated subjective assessments of "hard work" to justify withholding wages and devaluing workers. Manuel felt this particular sting when his employer said he wouldn't pay because the work was poor: "I come from work, my experience is as a worker. . . . I know how to work. Those are excuses."[61] Day laborers at once recognized that they might have avoided exploitation because of luck or fate, while they also emphasized the need to "work hard" when, as one day laborer argued, "there is no security." "Work hard and do a good job," like karma, God's justice, and faith, provided workers with a sense of dignity and agency where they had little control, as well as a grammar to articulate an expectation for justice even if it was not immediately forthcoming.

RESISTANCE AND *CONVIVENCIA*

There is debate as to whether day laborers' strategies and forms of resistance can be considered political. Sean Crotty argues that few day laborers see themselves as political actors; instead, they engage in "strategic visibility" to ensure access to the hiring space, ability to acquire work, and make day labor more bearable.[62] Such tactics can include developing selective social ties with other workers and regulating the behavior of others.[63] For example, the men waiting at the Federal site self-disciplined to stake a claim to a space where tensions previously existed with local businesses. A few years earlier, Centro's staff helped convince the city council to lift antiloitering ordinances and encouraged neighboring businesses to accept the workers' presence as long as they were looking for work. Workers accordingly governed each other's behavior.[64] They stressed that they kept the area clean—pointing to the nearby trash can—respected women, and didn't use drugs or get into fights. They were there to work. Still, the presence of the No Loitering or Standing Sign underfoot reminded them of their tenuous presence (Figure 10). One worker explained, "If you are Hispanic and you don't have papers, you always need to behave well."

Crotty points out that day laborers' strategies do not necessarily constitute resistance.[65] By competing with one another for scarce jobs and gov-

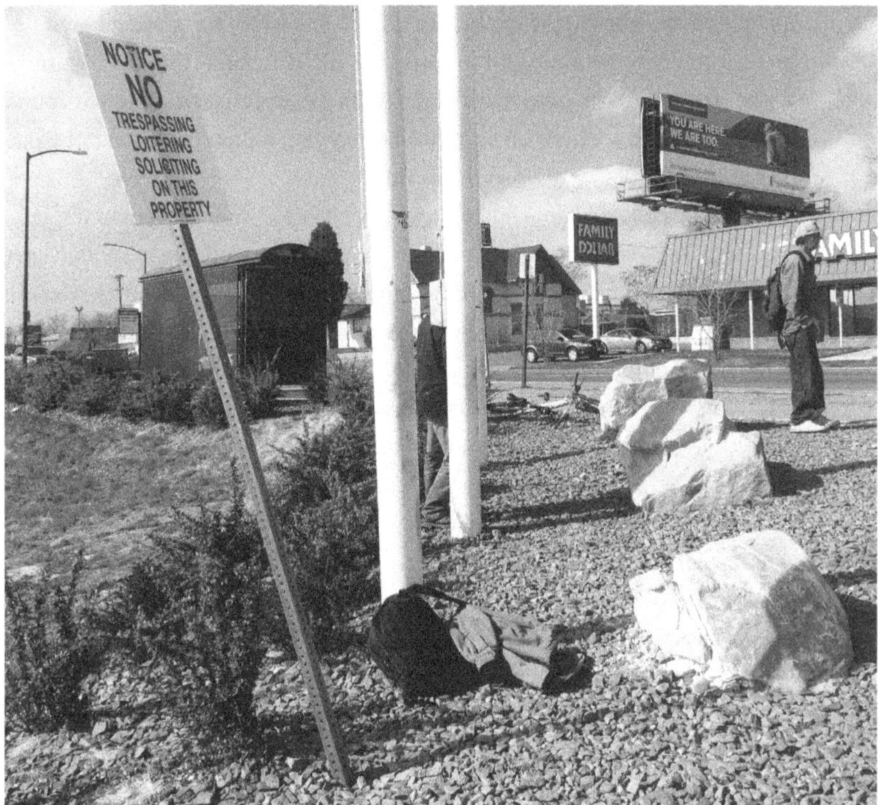

FIGURE 10: No Trespassing, Loitering, Soliciting on This Property sign at the Federal and 19th hiring site. Photo by author. Originally published in Galemba (2021).

erning each other's behavior to secure an employment niche, day laborers end up reproducing their "own exploitation as a low-cost labor source."[66] Yet such analyses can miss how sparks of solidarity can be found in everyday tactics to endure, *convivir* (coexist), and share their experiences with others. Nevertheless, day laborers guarded extending trust and friendship more carefully.

In addition to proximity and perception of employment opportunities, the other reason day laborers mentioned when choosing a hiring site was camaraderie with and knowing other workers. The strained solidarity at the *liebres* depicted in Chapter 4 provided the men with a sense of community and potential job opportunities, as well as warnings about particular employers. One man explained, "I have trust. I know how to work . . . with the people I know." He chose the Federal hiring site because he knew people there, who might also invite him along on jobs. Esteban shared his perception of community at the corner: "I am alone here. Here is my family [other workers]. We are all family members. We are all from different countries. . . . But those here we became countrymen although we are not from the same country. . . . [We] came to work."[67]

Still, others were ambivalent about friendships. Thus, most used the general term *conocidos* (acquaintances) or the general friendship of *compañeros* (companions) to refer to fellow day laborers, unlike Esteban who used terms like *family* and *friends*.[68] Strained solidarity and cautious friendship coexisted with competition and transience.[69] Comfort and companionship were not to be confused with trust, which posed liabilities whether extended to employers or their *compañeros*. One man explained, "There is competition [here], sometimes there are certain contradictions. We look for work, but we communicate good and bad news. There is a bit of everything [referring to kinds of people], the sincere and half sincere." Rather than trust, the tenuous forms of strained solidarity shared among day laborers contributed to what they described as *convivir*, or coexisting with their *compañeros*.[70] For day laborers, this offered a way to *seguir adelante* (to keep on going). Casimiro explained to Camden Bowman, "There are different *compañeros* who think one way, others [think] another way. But that's life. *Sigue adelante, sigue adelanete* . . . don't fall [down]. Right? That's how it is."

One brisker-than-usual August morning in 2015, I arrived at the Federal site and a man greeted me as he came to fill his coffee cup. He mentioned he hadn't seen me in a while and asked if any students were joining. I mentioned that more would come once school resumed in September. This was the day I met Claudio. He explained that if he was at the *liebre*, he would be happy to help with my research because many people wanted to tell their stories, but "some don't speak well or will not respond to questions the same way . . . so it's important to learn how to *convivir* with [others] here because people talk about things and respond differently." He had learned to "*convivir* with everyone." He continued, "Here [you] need to get used to *convivir*. . . . At first, we may be surprised and not understand." He then pulled out a cigarette, "Like I smoke but I'm also your friend. . . . [Points to another man] He drinks too much, but that doesn't mean he stops being a friend. I have learned to *convivir* with everyone here."

Learning how to *convivir* opened day laborers to opportunities and warnings and offered a way to pass the time and keep going.[71] It offered human connection, but guarded against the risk or fuller forms of friendship and trust that could lead to disappointment or exploitation, or prevent workers from landing scarce jobs. These forms of strained solidarity were not necessarily conducive to the types of collective action organizers envisioned.[72] However, as practiced by workers, they helped activate the human connection critical to sustaining workers' struggles and daily lives in the United States. It was telling that workers most appreciated when we came to *convivir*. They would tell us about their children, dance *bachata*, a popular Latin dance style that originated in the Dominican Republic, with Kendra, and tease Camden by calling him "*el Piqué*" after the famous Spanish soccer player because Camden learned Spanish in Spain. They preferred when we merely stood and chatted with them on icy mornings rather than when we came to hand out information about labor rights and ask more questions. While workers' relationships with my research and outreach team were quite distinct from what they shared with one another, they appreciated our companionship while also keeping us somewhat at a distance. They were keenly aware that it could be unwise to place too much trust in those who offered to help, but who lived lives far from their own and were usually a relatively transient presence in their lives.

Monforton and Von Bergen note that "building a community of day laborers is challenging . . . [but] talking about shared experiences can be empowering" to provide the seeds for worker power to grow.[73] Although day laborers' strategies end up being more survivalist than political or solidaristic, they help workers stake a claim to spaces in the city to make "spaces that work for them."[74] One man waiting for work in Aurora commented to graduate student Stephanie Renteria-Perez, "Respect [here] will help us succeed.... If we begin poorly, we will end badly.... We want to climb up, not down."[75] It is within these spaces, and by enabling day laborers to organize and inhabit them, that Crotty contends that workers can "begin to articulate their hopes for the future ... [so that they] will no longer simply exert a right to exist. They will exert a right to thrive. They will demand their right to the city."[76] As the man continued to tell Stephanie, "Little by little, we are growing and setting rules where day laborers can flourish."[77]

CONCLUSION

Today is cloudy, but there are days when it gets very beautiful in certain parts, the sky is clear. With the light of the Lord, who shelters us all, right?

—Man waiting for work at Federal and 19th

In winter 2019, graduate students asked individuals waiting for day labor employment at the Aurora corner, "Why do you think it [wage theft] happened?" They responded with a mix of explanations, but also framed the problem as a fundamental injustice. One man explained, "We are human beings and he [the boss] should pay. It is unjust. [It happened] because the boss was acting unjustly."[78]

Day laborers' compounding structural vulnerabilities were embodied as personal affronts to respect and justice. Workers drew on discourses of faith, God's will, and karma and cultivated an image as hard workers to express a vision for justice, center their own dignity, and foster human connection. They knew their employers were likely to do this again and that they might be victimized again despite their mitigation strategies. There was little change in day laborers' vulnerable structural position, which continued to make life and work unpredictable.

Although many resigned to leave their claims "with God" or did nothing, the fact remains that many had previously tried to do something. They had confronted their employers, found an attorney, and gone to court, the CDLE, or Centro. However, their ability to recover their wages, be treated with dignity, and exact justice was undermined by their structural vulnerability that facilitated wage theft in the first place.

A sense of justice animated by faith, restored via karma, or that can be steered by working hard and stressing one's own morality, might do little to prevent or redress wage theft. At worst, such sentiments rationalized, internalized, and sometimes perpetuated it. However, they also provided a grammar for understanding why bad things happen to good people, often again and again, while pointing to other frameworks for justice. These sensibilities articulated hope for a more dignified future where their marginal position in the world could be righted. In the moment, tactics to *convivir* enabled workers to form human connections and share experiences with one another, and even with researchers and advocates, but they cautiously guarded trust and friendship.

Before moving onto the next chapter, which details direct action approaches to worker justice, I present an interlude in which Severiano A. reflects on his wage theft experience with DAT volunteer Abbey Vogel.

SEVERIANO'S STORY

Interview conducted between Severiano A. and Abbey Vogel, May 12, 2021

SEVERIANO A. IS A DAY laborer who worked with the DAT to recover stolen wages in 2018. He won his small claims court case, but he was unable to collect on his judgment. In 2020, Severiano moved from Denver to Sylacauga, Alabama, with his family. Severiano came to the United States from Espita, Yucatán, Mexico, nineteen years ago. Severiano's wife is from California, and his 5-year-old daughter was a frequent guest at Centro while the team worked with him on his case. He shared his story over Zoom from the home he is renting in Sylacauga one weekday night after a long day of work.

I include Severiano's interview with Abbey Vogel, a former student and DAT volunteer, to illustrate some themes covered in the previous chapters. As demonstrated in Chapters 2 and 3, myriad contracting and labor brokerage arrangements and vague promises conspire to cheat workers out of their fair wages and strain their social connections. Like the workers in Chapter 2, Severiano had moved around in the hope of more work and lower living expenses, often to find conditions were not as promised. He had learned some strategies, though, to protect himself, based on his own experience and his work with the DAT. Like the workers in Chapter 6, he was hopeful for the future, had faith in some employers who had helped him (even if paternalistically) in the past, and had new plans in mind. Abbey reflects on Severiano's case in Chapter 7.

ABBEY: Did you arrive in Alabama to work for a specific person? Or to work on a specific project?

SEVERIANO: Yes—In my town [in Colorado,] a man came to look for me and he told me that we should come here [to Alabama] and that he would pay me $25/hour for regular work. We came, and in reality he only pays me $20. He also told me that he was a partner to a company, but really he is just their immigration partner. The company gives him a house, a truck, tools, they give him everything. In exchange, we have to give the company 40 percent of every project we work. . . . On one job,—he speaks Spanish very well—I went up to him and said, "Hey, [name redacted]; how much will the checks be for?" He was straight with me and said $8,300. . . . Then, I didn't bring in more than $4,500 at the end of the job. If he was a partner, then the checks would be split equally between all of us workers.

ABBEY: So you went to Alabama because this company promised you $25 an hour?

SEVERIANO: Yes, and they promised to provide a house.

ABBEY: Did they give you one? Did they give you anything else they promised?

SEVERIANO: They did give us a house, but . . . the problem is that it's a little illegal . . . it's like one that used to be used for farmworkers. There are eight bedrooms, eight bathrooms, and two kitchens. . . . We have applied for a house in Trussville, which is a city that will have more work, but the house is not free until the end of May.

ABBEY: For one year you have to do this? And then after that year you are free to go where you want?

SEVERIANO: Yes, but I am planning to leave early. I have already worked for him for nine months, and I can imagine that this would be sufficient for him to consider himself paid for driving my family and I the twenty-three hours it took to get here from Denver. This man who brought me is a general contractor; he is not a partner like he said. I have already told him that I don't feel comfortable continuing to work with this person. In Denver, I had my trusted little groups and my work, but it was all within my own company. I could work directly with the man who brought me, but not while this company is charging me for every job I work. . . . I have applied for an ITIN [Individual Taxpayer Identification Number, for those who cannot otherwise get a Social Security number to process their taxes] so that I can have my own company again. When everything happened during the pandemic, I did not have stable enough work to say, "Okay, I am making enough money." So, I gave up my own company for *el machetón* [this bossy know-it-all], and I do not want to continue paying him.

ABBEY: Have you told him you are planning on leaving? Is he kind to you, or will he be angry?

SEVERIANO: I haven't told him yet because this company is . . . how can I say it . . . well, two other people came from Colorado with me and they have returned. I am the only one left. . . . I do not want to return to Colorado because the rent is so high. . . . I guess I just have a different mentality than them [the people who left].

I do have some regrets about leaving Denver because prior to leaving. I was working with a company called Siding LLC [company name changed by author], and the boss would explain all of the projects and would give us tools, rides; he would pay for everything. All we had to do was show up for work. He would say, "There are regular clients, good clients, and bad clients." He would explain how much a job would cost to the clients and would say that if they wanted more details, more *cariño* [particular care or attention], that they would have to pay extra . . . he would explain everything.

ABBEY: So why did you leave this company?

SEVERIANO: *Por tonto.* Idiocy. I was told that they had better work and everything.

ABBEY: Does Siding LLC still exist?

SEVERIANO: Oh, absolutely. It's registered in Denver. The boss is still always sending me messages to come work. They just got a contract in Colorado Springs for $18 million.

ABBEY: But you won't return to work for them?

SEVERIANO: No, the rent is too high.

ABBEY: Were you working with Siding LLC when you experienced the wage theft case that you went to the DAT for help with?

SEVERIANO: When I had that problem with Hugo [employer name changed by author], I hadn't worked with Siding LLC. Some people had come up from Mexico, and they were a little problematic, so I left working with them to work with Hugo. After he refused to pay me my wages, it was actually the boss of Siding LLC who paid the rest of my rent that month because I didn't have any money. I was working at the time at [site in Denver] and [boss of Siding LLC] was there and said, "Come here. I want to see you." He said: "Climb up here." He was on the roof. So I climbed up and he asked me, "What's wrong with you? What a miracle that you're down here making friends with the poor folks." So I told him my story [about experiencing wage theft]. He was dying from laughter and said, "*Eres tonto.*" You're an idiot. He asked me, "Why did you go [work for Hugo]"? And then afterward, he said "*vamos para la troca*"—"let's go to my truck [colloquial phrasing in original]." We went, and he asked me how much I was short. I said a lot. He wrote me a check and said, "I am going to pay it all."

Things always happen to me like this—sometimes good, sometimes bad. Sometimes, sure, things are hard, but everything's okay.

ABBEY: But you and Hugo were friends and neighbors before the wage theft incident, right?

SEVERIANO: Yes, after it happened, he continued to live in those apartments, but afterward, I couldn't do anything and had to focus on making my own life better. Maybe he needed that money more than me.

ABBEY: Have you experienced any other instances of wage theft?

SEVERIANO: Only one time when I went to work for [someone] who owed me $8,000 and only gave $4,000. The owner of the house paid the remaining $4,800.

ABBEY: And did that end up being a fair amount for the work you did?

SEVERIANO: Well, really it was still $2,000 short because we bought materials from Home Depot . . . we had hung the materials when the owner of the house came home and said that the corner we had installed in her ceiling was not the color that she wanted, and that she wouldn't pay for the materials . . . we also lost a day and a half of work.

ABBEY: After that experience, have you had any others?

SEVERIANO: No, now I know to make a contract with whatever the person wants. . . . We decide to work together and then we write specifically what work they want, what are the costs, what's the color, everything is specified, that way afterward they can't say, "Hey, you didn't tell me what was going on or anything." Now, with a contract there, I get my money. . . . It's more secure.

ABBEY: So, you want to achieve starting your own company like Siding LLC, but in Alabama?

SEVERIANO: Exactly. It's because this boss [from Siding LLC] planted something in my mind. Just one thing: you can do it. I just have to focus mentally. It's not about saying "Can I or can't I?" I can. I am going to achieve it because I will. You always have to maintain positive thoughts, never negative.

7 THE DAT

Justice and Direct Action

Abbey Vogel, Diego Bleifuss Prados, Amy Czulada, Tamara Kuennen, Alexsis Sanchez, and Rebecca Galemba

USUALLY CENTRO HUMANITARIO para los Trabajadores (Centro) closes its building around one or two in the afternoon. On Tuesdays, however, shortly before 6:00 p.m., the Direct Action Team (DAT) coordinator reopens the doors. Volunteers make their way to the cramped back room of the building and pull up chairs to a communal table. They settle in, asking each other for the wireless password to pull up the meeting agenda, passing around paper plates and homemade fruit salad supplied by long-time volunteer Chris Wheeler, and keeping an eye on the door in case workers arrive to report an incident of wage theft or to share an update on an ongoing case. Workers rarely come alone. Sometimes they arrive with coworkers, a spouse, or children. The DAT coordinator always starts the meeting with an awkward ice-breaker, such as, "What is your favorite color grape?" or "What word do you hate the sound of the most?" to help new members feel comfortable in the space and cultivate a sense of community (Figure 11).

This chapter begins by describing the DAT's work, after which the remainder is coauthored by current and former volunteers, including myself.

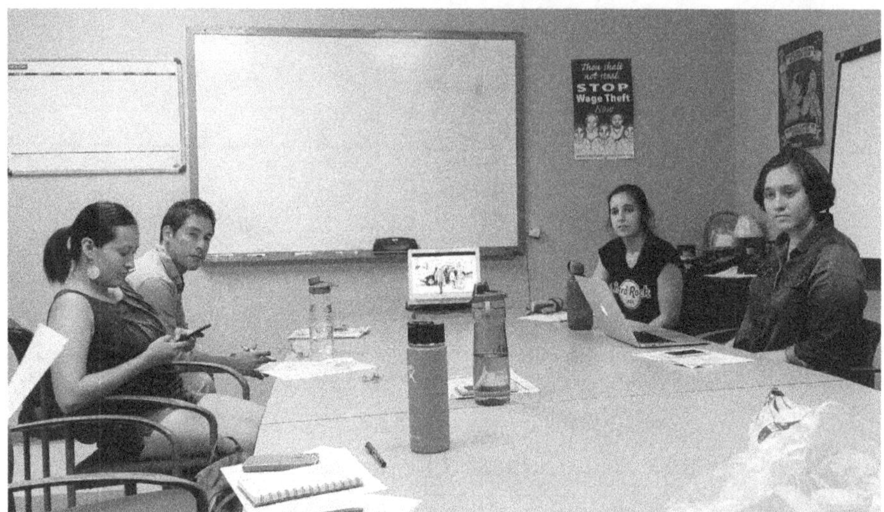

FIGURE 11: DAT team meeting. Photo by author.

We reflect on some of the challenges we have faced assisting workers with wage claims. Sometimes we struggled to reconcile individualistic forms of service provision with our wider goals of fostering worker empowerment. We also reflect on our own positionalities and the power dynamics that influenced our relationships with one another and with workers. Yet we come to argue that embracing these tensions in our work can highlight incipient ways to move toward a praxis that advances solidarity.[1]

THE DAT: ORGANIZATION, VISION, HISTORY, AND STRATEGIES

The DAT is a group of volunteers who use direct action strategies to help low-wage immigrant workers recover unpaid wages. Most workers who seek the DAT's assistance are Latino immigrants who work in industries related to residential construction, landscaping, cleaning, or domestic work. The DAT receives case referrals from Centro, Towards Justice, and outreach at day labor hiring sites and other workers who spread the word. The cases tend to be small, underdocumented, and sometimes convoluted, which makes them uneconomical for attorneys and challenging for workers to navigate on their own. The DAT also engages in coalition building with like-minded stakeholders to contribute to larger organizing campaigns and help advocate for policy changes at the state and local levels.

Long-time volunteer Chris Wheeler articulated a central motto to the DAT's work: "Never do for a worker what he (or she) is unwilling to do for him(her)self." The team is structured around a worker empowerment model, but in practice, existing hierarchies and the realities of providing assistance sometimes conflict with the team's broader vision for building worker power. Still, the worker is always central in determining what strategies to use.

The approach to direct action came from day laborers who were collaborating with Minsun Ji in the early 2000s before Centro opened. Direct action was inspired less by a specific theory of change than by, as Minsun reflected, the idea of "creat[ing] a sense of solidarity with the workers." Direct action meant finding direct ways to confront employers to pay their workers and providing basic legal education so workers could protect themselves, support each other, and organize. Direct action also birthed what became the first wage clinic initiated by then University of Denver (DU) law student Chris Newman[2] alongside Minsun. In the early 2000s, the only person at the CDLE who spoke Spanish was the receptionist. Newman and Doug Smith, his supervisor at the time, filed open records requests to conduct what they called "advocacy by inquiry." On the basis of their findings, they organized a direct action of workers to march into the CDLE's office to "sift through documents [and] force them to translate things." The clinic that emerged, as Newman put it, was a "blank canvas."

Marco Nuñez, who became Centro's executive director in 2012, began to formalize what became the DAT with the assistance of a community activist and retired political science professor, Chris Wheeler. When Marco left Centro in 2015, Centro was experiencing severe financial and staff shortages, which strained its ability to cover basic programs. Chris worried that the DAT could not be sustained, so he asked me to make us an appointment with DU's service-learning center for ideas. Over the next few years, we hired graduate students under my supervision (Amy Czulada and Diego Bleifuss Prados) or under Jim Walsh at the University of Colorado Denver (Alex Sanchez) to coordinate the team using work study funds. When Tammy Kuennen from DU's Sturm College of Law joined the DAT in 2017, she brought law students along with the potential to represent select cases.

Jim, Tammy, and I helped connect students in our classes to the team, some of whom stayed on as we helped build a volunteer base from like-minded community activists and some workers.

However, most students and even community allies fizzled out after a few months or when they moved onto other careers or moved away from Colorado. Only one worker, Davor, who sought the DAT's assistance for his own wage theft incident, has sustained involvement over time. Most volunteers tend to be white, college aged, and relatively privileged social-justice-oriented undergraduate, graduate, and law students.

New coordinators and students helped the DAT expand its tactics, diversify its volunteers, recruit worker members, and fundraise. Some infused the team with peers they knew from other organizing work with the Democratic Socialists of America or Abolish ICE. Over the next few years, the DAT became more independent, with Centro primarily serving as fiscal sponsor. Although now led more by volunteers than workers, volunteers were cognizant that their relative privilege could help tilt the power imbalances that promote wage theft and attempt to silence workers. Employers responded differently when we showed up at their door alongside workers and called them on the phone. Volunteers drew on their social, educational, and linguistic capital to help workers negotiate with employers, navigate legal bureaucracies, and fill out court paperwork to lower the barriers and costs of coming forward. When workers became disillusioned by attorneys and legal agencies that failed to help them or take their cases, volunteers offered an empathetic ear and new options. Although the DAT builds on a legacy of worker empowerment by ensuring that workers are central to the process, volunteers are concerned how they now play a larger role in leading the group than workers. These concerns figure prominently in the cowritten section of this chapter.

The DAT's direct action strategies employ stages of escalation to pressure employers. The steps tend to proceed as follows:

1. Gather information on the case from the worker.
2. Call the employer to get their side of the story and start negotiations.
3. Delegation: Volunteers accompany the worker to request wages at the employer's home or business.

4. Other forms of direct action. The team may distribute flyers to inform neighbors of an employer's behavior, run a call campaign, hold a protest, or reach out to coworkers, companies, media, lead contractors, or homeowners to find pressure points.
5. Legal options. When employers still fail to pay, the team may help prepare workers for small claims court to represent themselves, assist workers in filing claims with the Colorado Department of Labor and Employment (CDLE), or refer cases for legal representation to the Sturm Civil Litigation Clinic or Towards Justice. The team also combines legal strategies with direct action to pressure employers from multiple angles.

The DAT's vision is for workers to become active agents in educating and organizing other workers. Direct action flips the power dynamics that allow employers to commit wage theft with impunity as workers find a community of solidarity to recover their wages and shame offending employers. In practice, although many workers expressed interest in sustaining involvement with the team to assist others, they often lacked the time. Wage theft frequently exacerbated other forms of precarity in their lives. Their involvement with the team, and even on their own cases, therefore varied significantly.

WRITING AND REFLECTING ON THE DAT

The chapter now transitions to a collaborative authorship format with Abbey Vogel (former DU student and DAT volunteer), Amy Czulada (former DU student, DAT coordinator, and Centro staff), Diego Bleifuss Prados (former DU student and DAT coordinator), Alex Sanchez (CU Denver student, former Centro staff member and DAT coordinator, and DAT volunteer), and Tammy Kuennen (DU Sturm College of Law Professor and DAT volunteer).

The cowriting approach is intended to explore how anthropology can be practically put to work to foster the pursuit of worker justice, as well as how the collaborative writing process can advance theoretical understandings of justice.[3] The chapter draws inspiration from Bejarano and coauthors' invitation to "decolonize ethnographic research" by including different stakeholders as full participants in the knowledge construction process.[4] Our goal is not just to listen to participants or even just to provide them with tools to advance their own work, but instead to learn and reflect together on how our different positions and experiences shape and are shaped by our knowledge, relationships with one another, and ongoing praxis.[5]

Despite our attempts to invite workers to contribute to the chapter, this wasn't how they wanted to participate, at least not at that moment. Many workers gave us permission to talk about their cases, and in the cases of Severiano, Davor, and Diana, to use their first names. We acknowledge the limits of our own voices but argue that requesting a type of labor that is not valued by our interlocutors is far from inclusive, and at worst is a form of exploitation. Workers who wanted to recount their experiences, and even many volunteers and former students, did not have the time to edit multiple versions of a manuscript, and academic writing was not necessarily conducive to their own goals. Therefore, we lay bare the uneven social relations that undergird our attempts to be collaborative and focus on the complementarity that our different skills, desires, and contributions can bring to the DAT's work—not all of which can or should be accomplished in academic writing—while trying to avoid speaking for others.[6]

The cowriting process helped us reflect on the DAT's ongoing work and sought to nurture ongoing transformation in ourselves, blurring the divide between knowledge generation, volunteering, and activism.[7] Our particular positionalities and privileges are reflected in the tensions with which we grappled as activists and writers. Even through collaborative writing, we still fell into familiar trappings of power. At some point in the research process, Abbey, Amy, Diego, and Alex were paid research assistants or students under Rebecca's supervision, which infused inequities even when we tried to worked collaboratively.

The chapter embraces the messy sparks and disjointed conversations that we contend are generative for understanding worker justice. At times, we leave individual authors' words in block quotes and in other instances merge them into the text itself or note an author's specific contribution. Otherwise we write in one voice to create a cohesive narrative. We make these narrative choices stylistically while also making the labor that each author put into the chapter more transparent.

The process of writing and reflecting on our work helped us understand things we did not see in the moment, when we were consumed with helping workers recover unpaid wages. We highlight how the reflexive process is not an ornamental addition to contextualize research findings but can instead inspire new insights toward social change. We explore how our research and advocacy can cultivate the kinds of relationships, organizational forms, and values of justice we aspire to or, as Haiven and Khasnabish write, we "prefigure the world [we] would like to see," even if we are not quite there and missed it at the time.[8]

WORKER EMPOWERMENT VERSUS GETTING PAID

As volunteers, we often experienced a tension between helping workers receive their wages and the goal of building worker power. The demands of workers' lives often made it difficult for them to fully collaborate even on their own cases. Indeed, many came to us after trying other avenues on their own. When we got involved in cases, employers' actions occasionally triggered our own personal experiences or sense of injustice, which sometimes inspired us to act in ways that risked leaving the worker behind.

Kelvin's case provides a good example. Kelvin came to the DAT when he wasn't paid for work on a chimney by an employer named Todd. Todd had hired Kelvin through Centro's Employment Program. Shortly after his intake with the DAT, Kelvin called Alex to check if there had been any progress. However, he otherwise did not interact much with the team. When Diego, Alex, and Kelvin finally reached Todd to negotiate, Kelvin came but was quiet and standoffish. Diego grew frustrated by Kelvin's lack of input, though he also saw that Kelvin was clearly upset by the situation and obviously no longer wanted to interact with Todd. Still, Alex and Diego felt compelled to continue the case. They ended up settling for $200 of the $280 that Todd owed Kelvin. Looking back, they wondered if their own motivations eclipsed Kelvin's.

Although Alex first came to the DAT as a student through a class at the University of Colorado Denver (CU Denver), her passion to advocate for Kelvin was partly inspired by her personal experiences, and later by her staff role with Centro's Employment Program. When she joined the DAT, Alex described a process of coming to terms with her second-generation Mexican-American identity:

> I am quite obviously Mexican from first glance. My skin complexion is brown. So, when I got to the team I was asked to assist in translation during the intake process of a worker's claim, during our weekly meetings and even outreach work when speaking to day laborers on some of the gathering corners where they looked for work. I could have simply said I was not fluent in Spanish, but it bothered me very much and I found myself frustrated many times with learning and practicing again. . . . So I made a point to get better. I would wake up earlier than our scheduled times for outreach, before the coffee and the *conchas* from the *panaderia*, and I would practice what I was going to say. . . . From there, I would rewrite my "script," then practice until one day I didn't have to anymore.

Hearing workers' stories brought political consciousness to the injustices that had personally affected her family. Alex reflected, "Growing up in our home, we may have not had discussion of politics but we certainly had discussions around the injustices that my family experienced personally." She was frustrated by her father's silence about his own stolen wages:

> I remember as a child that when [my father's bosses] would ask my dad to get his hours together he couldn't stand the frustration of putting all that together. . . . He was far too exhausted from the endless hours on end he'd been working because that was his mind-set. . . . I saw this, but truly what I saw was guilt. He felt guilty that after all the effort he was putting in to support his family, it was not enough.

Growing up, Alex often worked alongside her father: "Working side by side, considering the amount of time we spent on these jobs and the effort we put in, I too felt cheated when he was cheated." She elaborated:

> From employers in larger companies to subs that were "helping" him out, [my father] somehow would walk away without the original wages he was promised or there was a change in his working conditions that did not benefit him. . . . More and more I became familiar with said "norms." For example, if his bosses were not paid, he quickly learned . . . that meant he wasn't going to be paid.

For Alex, helping Kelvin was a way of reconciling some of these tensions:

> My parents had always taught me to be outspoken and so I could not fathom why [my father] would accept what was going on. . . . He would simply reply, "That is how it is." We often fought about these kinds of politics within the industry because we did not see eye to eye on them. Ultimately, he was not the only one cheated or robbed either. It robbed our household of peace of mind that we would have everything that we needed . . . If he lost wages, his response seemed to always be, work more and work harder.

Upon later reflection, Alex became even more irritated by Kelvin's case because of what she had learned as a staff member with Centro's Employment Program. The program provides clear employer expectations, transparency, and accountability to hiring arrangements. So the fact that Todd hired Kelvin through Centro made the incident particularly egregious. When employers hire a worker through Centro, they must fill out a "Hire a Worker" form detailing the minimum hourly rate the workers are to be paid and insisting that workers be paid in cash upon finishing the work and no later. Even if an employer is not satisfied with the work, the form issues a disclaimer that workers must still be paid a minimum for their time. Although at the time, Alex knew less about Centro's program, the incident became particularly unnerving when she learned that Todd was more than aware of these expectations. She reflected, "I think this speaks to just how transparently open, intentional, and egregious this made the wage theft cases from Centro."

Some of us were motivated to work on a worker's behalf because of our positionalities as activists or because of an employer's flagrant behavior. Amy reflected that she may have felt this pressure because she had not yet fully come to terms with her class privilege, which sometimes caused her to prioritize winning for workers rather than ensuring they were active in the process. Amy recalled a case with workers Mariano and Fernando, who had also found their jobs with Drew through Centro. Drew had contracted the workers for a construction project and failed to pay them. Although the workers contacted the DAT for assistance, they seemed almost completely disinterested in participating.

Still, trying to recover their wages became an obsession for Amy, especially after she realized that Drew simply didn't want to pay the workers because he thought he could get away with it. Amy began calling Drew several times a day and leaving messages. The team then organized a calling campaign that recruited more people to call Drew. Finally, the team held a protest outside his home on a Sunday at 8:00 a.m. The workers didn't show up and had stopped answering Amy's calls before the protest. A group of about seven volunteers stood on the sidewalk outside the house and started shouting, "All Workers Should be Paid!" and similar chants that echoed in the streets (Figure 12).

When Drew heard the chanting, he quickly called Amy. He warned that they needed to leave or he would instruct his wife to let his dogs out. He even told Amy that he couldn't be responsible for anything that might happen to them. After the protest, however, Drew agreed to leave money for the workers at a nearby office complex. The team felt a sense of satisfaction upon receiving the checks, but when Amy met with Mariano and Fernando to give them their money, they seemed shocked. She had the sense that they

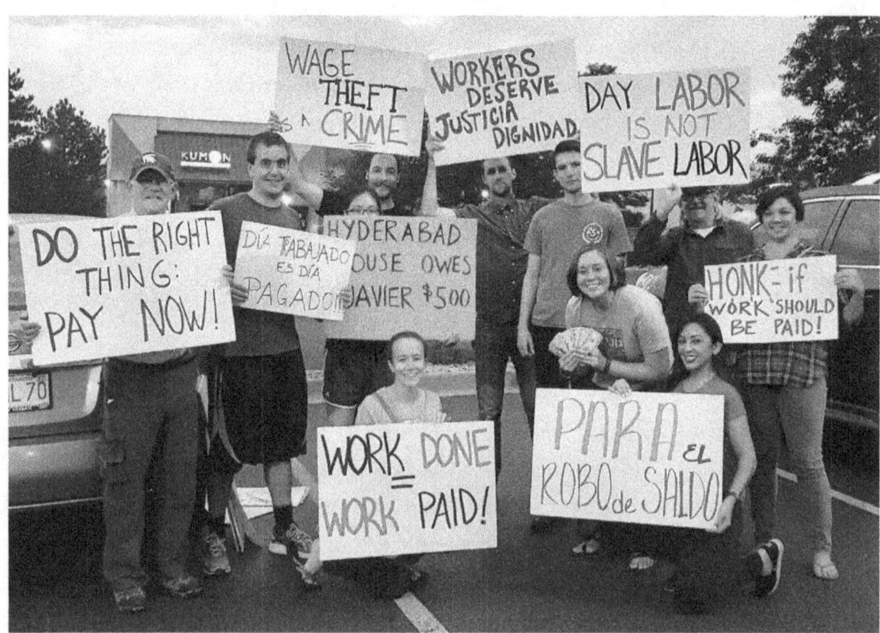

FIGURE 12: DAT wage theft protest.

had become so accustomed to not recouping money that they were surprised that anything had materialized.

In these cases, our efforts helped workers get paid, but they also undermined the goal of building worker power when our own frustrations overtook what workers were willing to do. The DAT attempts to level the power differential between employers and immigrant workers by accompanying workers in the process of confronting employers—many of whom otherwise think they can act with impunity. Yet acting for rather than with workers could reinforce power differentials between ourselves and workers. Amy reflected:

> While there are significant differences between me, a white woman from the suburbs with a lot of education, and day laborers working day-to-day in capricious labor, I think DAT has taught me that we are all at risk of being victims of wage theft and other labor abuses. . . . The most important and lasting piece of my work with DAT is how it shaped my class consciousness. It has informed my life's work, but has also helped me to recognize and deconstruct my privilege . . . on a daily basis.

We began to wonder if our expectations for workers to be active agents in their cases could be disempowering. Tammy asked herself:

> Why should I ask this worker to fill out their own paperwork when I can do it in a matter of minutes, and do it in a way that I know based on my experience will appeal better to the audience? Who does it benefit, the worker or the DAT?

Diana, a domestic worker who was owed wages, had already sent a demand letter to her employer for her wages but had hit a dead end. However, as soon as Tammy sent a letter on the law clinic's letterhead, her employer became willing to negotiate. It was more efficient for Tammy to fill out the papers but also dangerous to conflate empowerment with pursuing one's own case when the system clearly disadvantaged those who tried. By leveraging her own power and expertise, Tammy could help Diana overcome some of the power discrepancies embedded in the legal claims process that impede restitution.

Tammy recognizes that this dilemma is common to social change work of all types. When she represents tenants who live in substandard housing or survivors of domestic violence, she struggles with the same issue:

> How do you tell someone on the verge of homelessness, with an eviction court date pending, that they should organize the other tenants in the building, versus look for other housing or pack their belongings so that they won't be thrown out on the street? How do you tell a woman who is fighting for her safety and freedom, and that of her children, that the issue of domestic violence is a political, structural issue, and not just personal? When her spouse is abusing her and her children are at risk, the abuse is the most personal problem in the world. Larger social movement goals might follow, but are far down on the list of priorities. All I care about is getting her out of the situation, and now.

Our legal, educational, and, for most of us, white and class privilege could easily motivate us to rush to "fix" a particular situation rather than support workers to take control over their futures and organize collectively. Yet many workers came to the DAT precisely because they knew that employers, courts, and legal agencies might be more willing to listen to us because of our privilege and their relative lack of power.

LEGAL AND DIRECT ACTION PATHWAYS

The DAT often employs legal strategies in tandem with direct action. However, this relationship can also create tensions. For instance, many workers are more familiar with the concept of suing than organizing a call campaign. As volunteers, we often found ourselves resorting to legal options not only because the worker suggested it but also because we worried the employer would not respond to direct action. Direct action work can be challenging and sometimes uncomfortable—physically, emotionally, and ethically. It can also invite risks when volunteers and workers are wary about what kinds of attention direct action could invite.

In Davor's case, he invited Telemundo to televise his delegation to the employer's home to demand his wages (Figure 13). To avoid embarrassment, the employer paid a partial settlement right there and promised to pay the rest in two weeks. The attention spurred a relationship with Telemundo. Amy and Diego did information sessions on television, reporters occasionally followed us on delegations, and Spanish-speaking viewers called during televised call-in times hosted by volunteers. However, in one troubling case, a worker was fired after Telemundo showed up because the reporter interrupted his work. Amy reflected:

> In a few cases, [Telemundo] helped us to recoup money for workers. That added pressure . . . [and] was good leverage. There are limitations to bringing Telemundo as well. . . . Telemundo's main goal . . . is getting a good story, and at times that can interfere with DAT's goals. In one case when Telemundo came, the wife of an employer hijacked the conversation and started crying on screen, making herself appear as the victim.

However, when we merely handed cases off for legal representation or circumscribed our assistance to helping workers fill out court paperwork, it

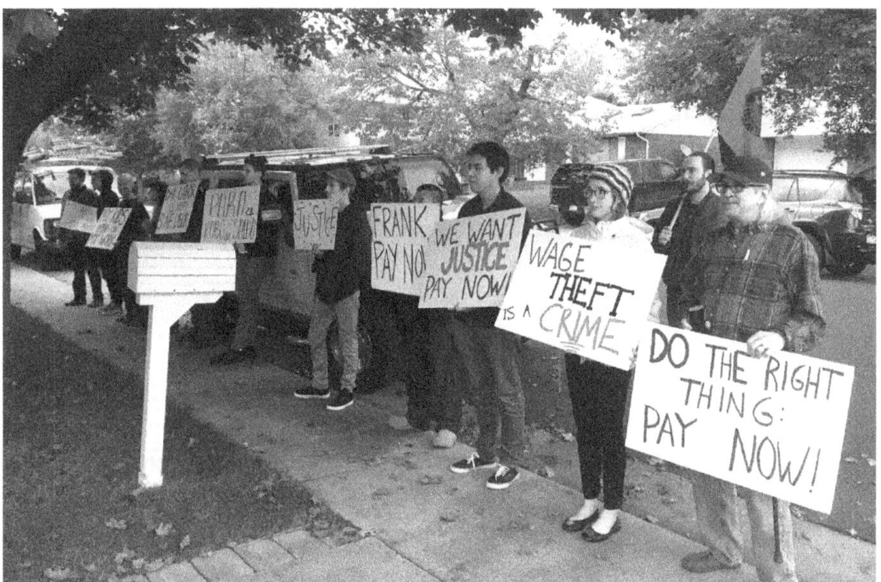

FIGURE 13: Protest outside the employer's home in Davor's case. Photo by Amy Czulada.

was more difficult to imagine creative solutions. As Chapter 5 showed, the legal system alone rarely yielded tangible or timely results for workers and did not prevent future incidents. Sometimes volunteers and workers also deferred to the expertise of attorneys in the group, which reinforced the epistemic privilege of legal experts. When we elevated the role of attorneys and legal expertise, we risked detracting from the larger transformative goals of social change and worker empowerment.[9]

Tammy's experience demonstrates the evolution, and shortcomings, of legalistic approaches. Tammy started collaborating with Centro in 2006, and she (alongside other attorneys) provided consultations along the lines of a traditional legal clinic. In 2008, she became inspired by a collaboration between two professors from City University of New York: a law professor, Sameer Ashar, and a political scientist, Saru Jayaraman. Their model was different from a traditional client-centered clinic. Sameer and Saru's model of community lawyering positions lawyers in the supporting backdrop while prioritizing community organizations and their members in the pursuit of justice.[10] In this approach, lawyers provide legal education for organizers and members to apply toward their movement goals. Tammy recalled what Saru shared:

> No one wants to organize, ever. Everyone wants an attorney; lawyers are not going to solve problems; they are the least effective of tools. If we just give every worker a lawyer, we're never going to get it. Lawyers should advise on larger issues and help strategize and educate about rights, but never be the most important player.

Saru and Tammy recognized that while lawyers could win cases, justice would never be achieved one worker and one lawyer at a time.

Tammy stepped back from Centro a few years later. However, in 2017, when Amy and Diego learned about Tammy's past connections with Centro through a law student volunteering with the DAT, they reached out and asked her to join. She quickly became hooked on direct action. While she had learned about similar models earlier, her own participation in direct action was new. Her experience prompted her to reflect back to Saru's comment:

> Saru's words really affected me. I think that her visit to Centro explains my reluctance, as the only lawyer on the Team, to be too influential within the team or to be seen as the authority on, well, anything. Yet my knee-jerk reaction, when it comes to just about any worker we meet, is "let's sue!" I am careful to not utter that thought aloud, or at least to not utter it very often. I know that in social norm change activism, filing individual lawsuits rarely does anything to change the status quo.

Although legal tools could push back against exploitation, they faced limitations given that the law otherwise tends to be anchored in the prevailing social order.[11] Moreover, when direct action tactics worked, they usually yielded much faster results than a legal process that could drag on for months. Direct action could also generate wider results by shaming employers and motivating workers to organize to come forward, spread the word, and assist others. Over time, we learned how to combine the threat of legal action with direct action; for example, we might deliver the employer a court summons at a delegation or protest to compel faster payment to avoid court and associated penalties. Using both approaches together often pressured employers to pay more attention than either action alone.

In 2017, the DAT relied more heavily on direct action tactics than legal ones. By 2018, however, we began to pursue cases in small claims court as a new tool. We hoped our efforts to prepare workers could lower the hurdle of small claims court—that workers have to otherwise represent themselves, known as *pro se*. The first case we helped file in small claims court was against an employer named Benicio. After we organized a protest and Benicio still refused to pay, the team prepped the worker for court. The worker won his case and Diego went to pick up a check from the employer shortly after. Diego reflected on this option (Figure 14):

> Reclaiming unpaid wages is a bit like trying to find loose change in a large house, with each room a different tactic. Discovering how the small claims court system worked, and that it could lead to a quick technocratic success, was like finding a new room in the house that we hadn't checked before. In the year or so that followed we flooded that room, hoping to win the cases we had been stuck on.

FIGURE 14: DAT volunteers, University of Denver students, and a worker pose outside small claims court after a win.

Small claims cases require fewer volunteers because we do not need to show up en masse for action. The court process allows workers to face their employer in front of a judge and set out their grievances, which can be empowering but also starkly individualizing. Still, the courts' limited workday hours, forms available only in English, and confusion about which jurisdiction to file in are difficult for volunteers, let alone monolingual Spanish-speaking immigrants with precarious legal status, to navigate.

When Alex analyzed DAT case data from 2018 and 2019, some of the problems with small claims court emerged. We helped clear the barrier of preparation, but the pro se requirement was not the only obstacle. The DAT helped prepare thirty cases that went to small claims court in 2018 and 2019 and won all but one. On paper this looked like a success. However, of these twenty-nine legal victories, only two workers were able to collect the money awarded by the judges from their employers. In contrast, over the same period, the DAT helped collect roughly $20,000 on behalf of workers through a combination of direct action tactics.

The one case we lost in court over this period (Cristian's) demonstrates how the legal system's technical requirements are not designed for low-wage immigrant workers and can discount their suffering. Alex attributed the loss to Cristian's inability to consistently present his story according to the format to which judges are accustomed.

Alex contrasted how workers must tell their stories to a judge versus how they communicate their stories to the DAT. The DAT's more conversational intake process allows workers to share their stories rather than having to "prove" what happened to them. However, once the worker is put in front of a judge, he or she must submit specific forms of evidence to make a claim. For Cristian, committing the exact dates of his work to memory to have a time line in his head to present in an organized manner was not important. What was important was that his employer had taken advantage and failed to pay. However, to the judge, the credibility of Cristian's testimony hinged on these technical requirements:

> His word . . . and tireless hours of work . . . were not enough to justify his wage claim. . . . This story is particularly disheartening because Cristian therefore walked away having felt he lost more than what he started with because a final decision was made regarding his experience and not in his favor.

Cristian lost not only his case but also the power to claim his experience. The demand for such scripted testimonies can be retraumatizing by encouraging individuals to perform, or become "experts in," their own suffering.[12]

After 2019, the DAT began to rely less on small claims court. Diego explained:

> Though we collected on a couple of small claims victories, there were thousands and thousands of dollars awarded that we never got. Employers refused to show up in court, refused to pay, declared bankruptcy, closed bank accounts on which we were placing writs of garnishment, avoided service or providing required information.

In a particularly illustrative case, eight workers were referred to the DAT by a representative from the Ironworkers Union in Arizona. They contacted the DAT because the work was performed in Colorado and the employer, Steve, was particularly hostile. Steve had threatened the workers physically and verbally, and they were afraid to confront him. Making little headway through direct action tactics, Chris and Diego helped the workers file in small claims court. Steve never showed up, so the judge issued default judgments to the workers, in their favor. But Steve still refused to pay. Chris filed interrogatories to find Steve's banking information to garnish the money directly, but Steve never complied. When we found Steve's bank information from one of the worker's old checks, we continued the process to try to garnish his account. However, when we tried to do so, we learned that Steve had drained the funds. There was nothing to garnish, and Steve disappeared.

Diego wondered about the banalities of the court process, which seemed to preclude justice by design:

> Going to courthouses to file the paperwork became difficult as only volunteers who had time off during the day and had cars could do it. For workers who were working all week and Spanish speaking, it wasn't really an option. The courthouse clerks told us conflicting information, the forms were wrong, the process would get bogged down in a bureaucratic slog, and the case would eventually die.

Small claims court unlocks a "new room," as Diego notes, to try to help recover unpaid wages. However, as Tammy admitted, "Law, except in rare situations, is a flimsy approach to structural issues." Doing direct action began to influence how Tammy came to see her role as an attorney:

> I recall that at my first DAT meeting, one of the members said he planned to call an employer to negotiate with him, and I remember thinking to myself: "Why would the employer listen to someone who is not a lawyer?" When I think back to that moment, I cringe. Upon reading the reflections of my comrades, and particularly upon seeing that my (and law students') membership on the team so heavily influenced our turn to law as a solution, at least for the year after I first joined . . . I

now make clear to my law students that an important lesson learned in any litigation clinic is understanding when litigation is *not* the answer.

Even when workers were successful in court and able to recover money, one victory did little to prevent further exploitation or deter employers in the future. The DAT has pursued a few renowned actors multiple times, often with different results. The DAT's repeat cases against Mr. Mendoza demonstrate this problem.

In 2018, two brothers (Ezequiel and Benny) and their father (Abelardo) brought a wage theft claim to the DAT against their employer, Mr. Mendoza, for painting work. We knew Mendoza from a previous case: Luis Angel's. In Luis Angel's case, Chris, Luis Angel, and Diego had negotiated a payment plan with Mendoza, but after a few payments, he stopped paying and tried to avoid us. The DAT then helped Luis Angel file in small claims court. He successfully made his case before a judge, who ruled in his favor, but was still unable to collect his money from Mendoza.

Shortly after, the DAT was back in court with Ezequiel, Benny, and Abelardo presenting a different case against Mendoza. Luis Angel came to support them because he understood their predicament. Their case would also present a good opportunity for him to speak with Mendoza because he had been dodging us and the money. Again, the judge ruled in the workers' favor. After the hearing, Mendoza, Luis Angel, and Diego went to the bank, and Mendoza took out the money he owed Luis Angel and paid him. Diego noted, "We thought this was a good sign that Ezequiel, Benny, and Abelardo's money would be forthcoming, but we were wrong."

Subsequently Mendoza filed for bankruptcy to avoid the several thousand dollars he owed other workers. Diego went through his filing and saw that Mendoza owed thousands of dollars to other creditors as well. Ezequiel even went to the bankruptcy hearing to advocate that he be paid what was owed, but his efforts were fruitless. Ezequiel was disappointed they never got their money, but he hoped Mendoza would think twice about stealing from workers again. Around two years later, Diego received a call from another worker who was owed money by Mr. Mendoza.

When workers present their cases in front of a judge, they make employers' threats somewhat less tenable in the future and gain confidence in their ability to assert their rights. However, because court hearings are relatively individualized and private affairs, they don't cultivate the group solidarity, social support, and community awareness nurtured by DAT actions like call campaigns, delegations, and protests in front of homes and businesses.

In contrast to using legal approaches, the process of coming together in direct action, whether in the backroom of Centro or protesting in front of an employer's residence, was transformative for us and for many of the workers who confront their employers with a team of support. The feeling becomes contagious. For Tammy, Tuesday night meetings are in some sense spiritual:

> Feeling a sense of belonging to this larger group that is committed to fighting for justice together, sounds to me like what I've heard people who attend church (or some churches) describe experiencing.

Yet we struggled with whether workers experienced similar feelings of transformation. Abbey added:

> The friendships that I built with the day laborers whose cases I worked on were transformative for me. Yet, I still feel like a passerby in the lives of these workers because, in the end, their material conditions and daily routines were not improved the way I would have hoped. We closed their cases, and moved on, but it did not feel like justice had been done, especially after all the time and energy the workers had put into their cases.

Still, solidarity emerged in more quotidian ways beyond delegations and court accompaniment. We built connections with workers from listening to their experiences while workers connected with volunteers who intrinsically believed their stories. In her work with sanctuary activists, Susan Bibler Coutin argues that "personal transformations that occur in the process of protest" are not irrelevant or merely instrumental to movements, but instead "constitute a significant part of the social change enacted by the movement."[13] Although we cannot say what these experiences meant for workers, they helped us provide a frame for our future actions. Some of us continue to work with the DAT, and while Abbey, Diego, and Amy moved away from Denver, they translated their experience to their jobs in worker organizing, economic and housing justice, and student debt advocacy.

QUESTIONS OF JUSTICE AND SUCCESS

Overall, we struggle to engage workers in a longer-term relationship with the DAT, whether to help other workers with cases or to join Centro as members, where they could collectively organize to upgrade working conditions and prevent wage theft. Sometimes it is even challenging to involve workers like Kelvin, Mariano, and Fernando in their own cases. We have tried multiple strategies to involve workers with the DAT: inviting workers to meetings and offering stipends to take on leadership roles, asking workers to help with street outreach or accompany others on delegations, and putting on social events for families. Each time, we had difficulty turning out workers or maintaining involvement over time.

We wondered if we, as volunteers, were overly determining a vision of worker empowerment. Worker empowerment looked different to workers themselves. When Abbey followed up with Severiano, he mentioned he had experienced better "luck" since his wage theft incident: he learned to better advocate for himself. Now he makes his employers sign a written contract clearly specifying the rate of pay and job expectations. Workers also returned to the DAT if they had cases in the future, talked to their friends about what they learned, referred coworkers to the DAT, and learned to better document their cases and insist on more transparent work agreements. For some workers, these more mundane forms of agency over their work arrangements, sharing of tactics, and referrals were seeds for building worker power. Yet these quieter forms of support were a double-edged sword because they also indicated that workers were still facing the same risks.

Some of the DAT's efforts evolved to target more systemic change through policy work and coalition building with allied groups. We helped prepare workers to testify to inform state and city legislation, hosted press conferences with signs downtown to draw attention to wage theft, shared data with stakeholders working on legislative proposals, and cohosted community information sessions (Figure 15). Some volunteers were also involved in other forms of social justice organizing and legislative battles to advocate for racial, immigrant, housing, and economic justice more broadly. With a wider lens, we built bridges with intersectional social justice initiatives and developed relationships that went beyond individuals' identities as "workers" or "immigrants" or our work on wage theft.

We often debated what constituted success and justice for workers. Was it the number of cases won, money collected, workers involved? Sometimes what workers considered justice was different from what we envisioned. Other times, our initial ideas, as well as what workers wanted, shifted as cases progressed. For some workers, justice simply meant getting their money so they could move on and avoid additional problems with the employer. By taking photos of workers with their money to share on social media, the DAT spreads the message that employers will be held accountable.

For other individuals, the meaning of justice was different. The wages became less important and in the long haul provided a shallow form of jus-

FIGURE 15: Press conference with the Southwest Regional Council of Carpenters, coauthor Diego Bleifuss Prados, and Towards Justice to publicize policy recommendations. Author's photo.

tice. Monetary restitution did not account for how employers commit wage theft again and again. Nor did it compensate for the widespread familial, emotional, and community harms that exploitation inflicts. In one case, we mailed $450 in owed wages to a worker after successfully negotiating with his employer. However, this wasn't sufficient. He was happy to receive the money but was more dissatisfied that nothing was done to punish the employer. In another case, a worker admitted that his unpaid wages were no longer a priority; he had found another job. But he continued to pursue the employer because he didn't want him to cheat others. In these cases, the larger indignities, rather than the immediate material necessities, mounted to weigh on workers as they began to address wage theft as an affront to their collective well-being.[14]

Leticia's case demonstrates the shortcomings of reducing justice to cases won and shows how the legal system can inflict injustice even when workers get paid. Leticia was owed wages by her employer, Camila, who owned a cleaning company. After the DAT's negotiations with Camila stalled, Leticia decided to file a small claims case. Tammy and Davor drove Leticia to court and helped her practice what she would say during mediation. When Leticia emerged from mediation, she had reached a settlement and was paid about $900 cash that morning. This result was good, but the process of mediation felt too coercive to Leticia. Tammy and Davor immediately let the court clerk and mediator know that Leticia's settlement was not voluntary, but Leticia did not want this either. She was happy to receive her money, but she felt as violated by the imbalance of power in the mediation—in which the language was not her first language, the mediator wanted a fast compromise, and Leticia could not have an advocate with her—as she did by Camila's initial refusal to pay. As in Cristian's case, the mediation constrained her experience into terms recognized by the legal system. The decision closed her case with a discrete decision and one-time payment regardless of whether she felt closure.

Tammy contrasted Leticia's experience with another case of four workers who actively participated in their case against repeat offender Billy. Tammy had joined the DAT about a week before a large protest the DAT staged outside Billy's daughter's home. The workers had been fighting alongside DAT volunteers to get their money for weeks, if not months, before Tammy met them. Eventually we helped them file a court case and obtained a judgment.

Tammy noted, "Though they never collected the money, their experience was not one of feeling reviolated." Instead, they felt empowered by the solidarity of the protest and the public shaming of Billy, not by the court judgment. Later, however, the workers wanted to collect on the judgment, but all attempts proved futile: they could not find the money. Tammy reflected, "By the end of our attempts to collect the money through the court process, all of us—attorney, law students, workers, and DAT members—felt a bit demoralized and disempowered." The strategies we use are often incomplete or can even be coercive to workers by encouraging them to interact with legal systems that are inaccessible and alienating, as Leticia experienced.

Pursuing justice was complicated when workers desperately needed the money, but also felt little reprieve from persistent risk. When conducting street outreach, some workers were hesitant to seek assistance because of the deep distrust they held for those who claimed to help. Alex reflected:

> Many workers would tell me they did not want our help. I later came to understand that workers felt robbed in many other ways beyond the lining of their pockets, but also of their faith and trust in advocacy work. [Speaking with workers at] the corners taught me how to build relationships with community members.

Amy added:

> Most workers are happy to receive the money they are owed by the employers. I would imagine that in most cases, [this] encompasses their conceptions of justice. If they felt that the employer was taught a lesson and that the employer would not commit wage theft again, I believe workers would feel an added bonus layer of justice. . . . If workers had the time and the energy to think about long-term solutions to the problem instead of swift reprieve from harm, we would arrive at similar points.

CHASING WAGE THIEVES

When we zealously pursued hostile employers like Drew, Steve, or Billy, it was not only difficult to compel them to take responsibility; we also realized we might be misdirecting our ire. In contracting chains segmented by race, class, and legal status, pursuing justice for one worker often meant relying on, and therefore reinforcing, the same oppressive social hierarchies that enabled wage theft. Pursuing an offending employer often entailed chasing an individual barely above the worker on the contracting hierarchy, discounting how these chains are designed to exploit workers with relative impunity. Because the DAT takes on small cases where work arrangements are likely to be informal, most of the disputes they see tend to occur at the lowest rungs of labor subcontracting chains.

Diffuse contracting arrangements made it difficult to identify whom to hold responsible. For example, Alex reflected that when she was the employment coordinator at Centro, despite their efforts to establish clear terms with employers, she realized that the employer with whom they entered an agreement would frequently not be the same person actually supervising the work. As more subcontractors came to the DAT with their own wage theft cases, we recognized that we needed to look higher up labor contracting arrangements, but we were also constrained. Subs may be owed money, but because of the nature of pressurized labor contracting, we could not be certain if they paid the workers under them, which otherwise might present a conflict of interest.

Abbey commented:

> It is difficult to identify who is actually getting richer when day laborers' wages are stolen because the true exploiters have been intentionally invisibilized by a convoluted web of economic arrangements that delegate the risk of doing business to contractors and subcontractors, while ensuring access to profit once the job is done.

Abbey, Amy, and Diego all noted that massive wage theft is likely going on at the bigger construction companies up the pyramid or hierarchy of the job site. However, the cases we saw usually involved employers at the bottom of that pyramid who were also struggling—they may be one dropped contract or stiffed check away from being unable to pay their own expenses. Workers who came to the DAT had a hard time locating the individuals who hired or supervised them, let alone any knowledge of higher-up arrangements.

Severiano's case demonstrates how chasing "wage thieves" can detract from seeing how labor contracting pits low-wage workers against their own social networks, making it difficult to know who to blame or from whom to collect. Severiano was not paid by one of his neighbors, Hugo. When Diego and Abbey went to Hugo's house with a demand letter, Severiano requested not to join them at the door because of his relationship with Hugo. He was concerned it would be awkward. Hugo came out of his apartment and told Abbey and Diego that he was never paid for the job either. Hugo even gave them the names of *his* employers who did not pay. We pursued action against Hugo's employers but also brought Hugo to court. The judge awarded Severiano $8,954. We successfully garnished Hugo's bank account to discover that he had less than $14.00 in it. While it is possible that Hugo emptied the account in anticipation of the garnishment, Abbey realized that it was more likely that Hugo did not have the money. By chasing Hugo, not only was the team unlikely to find any money but saw that Hugo was also a victim of labor contracting arrangements that offload responsibility down the chain and sometimes deep into teetering social networks.

The DAT often sees the smallest instances of wider systemic injustices at the bottom of extensive contracting chains. In doing so, we sometimes gain insight into larger culprits that rarely come to light, quickly settle, or whose business practices are usually considered to be perfectly normal or competitive. Amy asked herself, "What incentive do they have to follow the law when so many companies get away with it at an unbelievable scope?" She noted that in February 2021, Amazon settled a wage theft case for $61.7 million after stealing tips from their delivery drivers.[15] If one of the largest corporations in the world can get away with these practices or settle for a negligible amount considering their worth, how can smaller operators compete in such a tilted landscape?

Workers noticed these injustices. When students Avalon Guarino and Brittny Parsells-Johnson asked a worker at the Dayton and Colfax site why he thought bosses could get away with wage theft, he responded: "It happens for many years, over and over. And rich people get more and more money, so they can get away with more. Poor people can't do anything about it."[16] Rather than targeting an economic system that disproportionately concentrates profits, sculpts the law to its advantage, and incentivizes violations of workers' rights, wage theft incidents set workers against one another at the bottom of the market, forcing people to choose between paying their rent and keeping a business afloat or paying the friends they employed.

While the results of each case matter to workers, the process of direct action itself can ignite workers and volunteers. The process revalues workers' time, energy, and pride while instilling confidence for the future that small wins can add up over time. Perhaps, as Abbey suggests, "if we continue to meet workers where they are and do what they ask of us, more organic opportunities for longer-term system shifting will emerge. We're not sure what that would look like, but continuing to use direct action, in partnership with workers, to get money is a great place to start." Individual cases may only poke holes in the system, but as we experiment with new direct action tactics, push the law in ways it was not intended, and accompany workers, we generate a prefigurative struggle that insists on a different vision of justice.[17]

Abbey elaborated:

> While we are doing direct action, we are also learning how to organize. Even if we are not able to get the worker their wages, we are still building power for the future as we learn about organizing and fighting back against exploitation together.

We sometimes worried that we risked wading into murky territory. Were we providing unauthorized legal advice, taking prep too far for small claims processes intended to be pro se, or was it ethical to pretend we needed renovation work in order to ensnare an employer who was attempting to avoid us? We recognized that we had to concoct such creative schemes, be detectives, toe the lines of the law, and conduct continuous legal research precisely because prevailing arrangements of power made the limited options so absurdly inaccessible.

CONCLUSION

David Graeber describes how antiglobalization activists frequently don elaborate costumes and unusual gear, including "rubber ducky flotation devices," giant colorful puppets, and shooting water balloons and doughnuts, to protect themselves while engaging in direct action and to reveal the absurdity of the global order and its violent policing.[18] These actions are more than symbolic; they are meant to disrupt global capitalism through direct action, often at high-profile events like the Summit of the Americas in Québec, the World Trade Organization in Seattle, or the World Economic Forum.[19] Such disruptive interruptions provide tools that poke fun at while also providing a grammar that exists outside the current system. Our direct action work seems far from these broader movements, but these movements also often percolated out of small coffee shops and backrooms and cultivated creative mixtures of experimental tactics. Direct action movements may appear not to express a cohesive ideology, but this is precisely because "ideology is embedded in [their] practice," whereby the nonhierarchical, consensus-building, democratic organizing practices they develop "*is* their ideology."[20]

When we protest in front of an employer's home, business, or restaurant with signs, we come as ourselves or sometimes in red DAT T-shirts that feature a black cat and the words "Direct action gets the goods," an image and slogan borrowed from the anarchist and labor movement. Yet protests and delegations also interrupt the routinization of worker mistreatment and open it to public scrutiny. These actions provoke discomfort on quiet suburban streets, disrupt restaurant diners, or make a spouse complain that protesters disturbed their neighbors. These actions help point to how, as Diego phrased it, "wage theft is endemic to our economy, not by coincidence but by political choice."

The Romero Troupe, a social justice community theater group led by Jim Walsh at CU Denver, uses performance to center untold stories and transform participants and the audience (Figure 16). Many of their plays revolve around immigration, but they have also performed a skit about wage theft, including participants' own stories and some adapted from my research. Megan Carney's observations with Arte Migrante in Sicily similarly revealed how creative forums of expression can at once promote "social healing" and collective sharing that bring people together across differences.[21]

In another form of creative disruption, the Southwest Regional Council of Carpenters Union in Colorado altered an SUV to resemble an official state vehicle. It has lights on top and Colorado insignia, but inverts some state emblems to avoid liability. The car reads: Wage Theft Division, Criminal Colorado, and Payroll Fraud Division (Figure 17). It is clearly not an official state vehicle, but mimics one to alter the prevailing surveillance gaze. The vehicle circulates near worksites to warn employers that someone is

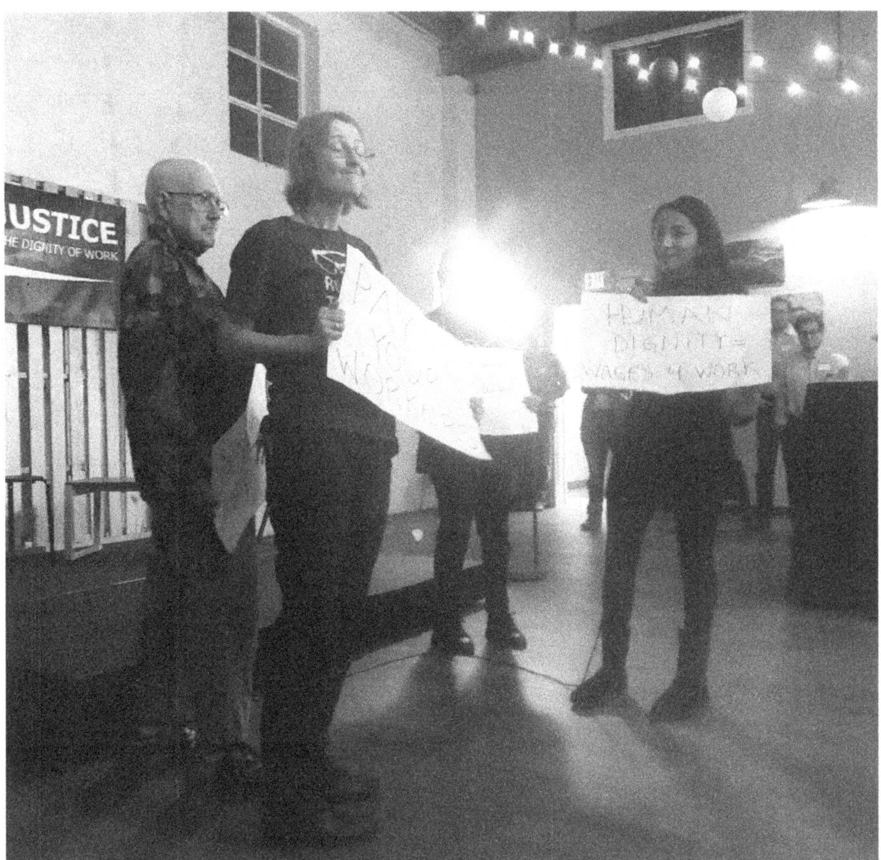

FIGURE 16: Romero Troupe play about wage theft at Towards Justice fundraiser. Photo by author.

watching *them*. The union even dubs it the "criminator." It prompts people to wonder, What if state enforcement mechanisms spent as much time pursuing unscrupulous employers as they do minor drug offenses, people suffering from mental illness, and even debt collection among low-wage workers and students? Protests, plays, and mock police vehicles are not just about informing the public and pressuring individual employers. They encourage people to critically rethink what they may have unconditionally tolerated, even if these disruptions may at first seem uncomfortable, irritating, or absurd. They shift the discourse around "immigrant criminality" about who is stealing from whom.

FIGURE 17: Author and Sarah Shikes, then executive director of Centro, in front of the Carpenters' Payroll Fraud Unit Vehicle. Author's photo.

The analytical division between mundane forms of service provision and social transformation is too often constrained by our own assumptions about what social change looks like. As we reflected on the tensions above, they became less troublesome and more productive for generating a theory and praxis of justice and solidarity. We struggled with how to reconcile helping workers navigate their current predicaments with our desire to reject and transform an economic and legal system that is fundamentally unjust.

By putting our power behind, or even serving, those criminalized and excluded by law, we push the system from within while we disruptively call out its absurdity and need for transformation.[22] For many workers, collaborating with the DAT, even when we were unsuccessful, interrupted dominant societal and legal arrangements that otherwise benefit from silencing immigrant workers, a power discrepancy on which wage theft thrives. Diana, as she describes in the interlude that follows, was appreciative of the help she received and recovered her wages. But to her, justice also meant being listened to and having people genuinely fight *alongside* her.

Our understandings about solidarity and justice are grounded in and emerged through our experiences, including practices of support, listening, assistance, and sometimes brief but loud disruptions. The dialogical process of reflecting on our experiences is part of the productive process of transformation, which is forged through and helps shape our future relationships, everyday practices, and their accompanying tensions.[23]

DIANA'S STORY

Interview conducted between Diana A. and Alexsis Sanchez, May 10, 2021

Transcribed and translated by Abbey Vogel

DIANA IS A DOMESTIC WORKER originally from Colombia who came to the DAT with three wage theft cases. This abridged interview focuses on her first wage theft case, when her employers paid her with a bad check. She received assistance from DAT volunteers using direct action and legal support from Tammy through the Sturm Civil Litigation Clinic. She eventually received her money.

Diana's interview with Alex, former DAT coordinator, highlights various themes in the book. As in Chapter 3, her experiences show how employers cultivate and exploit trust to cheat workers, which inflicts additional indignities and emotional harm beyond violations of wage and hour laws. Diana's wage theft experience and other forms of precarity compounded one another, stressing her relationship with her son and motivating her to take on jobs that made her susceptible to more exploitation. Like the workers in Chapters 4 and 5, Diana was also disillusioned by her attempts to file a claim with the Department of Labor. She found a sense of justice not just in the assistance she received from the DAT and the tactics she had learned for the future, but also through the process of building a relationship with volunteers who listened, learned with her, and took her lead, as demonstrated in Chapter 7. Much like the workers in Chapter 6, she also honed in on the character of the employers who cheated her while also hoping her victory would teach them a lesson. She was inspired to be strong, look to the positive, and move forward as she saw her son observing her.

ALEX: To begin, I think it would be best to begin with your first case of wage theft . . .

DIANA: Yes, well first of all, thank you. . . . Obviously without you all, there would not have been a solution for this case. . . . I had filed a lawsuit through the Department of Labor. . . . [They] kept telling me "they were going to think about it [taking on the case]."

You do not expect that the bosses are going to take that advantage of you, but it happens. You have to be prepared and thank God you [the DAT] are there to help because I investigated many places and there is no other help. . . .

ALEX: And speaking of your relationship with the children, how did you feel having this relationship and then receiving two paychecks which could not be cashed? How did you feel in this moment?

DIANA: Well, I dedicated myself to my work with them [the employers' children]. . . . And it was like being stabbed in the back. . . . Sometimes you think that people could never do that, but you never know who is who, or what they could do so you have to be ready, but it did hurt a lot.

ALEX: How did you get the idea to come [to the DAT]?

DIANA: I had to investigate and do something because it was a lot of money that I was losing. . . . I had been sacrificing my days to work, only to lose it [the money]. So, I said: "It can't be like this," and if they do this to me, they are going to do it to another person, not to mention that the bank where I turned in the check began to investigate me—as if I were a criminal, when it was never my intention in any moment to turn in a false check . . . This more than anything else inspired me to continue. . . .

ALEX: I wanted to ask you also how this experience affected you. I always see you with your son by your side, and how did it affect you and your son?

DIANA: Financially it is the hardest blow. . . . It means that [we] cannot do anything . . . as if he were being punished for something that doesn't even have to do with him. . . . Without money it is like, "No, my love. No, we cannot go out . . . we cannot do this." That, emotionally it hurts a lot. . . . The economic impact made me . . . realize that I cannot depend only on a single income and . . . it affected us not only emotionally but financially.

ALEX: How [did this] affect your trust and the relationships that you have with your employers?

DIANA: Now I save everything. I write [down] everything. I cannot receive money if it is not now on a payroll. . . . Unfortunately I do not trust anyone and if I see that they really will not pay the first week, I do not waste my time and just continue looking elsewhere. . . .

ALEX: So you are saying that before this experience, you [didn't say that]?

DIANA: Yes, I gave them the opportunity . . . up to a month was the most, . . . but now no. Not even one day. Either you pay me or I don't come back, and that's better.

I have taken care of kids for thirteen years and until this moment I never had any problems. Maybe for this reason I had the trust I did. It was a surprise because I thought that checks were something simple. I didn't know they could not have funds.

ALEX: When was the moment that you understood that it wasn't a situation of not having the money?

DIANA: After a month and a half was when I said, okay. That's enough. It became abusive. . . . When I told her that the check you gave me bounced and I need you to pay me, she said that she was going to talk with her husband to see what he says. I said that this is nonnegotiable. . . . She does not have to ask anything of her spouse. Either she wants to pay me or she doesn't want to pay me. . . . It's like it was not important to her that I had problems at the bank. . . .

ALEX: And so when you finally received the pay, how did you feel?

DIANA: It was justice. They finally understood that they can't play around, and for me the thing that made me happiest was that she wasn't going to do it anymore. Or at least that she was going to think twice and be more careful. . . . I lost in the end because I still left a lot of things there [at their house,] but I will not return anymore. I lost the love of their daughters, and in the end I lost the money that I had to pay to the bank [because of the bounced checks] but I did not have any debt from the bank. . . . I felt happy, as a result of having this check; it gave me a breath. I was able to breathe.

In addition to the bad checks, Diana's employers also tried to change the nature of Diana's work and renegotiate the price.

ALEX: What did you think and how did you feel . . . when she changed the [price and] conditions of your work?

DIANA: Although I took care of the girls . . . I cleaned the house, I folded the clothes, I provided extra help. . . . She didn't value this. . . . Children are the treasures of the family and I was the one living for the kids. . . . For me, this was the saddest part. . . . If they don't think who is taking care of their children for two or three cents difference, . . . what type of society are we going to have . . . ? Nothing good will come from this.

ALEX: Thank you very much, Diana

DIANA: You're welcome. Thank you all for taking time to chat about my necessities, because I am usually left without a voice because no one listens. . . . After lining up for two hours at the Department of Labor and Employment and after turning in all my papers, the young women there . . . tell me, "Okay, we'll get back to you after six months. We are going to look over the case." There is no rush, and it's worse for immigrants who are afraid because of the same laws and obviously because of the injustice [they face].

ALEX: What does it mean to you to receive justice as a worker when something like this happens?

DIANA: To be listened to and take the side of the person . . . who is the most honest. That is justice for me. . . . Justice is being listened to and giving a voice to those who are right, but are being judged. . . . I demanded justice to teach them a lesson. . . . But they say that a person who is bad will never learn how to be good.

ALEX: I admire you a lot because in all your answers, I have heard that you are finding the positive in these situations. . . . How did you find that inspiration?

DIANA: There is someone who has always been watching what I do—my son is seeing this example. . . . I think that if I were alone . . . I would not have done anything [about wage theft], but I think that with my son I have decided that he has to see someone strong who is not going to allow their rights to be violated, so we have to get him to see the positive. . . . If we do not overcome that first stone on the way, we will not overcome the second or the third. and I think that life is a process of falling and getting up stronger.

I believe that the United States taught me that. . . . In Colombia, I was the girl of rich parents who were not at home because they had us cared for by a service woman—we had everything. . . . When I got here [to] the United States . . . [as a nanny] I learned to value the work that parents do. I learned what my mom and dad taught me about going to work every day . . . , and more as an undocumented [person], that you have nothing, not even a neighbor who is honest with you . . . that hurts a lot. So I learned to create that armor on my body to be strong and teach my son to be strong. I learned that here in the United States—[this was] a lesson that I had to overcome and move forward because what else can I do?

ALEX: Thank you very much for your time and for sharing with us. I want to tell you that . . . we, the Direct Action Team, learned something from you, too, and that I love to see the members of the community who are leaders like you and I admire them and see them as my teachers, so thank you very much.

DIANA: Life is the process of learning, and each one has their own speed is what I think. So I am very happy that you have learned with me; we all learn in this transformation of life.

CONCLUSION
SÍ, SE PUEDE

I love to work one-on-one [on cases], but I know you have to have the larger structure to change. What you have to do is find some crack in the system and then push it open, that's when you can make major change.

—*Chris Wheeler, activist, DAT volunteer, and retired political science professor*[1]

IN MARCH 2018, THIRD-YEAR LAW student Katie Brown won $15,000 in unpaid wages and damages in Arapahoe County Court on behalf of four immigrant workers who had not been paid by their employer.[2] Katie became involved in wage theft work as a volunteer with the Direct Action Team (DAT) and with Tammy's Civil Litigation Clinic at the DU Sturm College of Law. Towards Justice originally referred the case to the DAT after the workers came in for an intake. The case was too small for an attorney, but the workers were motivated, which made it ideal to refer for direct action tactics.

A few weeks after the court victory, Towards Justice organized a press conference at the Sturm College of Law to raise awareness around wage theft. Through the process of organizing the press conference, we realized that student surveyors had originally encountered these workers on a Denver street corner as part of my research. The workers used the contact information on the know-your-rights cards we distributed to contact Towards Justice. When Towards Justice referred the workers to the DAT in fall

2017, the case came full circle because many surveyors were also volunteers with the DAT.

The DAT, coordinated by Diego at the time, first attempted direct action techniques. They called the employer and visited his home multiple times, but he remained resistant. The team then got the workers' permission to allow Katie to represent them in county court under Tammy's supervision. Not only did Katie, as a law student, have more time and energy than most attorneys to prepare the case, but the workers had more evidence than cases the DAT typically receives. The workers had time cards, their intakes from Towards Justice, and even a photo of a whiteboard from the employer's garage that depicted the workers and their hours, somewhat akin to a NCAA bracket.

The press release celebrated the collaboration.[3] One worker reflected, "I am so happy that we could get the money we earned. . . . I am also happy to see that we are part of a bigger effort to make the system more fair. But mostly I am grateful to Katie Brown and the DU Civil Litigation Clinic for their work on my case and for believing in me." Katie added, "I am honored to support these workers and help enforce wage and hour laws in Colorado. It's also great to be part of a dynamic network supporting our most vulnerable workers." Diego commented, "I am inspired by [name redacted] and his colleagues for standing up for themselves and insisting on justice. . . . It is their bravery and insistence on justice that makes this all possible."

Advocates have pointed out that government enforcement agencies, even when sufficiently resourced, cannot tackle wage theft alone. This is especially so when workers do not believe that state agencies work in their interest or are fearful to submit complaints.[4] Increased public enforcement and investigators are necessary to deter wage theft, but it is also not enough. Instead, scholars advocate for co-enforcement schemes, whereby worker organizations, high-road employers, attorneys, and unions can partner with enforcement agencies to investigate and target particular industries, channel claims, monitor compliance, and organize workers.[5] Still, alliances depend on each actor having sufficient capacity, political support, resources, and will from government agencies, as well as mutual trust and communication. Such strategic partnerships are still relatively uncommon in the United States.[6]

This case looked like an ideal celebration of such strategic collaboration around wage theft. Not only did the victory lead the workers to feel individually validated by a system that rarely heeds their concerns, but the workers saw themselves as part of something larger. This was just one victory for four workers—relatively insignificant to poke at the scale of wage theft and worker mistreatment. Yet it did represent one of the cracks to which Chris referred, which can perhaps be pried open. However, as the months passed, we were dismayed to learn that the workers were unable to collect their money from the judgment.

Katie's case reflected many of the tensions demonstrated in this book, as well as the challenges of applying anthropological research to advance workers' rights. We leveraged the tools of research, outreach, and strategic collaboration to produce a victory for the four workers. But Katie's case raised the nagging question: Could cases like this stimulate public attention to shift societal consciousness around wage theft to create space to promote worker-friendly policies, motivate workers to organize, and create synergistic partnerships among private and public enforcement entities, workers, and advocates? Or did we risk getting caught up in small victories that merely rippled off the surface of waves of systemic injustice? At the end of the day, did these wins help workers receive their money, achieve justice, or prevent future exploitation? Or on the more positive side, could such a case offer advocates the opportunity to recognize the gap between the law and its utility and devise policy solutions to more holistically address the shortcomings? Small collaborative wins could begin poking at injustice, but the struggle was also much longer, winding, and difficult. Even if minor, small wins along the way help inspire participants to maintain momentum when the demands of the longer struggle may seem insurmountable.[7]

Throughout this book, workers and advocates trouble the limits of legalistic approaches to justice so long as immigrant and low-wage workers occupy a subordinate position in society that devalues their labor, bodies, time,[8] and worth. In contrast, the mural on the side of Centro's purple warehouse artistically depicts what the struggle for justice demands (Figure 18). It requires strength from multiple vantage points to collectively break the chains that choke the earth and strangle its heart. The mural was created around 2010 by Brenda Clearly, an art teacher at the Tlatelolco School, a

Denver alternative public school whose mission centered around instilling cultural pride and leadership among Latino youth. The school emerged from Denver's vibrant Chicano movement, opened in the early 1970s, and was founded by activist Rodolfo "Corky" Gonzales who led the Crusade for Justice.[9] The mural's creative process began between Centro members and Latino, Chicano, and indigenous students as they shared dialogues about "common stories, dreams, and hopes." Their conversations inspired a mural design that centered themes of "ancestral pride, justice for workers, women's rights, freedom, liberation, peace, hope." To inaugurate the mural, Centro hosted a press conference with an Aztec dance group that blessed the mural with a ritual and dance.[10]

My 2020 photo of Centro's building depicts the construction cranes that have hovered over the mural horizon for the past few years. The foreground became dominated by homeless tents that began to converge in the area

FIGURE 18: Mural on the side of Centro with homeless encampments that began to surround it in 2020 and 2021. Photo by author.

in winter 2020 and grew more pervasive as the COVID-19 pandemic took hold. Struggles for immigrant and workers' rights are intimately bound up with wider demands for dignified livelihoods, racial justice, education, housing, and health care.

After summarizing the book's main arguments, this conclusion uses Katie's case and my first wage theft delegation—a group visit to an employer's home to demand wages—to delve into the ethical ambiguities raised by conducting community-based research centered on immigrant worker justice from a position of privilege in my own city. I offer that learning how to *convivir*—coexist alongside—is a step toward solidarity and justice waged from standing with workers on common, even if uneven, ground.

THE NEW NORMAL

Laboring for Justice has argued that immigrant day laborers' subordinate structural position, exacerbated by the degradation of workers' rights, pervasive labor contracting arrangements, discrimination against Latinos, and rising interior immigration policing, makes them particularly vulnerable to wage theft and hesitant to seek recourse. Chapter 2 detailed how racially and legally segmented residential construction chains not only offload risk down the chain, but weigh on low-wage immigrant workers' often fragile social networks. Instead of benefiting from Denver's postrecession construction boom, industry pressures and dynamics led to a familiar story of increased exploitation amid limited decent work. As Chapters 3 and 4 demonstrate, wage theft has become a patterned and intentional way of doing business that is not exceptional, but instead indexes a wider deterioration of work that reinforces worker insecurity. These chapters demonstrate that even when workers know their rights, weak enforcement, discrimination, fear of retaliation, power imbalances with employers, and scarce employment prospects encourage many workers to take a chance on risky employment and move on rather than pursue redress when they experience exploitation.

Chapter 5 delved into the legal maze to illustrate how well-intentioned legal remedies tend to rely on individualized and reactive approaches, which fail to recognize wage theft as a structural crime that thrives on power discrepancies. The state's failure to proactively address wage theft serves to entrench workers further in the sectors of the economy least protected by labor laws while reminding them of their subordinate inclusion into society. In response to these challenges, the chapter points to more recent policies and frameworks that have greater potential to strengthen workers' rights at the local level. Chapter 6 complicated accounts of exploitation to reveal how workers engage in more subtle, indirect, and sometimes even insurgent or violent tactics to exert agency over their lives, assert moral claims, share collective experiences, and uplift their subordinate position. Coauthored Chapter 7 examined how volunteers leverage direct action strategies to accompany workers and help them recover unpaid wages. With coauthors, we reflect on the tensions we faced between direct action and more legalistic approaches, working alongside versus on behalf of workers and our own goals versus workers' desires and demands.

I conclude by insisting that wage theft's structural and systemic underpinnings demand more radical shifts toward revaluing the lives, rights, and labor of immigrants and workers, regardless of where they happen to be born or what employment arrangements classify their labor. Any examination of wage theft committed against immigrant workers like day laborers must take into account the unjust sociostructural position of unauthorized immigrants in US society, which cheapens their labor and renders their very presence tenuous. Justice cannot be circumscribed to reclaiming unpaid wages, but instead must envision broader forms of solidarity whereby labor and political rights are not constrained by national borders.[11]

This book has highlighted the experiences of one of the most vulnerable populations in the United States: immigrant day laborers. In fact, the lessons go beyond day laborers, immigrants, and wage theft. I argue that if we understand how employers cheat day laborers with relative impunity, we gain a glimpse into the wider unfolding of racial and economic inequality and the exploitative labor practices that sustain it, most of which are legal. When the most vulnerable workers are afraid to organize for better conditions or report exploitation, all workers suffer.[12] However, historically, efforts by immigrants, labor activists, and their allies have often spearheaded larger societal shifts.[13] Chris Newman recalled from his research into the history of legal aid that the idea of free legal services initiated with wage and hour clinics created by US German immigrants in the 1800s, as well as through Jewish and German immigrant mutual aid societies.[14] Struggles around immigrant workers' rights are instructive to wider immigrant and worker justice movements.

Attorney Raja repeatedly pointed out that wage theft is the "new normal" across many industries. Attempts to reclassify workers as independent contractors and remove firms and employers from responsibility over working conditions is visible in the proliferation of the gig on-call economy, but it is by no means exclusive to it. Construction is instructive because Erlich terms it the "original gig economy."[15] Multiple layers of contracting, misclassification, and cash pay off-the-books became routine, degrading pay, benefits, working conditions, and enforcement of violations.[16]

As more industries and employers seek to reduce costs, rearrange work arrangements, and reduce obligations to their employees, more employment resembles day labor. Albeit the stark livelihood impacts may be easier to spot in the extreme precarity of day labor, these conditions should inspire a general wake-up call.[17] Instead, the public, policymakers, and even advocates tend to treat the plight of immigrant day laborers as an extreme exception. Their living and working conditions may alternatively provoke pity and compassion or its flip side, derision and deflection of blame for social and economic inequality and the decimation of social and state supports onto the most vulnerable. Wage theft inheres in the trajectory of neoliberal and racial capitalism. It is far from an aberration to how the economy operates. Despite some improvements and wins, federal and state-level labor rights enforcement largely continues to trail far behind the changing nature of work, in effect normalizing and legalizing it.

It is therefore necessary to open wider critical scrutiny into what constitutes wage theft amid the broader erosion of working conditions and the dehumanization of immigrants. I insist that a broader view of wage theft challenges the preconception that low-wage, unskilled work even objectively exists. Instead, deliberate employer strategies to justify cost-cutting and boost profits, alongside immigration restrictions and racial discrimination, create the category of the low-wage, unskilled worker and the devalued notion of "immigrant jobs." The justification for the existence of low-wage work is reinforced by public, political, and media discourses that devalue the labor of those who concentrate in low-wage industries. Job insecurity, lax worker protections, and insufficient income increasingly extend beyond low-wage jobs to encapsulate more workers and workplaces, extending into the alleged "middle class."[18] As an example, construction jobs once provided a road to the middle class with decent wages, benefits, and occupational mobility, but a recent national report found that 39 percent of construction worker families currently participate in at least one safety-net program, receiving $28 billion a year in federal assistance; moreover, construction workers are three times less likely than other workers to have health insurance.[19] Moreover, 31 percent of all workers across US industries have a family member on public assistance.[20] These forms of devaluation, deprivation, and wage suppression are also forms of theft that should concern us, even if they do not qualify for any legal remedy.

Wage theft is not new. The plight of immigrant day laborers is a symptom of a society founded on and fueled by theft. The United States has devalued and expropriated the land, bodies, and labor of immigrants and racial minorities to extract profit through settler colonialism, imperialism abroad, enslaved labor, and ongoing racial capitalism.[21] A racist history of theft continues to inform why employers believe that immigrants can be paid less or not paid at all. Or why certain occupations that heavily rely on the labor of women and people of color remain low wage, and some industries, like agriculture and domestic work, are still excluded from various labor protections. Narrow legal definitions of wage theft leave these foundational, racialized, and routinized forms of theft intact even as they ground and perpetuate racial and economic inequality in the United States. Day laborers' experiences with wage theft and attempts to recover their owed money raise larger questions about who is stealing from whom.

Instead of exceptional, theft is foundational. In this book, I therefore challenge societal rationalizations that associate occupational and economic mobility with individual drive and hard work. Instead, attuning to unjust wages and work highlights the deliberate industry practices, legal architecture, policy decisions, and racist ideologies and actions that create and maintain bad jobs and stagnant wages, including a federal minimum wage that hasn't budged in over a decade despite escalating costs of living, as the normal workings of the economy.

COMMUNITY-BASED RESEARCH AND ITS DISCONTENTS

Insights about wage theft and struggles for immigrant and worker justice are intimately interwoven with the ambiguities and labor politics of conducting community-engaged ethnography in my own city, which I occupy as a settler on indigenous lands. The aftermath of Katie's case was just one example that led me to question whether my attempts to help workers through activist and community-engaged research could be patronizing and short-sighted. I returned to a reflection that former student Claudia Castillo submitted after completing surveys at Dayton and Colfax. There were no "boxes" to capture what she felt:

> Yesterday at Dayton and Colfax while I was approaching my first survey . . . I was stopped by two laborers with questions about our organization. [One] was very upset and came to me in a very aggressive manner. He, in several ways, expressed the sentiments below:
>
> 1) I'm not sure what benefits you get for taking our information, but we get nothing.
> 2) Not one person here has been helped by your organization
> 3) You come here and lie to us that we can get our money back, but you don't do it.
> 4) Stop giving out cards with numbers and help us.
> 5) I am going to tell everyone here to stop talking to you all because what you say are lies.

Claudia was taken aback by this encounter. She often felt these cases personally from her father's experience as an immigrant day laborer in Texas during her childhood. She concluded, "I was quite upset, but knew this would happen someday." She learned that the worker had never called any of the numbers on the card. But it also didn't matter. So many individuals claimed to help day laborers—students, researchers, attorneys, Centro, other nonprofits, and churches and missionary groups—that they all began to blur together while day laborers' predicament largely remained the same.

My goal was to iteratively combine research with policy advocacy, activism, community collaboration, and direct worker assistance to more fully understand wage theft while contributing to building policies and worker power to tackle it. Yet I, as well as my community partners, continued to struggle to involve workers in the DAT or as research partners. Because low-wage immigrant workers face a myriad of daily challenges, I wondered if demanding the kind of activism we expected of ourselves was harmful to the larger struggle. Did envisioning possibilities for transformative change actually help workers receive the money they desperately needed now? On the flip side, did getting one worker his or her money actually change anything? Workers are correct to suspect not just government agencies and nonprofits but also well-intentioned allies and researchers whose careers benefit from their suffering as their subordinate position remains unchanged.[22] As Eve Tuck observes, historically oppressed communities have been overly researched but still remain invisible.[23]

Despite my intention to work collaboratively, I occupied a position of power as the lead investigator and author. Researchers who claim to partner with the communities they aim to serve often discount inherent inequities in who sets the research agenda, structures the partnership, controls budgets, asks and analyzes questions, writes, and speaks for whom.[24] In doing so, such partnerships can reinscribe colonial dynamics of knowledge production and power rather than offering space for social transformation. These very power discrepancies are otherwise what make day laborers vulnerable to exploitation and hesitant to speak up.

Yet such pessimistic assessments can also obscure the kinds of agency workers engaged in each day and the trickling impacts of outreach and organizing efforts, whether through workers' discussions, advice, and gossip with one another, their silent or sometimes loud shunning of bad employers, their participation with the DAT team and other advocates, or even more violent refusals to submit to employers' whims. Even if they discontinue their participation with Centro or DAT, individuals like Severiano and Diana took the skills they developed with them and shared what they learned with others.[25] These small sparks may be less visible but constituted ways for workers to forge a sense of a more just future or even just more tolerable tomorrows in conditions of extreme precarity. One worker at Dayton and Colfax simply told us that when people who claim to help actually pay attention, trust can be built. Perhaps these were the more subtle transformations of coexistence, sometimes simply to *convivir* and listen, to which we needed to direct more attention. While writing press releases, passing new laws, and even holding demonstrations could draw more attention to wage theft, more everyday forms of *convivencia* were foundational to ensuring that any of these actions actually mattered to, and are ultimately led by, those they intend to benefit. As Dakota scholar TallBear offers, "standing with" is an ethical stance that should also motivate us not to "inquire [from a] . . . distance, but based on the lives and knowledge priorities of subjects."[26]

ARTURO'S CASE

The process of learning and listening to workers and collaborating with stakeholders, rather than the result of any one case, was prefigurative for expanding our vision of what is possible. Collaborations between stakeholders over the past few years have also informed policy advances at the state and city levels, and advocates have worked together to ensure they are enforced and held accountable. Cases like Katie's may have resulted in disappointment, but each instance of collaboration provides a way for advocates to learn both in terms of the process for how they can come together and the substance of what can be achieved. My experience on my first wage theft delegation with Arturo to his employer's home to demand his unpaid wages highlights the tensions between the potential offered by sharing experiences and building partnerships and the realities of tragic and systemic injustice. It further probes the ethical dilemmas raised by community-engaged research and teaching.

Triumph

It was May 18, 2015, at 6:00 p.m., just beginning to turn to dusk, as I buckled my then almost five-year-old daughter into the car. Chris Wheeler had invited me to join him, other DAT volunteers, and Arturo on my first wage theft delegation to Arturo's employer's home to demand his unpaid wages. Arturo was a masonry worker originally from Oaxaca, Mexico. At the time, he had lived in Colorado for over a decade. His wife was a US citizen, but Arturo had been unable to adjust his status. He was hired for stucco work on a house by a man named Samuel, who had been subcontracted by a contractor in charge of building the home. Arturo worked for a week in August 2013, but Samuel didn't pay him. He was owed $3,400. Although Arturo was never paid, he nevertheless paid the two workers who assisted him. Meanwhile, Arturo's mother awaited knee surgery in a hospital in Mexico City. They would not operate until payment was received, and Arturo had still not been paid. He had been trying to recover his unpaid wages for nearly two years.

Arturo knocked on Samuel's door. No one answered, but Samuel's truck and car were parked outside so we assumed someone had to be home. A few minutes later, Samuel opened the door. Given his resistance thus far, the team did not expect him to do them any favors. At first, Samuel appeared friendly, but then he turned defensive and kept changing his story. He started by saying that he didn't owe Arturo anything, but then said he only owed him for twenty-nine hours of work at $12 per hour, significantly below their verbally contracted amount.

Samuel then claimed that the contractor who had given him the job had not paid him. Like other cases throughout this book, Samuel attempted to hide behind murky subcontracting chains. But his excuses didn't hold because Chris had already spoken with the head contractor who supported Arturo's claim. Samuel grew frustrated. "Then prove it," he retorted. The volunteers responded okay and handed Samuel a summons for court for July 2.

The case proceeded to court and Arturo prevailed. The judge gave Samuel ten days to pay or submit financial information to the court, after which the team was preparing strategies to garnish Samuel's bank account should he continue to prove recalcitrant. The day before this information was due, Samuel called Arturo to ask him to come over. Volunteers worried whether Samuel was setting him up, perhaps to provoke a confrontation. To their surprise, when Arturo arrived, Samuel opened the door, handed him a check for the entire amount, and shut the door!

The team took pictures of Arturo with his money, and Arturo recorded a short video about his victory. He thanked the team for helping prepare him for court, including his testimony, evidence, and support from the contractor. Arturo even donated $400 of his win to Centro to help other workers. The case was a success: it produced a win for Arturo and accountability for the employer, and it generated wider impacts when Arturo was inspired to stand in solidarity with other workers.

Judith Márquez, then staff member of Centro and DAT volunteer, summarized the outcome in the DAT case log:

> The first win was the small claims court judgement, and the second, collecting his wages. Judith finished the case summary with the popular refrain, *Sí se puede*—yes, it can be done.

Sí, se puede resounded through the immigrant rights mobilizations across the country in 2006 and 2007, but the phrase had emerged earlier from Latino workers' struggles popularized by César Chávez and Dolores Huerta's efforts to organize farmworkers to demand better wages and working conditions.[27] The DAT's work is one small part of this ongoing struggle.

Tragedy

When fall 2015 came around, I had a new group of graduate students enrolled in my qualitative methods course researching wage theft in Colorado. Students suggested that Arturo be a keynote speaker at their final presentation event after they had gotten to know him by working with the DAT. We gathered a modest honorarium for Arturo, hired a translator, and purchased tamales to be served from Centro's women's catering cooperative.

A week before the presentations, I received a disturbing email from Chris who had just heard that Arturo's wife was in a terrible automobile accident. A driver had run a red light and totaled her car. She was recently released from the hospital but in a wheelchair. She had serious back injuries, was still in a lot of pain, and could not work.

Their troubles began to spiral. The owners of the house that Arturo and his wife were renting were preparing to sell it, so they had to move. They found a new place but could not manage the move. They were financially stressed because his wife was unable to work. Chris wondered if Centro could return his donation even though Arturo never would have asked. This didn't turn out to be possible, and so they helped organize a GoFundMe request, the paltry way of offloading US failure to provide universal and affordable health care onto individuals' social connections.

Arturo's situation led me to reconsider his involvement. Would it be traumatizing and unethical to expect him to share his story at such a time? But Arturo was grateful to Centro and insisted on telling his story, which he hoped could help others. For some workers, the very act of talking about what happened with others was personally therapeutic and transformative. Marco had told me that recovering wages is not just about the money or even about holding an employer accountable. It also transforms individuals in the process—workers and those who assist them. Immigrant workers stick up for themselves, find a community of support, gain recognition from the system that so often excludes and even criminalizes them, and share their experiences with and advocate for others.

Celebrating victories felt good, but was this just a brief respite from Arturo's ongoing precarity? His case was much like Katie's and many of the other "victories" depicted in this book, which were nested within and revealed larger systemic injustice. Volunteers, advocates, and I experienced similar disappointments when workers won their cases in court but couldn't collect their money, when we garnished an employer's account and found no funds, when we pursued an employer to learn they were likely being exploited along larger subcontracting chains, or when recovering wages did little to address the multiple vulnerabilities that continued to impinge on workers' lives. Nor did victories necessarily prevent future exploitation.

Arturo's wage victory did little to address the factors that continued to make individuals like him vulnerable not only to wage theft but also to myriad forms of exploitation, discrimination, injury, housing insecurity, illness, and poverty. One man waiting for work explained to student Claudia Castillo that the workplace abuses he experienced were not fully captured by the survey question on wage theft. He expanded to elaborate on the "yelling, threats, you have no idea what I had been through, much abuse, a lot of suffering. It is not right." He continued, "I was helped by two Honduran laborers [when his wages were stolen] and I try to do the same [for others]. But no one can stop it." Similarly, Arturo might be better prepared on the next job. He might keep better records, get a written contract, and collect more information on his employer. In fact, many of the workers who listened to outreach presentations or worked with the DAT learned to keep better records on their employers, worksites, hours, and wages. But would this preparation improve Arturo's economic security or prevent another employer from taking advantage? His structurally subordinate position remained unchanged, whereby any hiccup, stroke of bad luck, let alone catastrophic event—whether illness, wage theft, injury, a traffic stop, death of a loved one, or loss of work—could rapidly escalate into an emergency. When Arturo's wife was injured, it not only imperiled her physical health, but the entire household's emotional well-being, financial stability, and housing security. Even the inconvenience of moving boxes into a new rental turned urgent.

In a matter of days, Arturo's situation deteriorated. Shortly after, we received the shocking news that not only was his wife not getting better, but when they conducted further x-rays on her injured spine, they found cancer, which had spread. As we continued to raise money for and check in on Arturo, before I could even get a response, I learned from Chris that his wife had passed away.

RECKONINGS

For more than seven years of research, policy advocacy, and activism alongside immigrant workers and partner organizations in Colorado, Arturo's case has stayed with me. It was particularly tragic, but also all the more disturbing for not being that uncommon as workers' stories throughout this book illustrate. His story prompted critical reflection, as well as frustration: frustration for his terrible misfortune, frustration at a system that exploits immigrant workers with impunity, frustration that victories can shroud broader failures, and frustration with our inability to do anything. Although his case illustrated central theoretical tensions in this book, it further compelled me to reflect on dynamics of vulnerability and power as I continued to occupy the same city as individuals like Arturo. Here I reflect on the possibilities of dismantling colonialist conceptualizations of fieldwork and participant observation to encourage humility, mutual recognition, and accountability.

Although my students' situation was far from Arturo's, as they began learning about and researching wage theft in my class, they widened their critiques of an economic system where any alignment between wages, value, and costs to sustain livelihoods is dramatically unhinged. Each time I teach my methods course, a few students realize that they also experienced wage theft. As graduate students, many work multiple part-time jobs to make ends meet, including in restaurants, bars, child care, and underpaid internships—industries all prone to wage theft. I learned from students to expand my own lens on theft as skyrocketing student debt threatens to steal their futures.[28] Wage theft is indeed a canary in the coal mine of the evisceration of work, as its normalization and our own silent complicity—even when it does not benefit us—make it difficult us to think and act otherwise. I also benefited from students' labor for this book, and no amount of course credit, citation, or paid assistantships can compensate for the labor inequities underlying most academic research. Yet by engaging students in a collaborative research and teaching model, I insist on the need to reinvigorate a type of anthropological pedagogy that evaporated in the 1980s as mentors largely left graduate students to their own devices, often with little training or ethical guidance as they exalted the figure of the lone ethnographer over more collective forms of knowledge production (Figure 19).[29] Even so, collaborative and even activist projects cannot escape the power relations in which they are embedded; at worst, they assuage them via discourses of partnership.[30] Berry and colleagues insist that "[a]ctivist research that does not pursue epistemological decolonization will . . . inevitably reproduce the very hierarchies of power that it seeks to help dismantle."[31] Recognition and critical scrutiny are required for more liberatory approaches to engaged research, but far from sufficient.

Working in my own city raised additional considerations about anthropological fieldwork. Through the objectification of the "field" and "field-

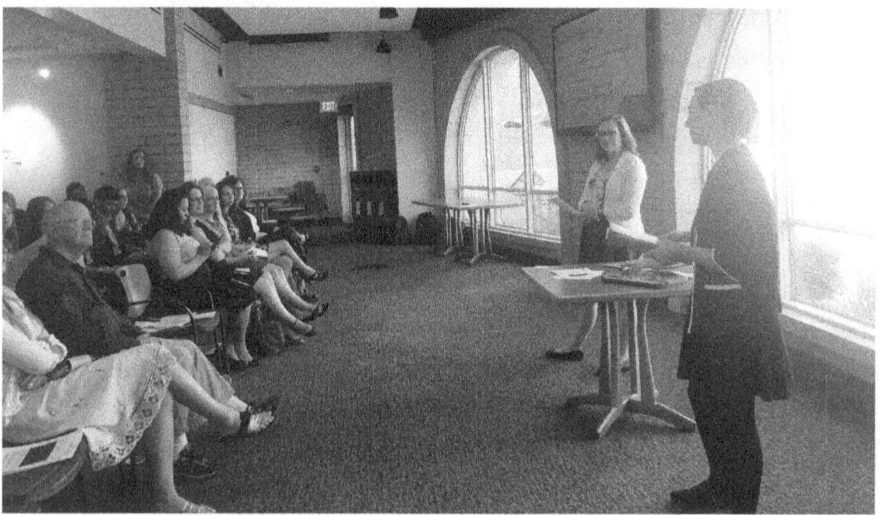

FIGURE 19: University of Denver graduate students Abbey Vogel and Pamela Encinas (with Stephanie Renteria-Perez, Sierra Amon, and Cecily Bacon not pictured) present their group's research on day laborers at the Josef Korbel School of International Studies, June 1, 2018.

work," ethnographers bound complex geographies and social relations into discrete places and timetables that can be objectively observed, which in turn "become spaces saturated by the fantasies of outsiders."[32] The "field" concept enables ethnographers to arrive and detach themselves according to convenience or funding parameters and distinguish, distance, and elevate themselves from "their informants." This colonizing gaze obscures the researcher's role in shaping, extracting, and legitimizing what comes to be valued as "knowledge" about gendered and racialized "others" in "other" places.[33] Perhaps so many anthropologists have been encouraged to study distant cultures from a neutral and objective vantage point not only as a legacy of a discipline that once believed that the search for cultural difference could only discovered "elsewhere,"[34] but to avoid their complicity in the systems of oppression they study and to cloak and preserve the racialized, gendered, and classed expectations undergirding what constitutes expertise, who is presumed to offer it, and from which particular social and geographic locations.[35]

My class, racial, and academic privilege afforded me the ability to shapeshift that most day laborers lacked by opening spaces to interview workers on the street but also to talk with attorneys, developers, and politicians, some of who occupied social networks close to my own.[36] This dilemma became clear when workers' testimonies were not sufficient, and sometimes suspect, in courtrooms, legislative hearings, and employer negotiations. Legislators were often more swayed by statements from white workers, advocates, or researchers with whom they more readily identified—like the testimony of a white brewery worker or a young white female waitress—whose stories helped inform the Wage Protection Act and the revision of Colorado's felony theft statute. Policymakers, community organizations, and state agencies asked for reports from my research to help validate what workers were already telling them. I could use my white and class privilege and academic credentials to draw attention to a problem that thrives off these very power dynamics, which could help pave the way toward addressing them and remove the burden from workers. But I was also inscribed in them by virtue of my own position.

CONVIVIR: ACCOMPANIMENT AND SOLIDARITY AMID PRIVILEGE AND PRECARITY

As they wrestle with how to position their relative privilege and power in the pursuit of social justice, ethnographers have begun to draw from a Latin American tradition of solidarity known as *acompañimiento*, or accompaniment.[37] Accompaniment and activism may come together, but can take different forms. As Whitney Duncan[38] notes, "*acompañimiento* conveys . . . forms of relatedness and nonjudgmental care" in response to institutional and systemic violence. As a methodological and ethical approach, *acompañimiento* unites people "in a strategic relationship of being and doing with those on the margins" to aspire toward social change.[39] In so doing, it centers human relationships and "create[s] a sense of belonging . . . acceptance," and community.[40]

Collaborating with the DAT and conducting research and outreach at street corners often involved literal accompaniment as my students and I joined workers to confront employers, students prepped workers for court cases, or we stood at street corners to listen to workers' stories without a set list of questions. Accompaniment emerged in the form of relational solidarity cultivated as we listened to workers' lives and concerns beyond wage theft incidents.

Accompaniment and solidarity require going beyond wage theft and workers to understand individuals' lives on their own terms. Yet these sensibilities must address the uneven sociostructural terrain on which they operate, as well as the inequalities between differently positioned allies and those with whom they attempt to forge solidarity. Sara Ahmed writes,

> Solidarity does not assume that our struggles are the same struggles, or that our pain is the same pain, or that our hope is for the same future. Solidarity involves commitment, and work, as well as the recognition that even if we do not have the same feelings, or the same lives, or the same bodies, we do live on common ground.[41]

Megan Carney, in her work with migrant solidarity movements in Italy, argues that solidarity, in contrast to mere compassion, is inspired by the desire to enact "radical structural shifts."[42] In practice, she depicts solidarity as an "aspirational project" within which differently positioned actors negotiate alternatives as well as their own unequal positionings within the system they attempt to bridge and transform."[43]

Accompaniment and solidarity strive toward aspirational futures, but are not sufficient if they do not motivate actions that transform the structural conditions of power and violence to which they otherwise respond.[44] *Convivir*, or coexisting side-by-side, in contrast, troublingly suggests wading within that status quo. Yet to *convivir* acknowledges the constraints workers face competing for work every day at the corner with their desires for companionship and solidarity with one another and with activist researchers. I offer that wading alongside workers as an everyday practice of being and doing is a necessary step before deciding what accompaniment and solidarity should look like, which are frequently defined from the standpoint of well-intentioned advocates rather than workers.[45] My students and I truly connected with workers when we put our interview questions and wage theft cases aside and learned to *convivir*. However, researchers must also take responsibility for the vast unevenness of the "common ground" they seek to cultivate.[46] Some days at the corner, we were welcomed only if we intended to *convivir*, not to conduct interviews.

EL CIERRE: CLOSURE AND RENEWAL

January 20, 2022. I am almost done with revisions for this book, but I am finding the task of concluding challenging—a common problem that plagues the bounding of the life experiences of others into a discrete written product. I'm waiting in my car across from Centro's former building for students I will accompany on a community mapping assignment for my qualitative methodologies course. I've done this assignment every year, but this time was different. I hadn't been to the area since the building was sold that past October. Across at Stout Street, a handful of workers still hoped to find work and greeted us with pleasantries when we walked by. I felt something I couldn't pinpoint: nostalgia, despair, or maybe it was just the piercing cold in my fingertips as the Denver winter finally caught on despite its late start.

I knew Centro made the right decision to sell the building—the area was changing and costs were adding up, especially as the pandemic continued. I understood these decisions more acutely after I joined Centro's board of directors in early 2022. Staff were connecting workers with jobs and trainings remotely and were expanding outreach through Centro's role as a partner with the Left Behind Workers' Fund. This fund, a public-private partnership, was initiated to disburse funds to individuals who lost jobs and income because of the pandemic but were ineligible for state or federal forms of unemployment and stimulus funds. The fund relied heavily on trusted nonprofits like Centro to reach eligible participants and distribute payments. But where would workers go to store their belongings, share stories about employers, talk about their children back home, use the computers, chat over warm coffee, and *convivir*? It was this aspect of *convivencia* that drew me back over and over to Centro—the community established through talking with workers, attending tamale lunches, and participating in the yearly Christmas celebration where we went around sharing our hopes for the new year and for the future.

The sun was finally starting to peek through by 9:00 a.m. The building's purple paint continued to chip and it was hard to decipher where the mural cut off and graffiti began. A black and white sign advertising the building's sale as restaurant/retail space, the square footage, and telephone number of a real estate group was plastered above the graffiti. The homeless encampments I had seen over the summer, which made walking down the street difficult, were eerily gone with just a few scattered tents owing to ongoing city sweeps. Meanwhile, the apartment complex behind was nearing completion and the crane turned reliably overhead, extending outward from the building over me, as if to index a landscape simultaneously characterized by growth, the violence of eviction and cultural erasure, and disrepair—at once a familiar continuity and a brief temporal moment.

I perhaps felt this mixture of emotions because of my growing distance from the site. Working, teaching, and living not far from my research sites always created a sharp juxtaposition between morning fieldwork, the afternoon classroom, and home. I was troubled by how research problems, writing schedules, and funding cycle calendars circumscribed and blunted the longer, more circuitous path that social justice struggles demand.[47] Yet my very sadness upon witnessing these changes also reflected how I could easily distance myself.

Leisy Abrego reflects on how standard qualitative methods training guides students to see "good qualitative research [as having] a start and end date, with the goal of entering and exiting 'the field' in ways that minimized emotional entanglements."[48] Writing from her social location as a Salvadoran immigrant scholar, these disconnections for Abrego were not only untenable but interfered with the insights that emerge through emotional and embodied experience.[49] In contrast, my own social location as a white woman professor from a privileged economic background granted me the choice to turn away, become frustrated, or even to sustain my research, policy advocacy, and activism amid obstacles. Sometimes I had trouble understanding how the merging of the personal and professional drained some of my differently positioned collaborators, leading them to take much-needed breaks for disconnection. Sharon Welch argues that the impulse to frustration or cynicism when social justice struggles become difficult is a "despair cushioned by . . . and grounded in privilege." This becomes an option only for those otherwise comforted in and by the present.[50]

I soon learned that my despair might be a reflection of my own personal and professional shortcomings in this work rather than what my collaborators were experiencing. The sale of Centro's building and the pandemic were not all negative. For some, they signaled renewal and new possibilities. Without being weighed down by monthly building payments and tied to a fixed location in a rapidly gentrifying neighborhood, Centro became more nimble to think and act creatively. Its leaders developed new digital organizing strategies, and workers learned to use Zoom and found ways to build community less dependent on a physical space. Meetings once attended by the same in-person twenty to thirty people began to grow to over eighty on Zoom, including original and new participants. Through their role of helping to distribute funds to immigrant workers in Denver on behalf of the Left Behind Workers' Fund, Centro pivoted to a model of *conectoras*. A mobile outreach model allowed it to reach over three thousand immigrants across the city in connection with the fund, many of whom expressed interest in learning more about their rights as workers. Centro found opportunities to expand its base and organizing kit.

The pandemic exacerbated low-wage immigrant workers' long-standing anxieties around health care, illness, and workplaces prone to health and safety violations, and some experts expect that the pandemic-induced recession will intensify both wage theft and workers' reluctance to report it out of fear of losing their jobs.[51] The pandemic revealed the disproportionate consequences borne by the most vulnerable,[52] but some immigrants became more interested in learning about their rights as workers precisely because of these impacts.[53] Moreover, the emergence of new digital tools; growing public attention to racial injustice, health inequities, immigrants' contributions to essential industries, and the quality of work; and more immigrant workers eager to assert their rights could also offer new visions for opening a policy climate more ripe for building coalitions to advance worker power and immigrant justice.[54]

I continue to wrestle with my role as I advocate for policy and social change. My trajectory departs substantially from the post-2008 recession lives of the day laborers who appear in these pages. I originally moved to Denver with a one-year academic contract after a different three-year temporary position as I struggled with the continuing impacts of the Great Recession and the bottoming out of the academic job market. My own contingent position was challenging and at times demoralizing but less financially critical because of my spouse's new job. My ability to persist and eventually climb the ladder into a tenured position was a testament to how much the system is built on existing privilege rather than merit while the majority of academic positions are increasingly contingent, bereft of benefits, and pay not only below qualifications but often less than what individuals and their families need to sustain themselves.

Because I moved to Denver in 2012 at the height of the postrecession boom that drew me into this project, I was complicit in the rapid construction and remodeling that displaced long-term residents. I watched new houses go up in my neighborhood and gave out leaflets on labor rights to workers as I sat comfortably in a house that may have been constructed under similar conditions. My students also reflected on the personal implications of Denver's postrecession rise; many were part of the influx of young students and educated professionals contributing to displacement and gentrification, but these dynamics made it difficult for many of them to live close to school and afford to live in Denver after graduation.

My own proximity to capital offered me the flexibility to write most of this book from home during the pandemic as most of the workers depicted in these pages kept going to work as "essential workers" in underprotected industries.[55] Indeed, Sarah Horton depicted COVID-19 and its starkly uneven distribution of risk as an "occupational hazard."[56] Even as

I struggled to manage months of primary care and remote-schooling responsibilities for my two elementary school-aged children with writing, I sat un/comfortably close to capital given the topic of this book, cushioned by a half-paid sabbatical, a spouse with a private sector job, and a class background that did not burden me with student debt. In contrast to the occupational hazards experienced by many workers during the pandemic, I enjoyed an occupational privilege to work from home and sustain a career that took years to make economically viable.

I argue that research methods, analytical insights, a reflective accounting of my position, and advocacy and activism cannot be disentangled. They are as intimately bound up in each other as they are with my own day-to-day praxis and the wider systems in which I am invested. In the end, I struggle with whether *I* should be the one to write this book about immigrant labor rights—a struggle that I learned about through listening and activism, but that I was otherwise not positioned to experience myself. Whitney Duncan wrestles with the fact that while allies are critical to the immigrant rights movement, "we cannot possibly understand in an embodied way what is at stake."[57] I've settled on the fact that more scholars need to become comfortable writing about and confronting our discomfort and not tidying it away to feign objectivity or even try to reconcile it. Those of us with power, as well as the security of tenure, ought to critically and reflexively apply it to advance the issues we research and claim to care about even if we make mistakes along the way.[58] We should transparently disclose the social relations conditioning the production of our work and lay bare the chasms between our "discursive claims . . . [activist proclivities] . . . and [our ongoing] material practices" even if it opens us to critique.[59]

Sí, se puede requires more than immigrants, workers, and allied coalitions and communities to organize, dismantle oppressive systems, and insist on change. It demands that more sectors of the public, including people like me and my students, realize we must. A first step may be withholding our own questions, policy advocacy, and even activism to listen and *convivir*, especially if we want to begin to understand a struggle when it is not ours and recognize that our interlocutors might rightly guard what they share. The mundane forms of *convivencia* forged with workers stimulated innovative ways for nurturing solidarity that transformed me, the research, my students, advocates, workers like Arturo, and even policymakers. However, the long-term process of engagement revealed the unevenness of these transformations and their limitations as they continue to be wrought within the context of our existing yet intersectional and sometimes shifting positions. In itself, *convivencia* cannot necessarily address the broader social, political, and economic shifts required to tackle wage theft and immigrant worker justice. Yet it can offer a foundation for cultivating the kinds of relationships and coalitions that shift the terrain to rethink what is possible and advance a more just future.

Appendix A
Methodological Supplement

This appendix provides a transparent account of the qualitative research and survey strategy conducted at day labor hiring sites to contextualize the results, explain challenges, and provide access to the process, methodology, and approach underlying the results so that other researchers can learn from it. The qualitative and survey phases were approved under separate IRB protocols (numbers 684443 and 945425, respectively) by the University of Denver.

In winter 2015, building off my classroom partnership with Centro Humanitario para los Trabajadores (Centro), I began a larger qualitative study to understand day laborers' experiences with wage theft across the five sites in coordination with Raja Raghunath's Workplace Rights wage theft clinic at the University of Denver's Sturm College of Law. I structured the initial research around participant observation and informal conversations about workers' lives rather than focus on wage theft, which could be alienating to workers. We brought coffee and bagels and spent two to three days each week at street corner hiring sites (*liebres*) and at Centro getting to know workers.

By the summer of 2015, I had developed a list of unstructured interview questions to understand workers' migration histories and work experiences, including questions about good and bad employers and jobs. The qualitative findings revealed workers' experiences with wage theft, the precarities of day labor, how immigration fear influenced their lives, relationships with family members abroad and in Colorado, migratory trajectories, and how workers attempted to protect themselves and make a living in the United States. I devised a loose guide for questions so that student researchers and I could weave them into more open-ended and natural conversations. We did not ask every individual every question because we wanted them to take the lead. Interview structure and depth depended on the flow of conversation and the dynamic nature of the hiring sites. Workers were first and foremost seeking work, and we made clear that conversations could be halted at any time. We then began to track population counts and wage theft experiences at each site to better diversify site selection and avoid oversaturating smaller sites and underexamining larger and more diverse ones.

From 2015 to 2016, my students and I interviewed 170 workers, but interviews ranged in quality and length as we stressed open, and sometimes held group, conversations. I trained student interviewers through my master's-level methods course or as paid research assistants in standard field note formatting and processes to establish consistency. We wrote short reflective and analytical sections to accompany field notes to spur further questions and compare insights.[1] Some interviews were taped and transcribed with worker' oral consent, but because of the informal atmosphere, the majority of notes were handwritten and then later fleshed out, typed up, and uploaded into Dedoose coding software. Dedoose's flexible secure online format allowed for group coding and checking, as well as for different students to rotate on and off the project. Data were coded either by myself or a lead research assistant under my supervision. When students conducted their own ethnographies through my methods course, they coded their data in separate Dedoose projects, but shared the data with me for inclusion in the larger project's database. Each student gave permission to use their data in this book and to be credited where applicable.

When students in my qualitative methods course, or other new research assistants, joined the project, I or a lead student assistant with established rapport would accompany them to the hiring sites. Graduate student Camden Bowman was instrumental as the first lead research assistant on the project, after which Kendra Allen, Morgan Brokob, and Amy Czulada took on these tasks. Camden established significant rapport by conducting independent research at hiring sites for his master's thesis in 2015. Over time, I supervised additional students to help me interview attorneys, advocates, politicians, employers, and collaborate with the Direct Action Team (DAT).

Still, owing to the demographics of a predominantly white, expensive private university, the majority of the students going out to street corners were white, relatively privileged, highly educated, and female owing to the demographic tilt of my students. Nevertheless, because we maintained a consistent presence at the corners over time to *convivir* and students pursued a more open-ended approach to fieldwork, most day laborers welcomed me and my students. Some workers relished the opportunity to speak with young people interested in listening or wistfully commented that students reminded them of their daughters back in Mexico or Central America. Life on the corner, we realized, was otherwise long, monotonous, and often demoralizing. One day when graduate student Amy Czulada and I stood with workers at the Federal site for three hours on a snowy February morning, workers commented that now we knew what it was like. Still, we were critically aware that even as our feet froze and it became difficult to hold our pens, we would soon get into our warm cars and drive to our classrooms and homes.

Quantitative Phase

After a year of qualitative research, I collaborated with demographer Randall Kuhn, a colleague at the University of Denver (before he moved to UCLA), to develop a survey instrument. The survey used the qualitative insights and knowledge of the street corners to develop questions and the sampling strategy. The survey aimed to more systematically assess day laborers' demographics, migration histories, retrospective five-day work histories, work experiences, wage theft incidences, strategies for wage theft prevention and redress, and legal knowledge and awareness.

Students were also instrumental in designing the survey approach. Graduate students in my qualitative methods course, under my supervision and Institutional Review Board protocols, helped gather more qualitative data and conduct interval counts at each hiring site to systematically assess each site's population rhythms at different times and days of the week to construct a sampling frame. Students in Kuhn's master's-level community-based research methods course helped draft survey questions, sampling design, and REDCap electronic capture software.[2] During summer 2016, undergraduate student Eloy Chavez and I piloted the survey modules at Centro and other hiring sites, and I then edited accordingly. I next recruited and trained bilingual students, many of whom came from Latino immigrant families, to orally administer the survey in English or Spanish, depending on the worker's preference. After each survey, workers were given a $10 grocery gift card and a know-your-rights card on labor rights. Surveyors were also trained by Centro staff to conduct know-your-rights workshops at these sites on days when surveys were not being conducted. We then incorporated a survey question assessing if workers had listened to these presentations or received a card.

It is inherently difficult to construct a representative sample of a transient, hidden population for which there is no known population parameter from which to draw a sample. Street ethnography and scouting improved the sampling design while we also incorporated techniques used by the National Day Labor Survey (NDLS) in their 2004 day labor study to account for a quintessential problem—the fact that the outcomes of interest—work and wage theft—were a function of the sampling venue.[3] This posed two problems: by design we missed workers who were working because we were sampling where workers were waiting to be hired (and thus did not have work) *and* exposure to wage theft is conditioned on exposure to working. Without accounting for propensity to work, the sample would bias toward workers with a low likelihood of working. These were all adjustments that Kuhn incorporated into the weighting strategy. We also distributed the survey into quarters over the course of a year to understand seasonal variation with the goal of collecting one hundred surveys per season for a total of four hundred. We knew that work was more plentiful in the summer and slower in the winter. Yet seasonal variations were not straightforward. Snow produced work opportunities for shoveling, whereas mere cold did not. Attorneys also informed me that wage claims were often suppressed in the summer because workers were busy working. Workplace abuses that occurred during the summer were often filed months later when the pace of work slowed.

In total we surveyed 411 workers across five hiring venues, including the four street corner sites and Centro between October 2016 and August 2017. The reported weighted results refer to a sample of 393 after culling exclusions, which included respondents coded as having great difficulty answering questions and suspended interviews and surveys with missing data on more than one question or that could not be connected to the sampling paradata.[4] To respect privacy, we did not collect last names and requested only first names and an initial, but we also allowed individuals to provide a nickname or fake name instead. We secured this information with REDCap electronic capture software to protect and track participants. In the field, surveyors conducted the surveys orally and filled them out in paper form, which they then distributed to me or student assistant Jordyn Dinwiddie to digitally enter into REDCap. We followed up with surveyors for any queries and accounted for individual surveyor effects.

First, using the presurvey and population accounts, Kuhn created a survey calendar for each season with dates, assigned locations, and assigned surveyors. For each outing, two surveyors went to one site with the goal of collecting four surveys (two each). We designed survey windows to account for time-of-day effects to assess whether earlier respondents were more successful at obtaining work. Surveyors were instructed to each collect one survey in the first time window (7:00–7:30) and a second in the second interval (8:30–9:00). At each survey outing, the two surveyors conducted an initial head count, then used a modified K-ish table (a grid of randomly assigned numbers used to select respondents) to select the *n*th worker to be surveyed to approximate random selection. Although surveyors always counted workers in the same manner or direction at each site, this was difficult because workers moved around and we often had to recount if we received more than a few refusals. At the Kentucky and Sheridan site, some workers remained in their cars, which made consistent counting difficult. In contrast, workers at Dayton and Colfax, Stout Street, and Federal and 19th tended to wait more in linear fashion down the street. After both surveyors completed their first survey, they took another head count and repeated the random selection to choose their second respondents. They took a final head count before departing. Survey cover sheets allowed us to track sites, surveyors, the three interval head counts, and refusals. We also asked workers to fill out duplicate forms if they were selected and had already taken the survey. As part of a work module, surveyors took workers through a five-day retrospective employment survey to assess their likelihood of working and being present at particular hiring sites on certain days. The interval head counts, duplicate sheets, refusals, and the five-day work histories were used to design each subsequent quarter's survey calendar and to weight results—especially to account for workers' propensity to work.

The head counts and duplicate forms allowed us to perform capture-recapture to estimate the total population size.[5] Although this process was subject to some error, duplication, and manipulation, the rate at which repeat individuals surfaced rose throughout the survey period as expected, establishing the limits of the population's true size.[6] Across all sites and days, we counted 6,251 workers, with the recapture revealing a total population estimate of 1,400 to 1,600 day laborers.[7] The 19 percent recapture and 18 percent refusal rate narrow the true population to 1,554.[8] If these five sites are the only major recruitment sites in the Denver metropolitan area, then the survey sample of 393 constitutes a 25 percent sample of the day labor population.[9]

I trained and selected student surveyors based on their prior work on the project and Spanish abilities, and with attention toward compositionally diversifying the research team in contrast to the qualitative research phase. Still, because they were students and their schedules frequently changed, many surveyors rotated on and off the project over the course of the year. Most workers accepted the opportunity to participate, but we did encounter refusals, especially at the Dayton and Colfax site in Aurora, where we learned that one reluctant individual could alter the willingness of others present. Interestingly, surveyors seemed to receive more pushback than during the qualitative phase, where we encountered few refusals. Even when students shared cultural and linguistic backgrounds—some students came from immigrant families and all spoke fluent Spanish—the students' lives still seemed worlds away.[10] The stricter structure of the survey was potentially more alienating and demanded more of workers than the more open-ended qualitative research. Surveys were relatively short to respect workers' time—about fifteen minutes. This meant that two surveys and debriefing could occur in about two hours, leaving little room for the kinds of camaraderie we had cultivated at the corners in the earlier phase. The survey data were statistically weighted and analyzed by Kuhn and student assistants under his supervision at UCLA. We compared the quantitative findings with the qualitative insights to explore themes, explain surprising results, and generate questions for ongoing research.[11]

Taking into account surveyor error, inaccuracies that can emerge when surveying street corners over four seasons, and the difficulties of sampling and surveying a mobile and relatively hidden population long suspicious of research or interventions, the survey sample is as close an approximation of a representative sample of day laborers in the Denver area that was possible given the resources available.

Appendix B
Figures and Table

The following table and figures show results from the survey that are referenced throughout the chapters.

TABLE 1: Mean of employment outcomes, wage theft, and self-protection. Data analyzed and table by Randall Kuhn. Reprinted with permission from Galemba and Kuhn (2021).

		Duration			
	Total	**0–9 years**	**10–19 years**	**20+ years**	**US-born**
Day labor activity					
% of days look for/had work	54%	64%	54%	54%	44%
% of days worked	40%	56%	44%	35%	28%
Hours worked					
On average working day	7.0	7.8	6.7	6.8	6.9
On all days	2.7	4.4	2.8	2.4	1.8
Wages and earnings					
Average hourly wage	$15.60	$14.74	$15.59	$16.27	$14.46
% of workdays below minimum wage	7.3%	8.1%	4.2%	5.6%	21.9%
On average working day	$107.80	$117.34	$103.58	$108.60	$98.22
On all days	$42.38	$63.59	$46.23	$38.01	$22.43
Wage theft					
Ever experienced	62%	53%	66%	61%	68%
Last six months	19%	31%	22%	11%	15%
Total owed (if any episode)	$348	$305	$337	$303	$564
Self-protection					
Knows minimum wage	22%	19%	21%	22%	33%
Knows Fair Labor Standards Act	14%	8%	17%	13%	22%
Knows Colorado Wage Claim Act	12%	8%	10%	12%	18%
Collects employer contact information	41%	41%	31%	44%	49%
Records days/hours worked	64%	60%	63%	65%	69%
Knowledge score (of 8 points)	2.4	1.9	2.3	2.4	3.0

FIGURE 20: What can you do to make sure an employer pays you? Originally published in Galemba (2021).

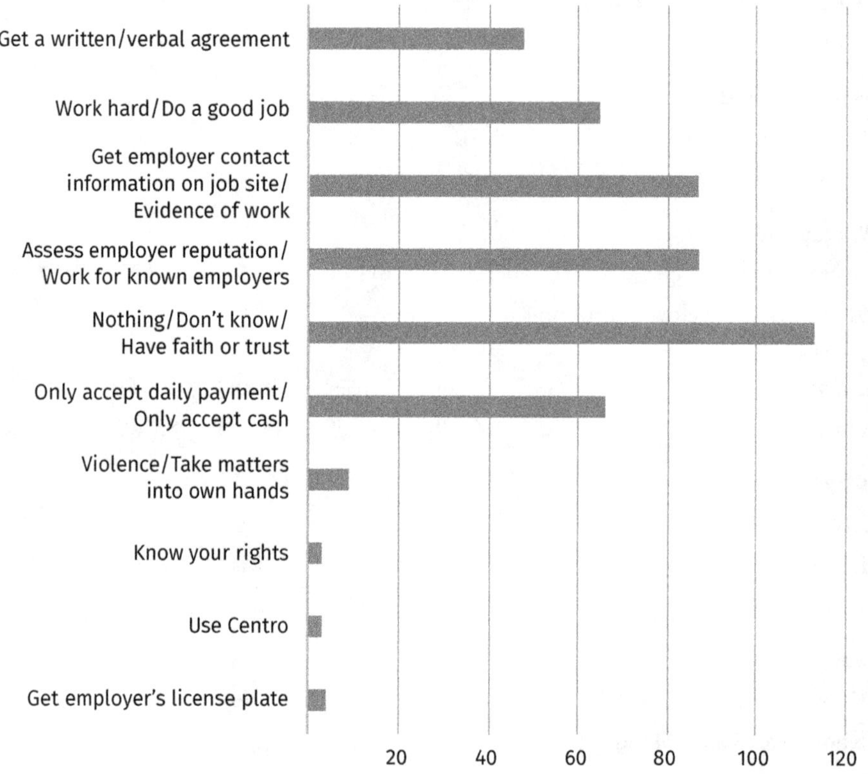

Note: $N = 411$. Open-ended questions allowed multiple answers per informant.

FIGURE 21: What would you do or who would you call if an employer did not pay you what he or she legally owed you? Originally published in Galemba (2021).

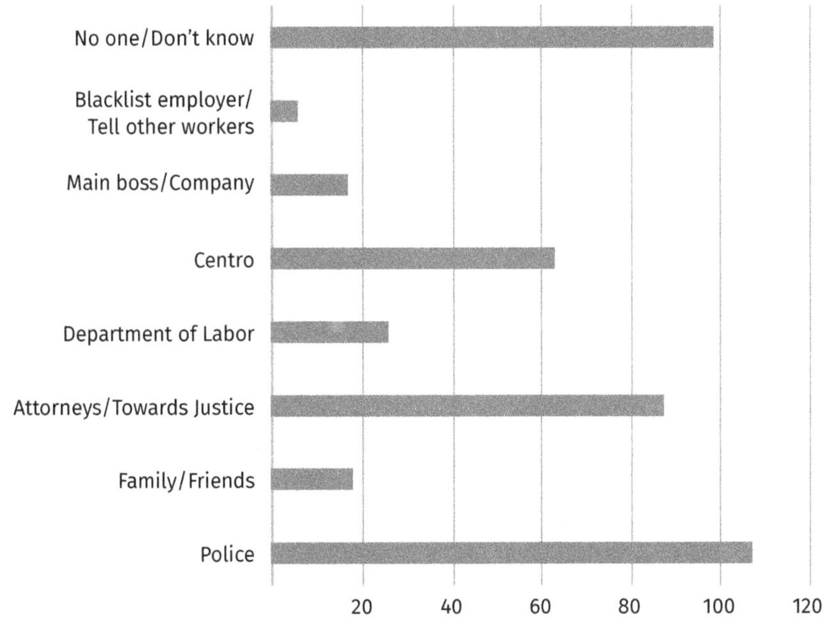

Note: N = 411. Open-ended questions allowed multiple answers per informant.

FIGURE 22: Who did you ask for help? Originally published in Galemba (2021).

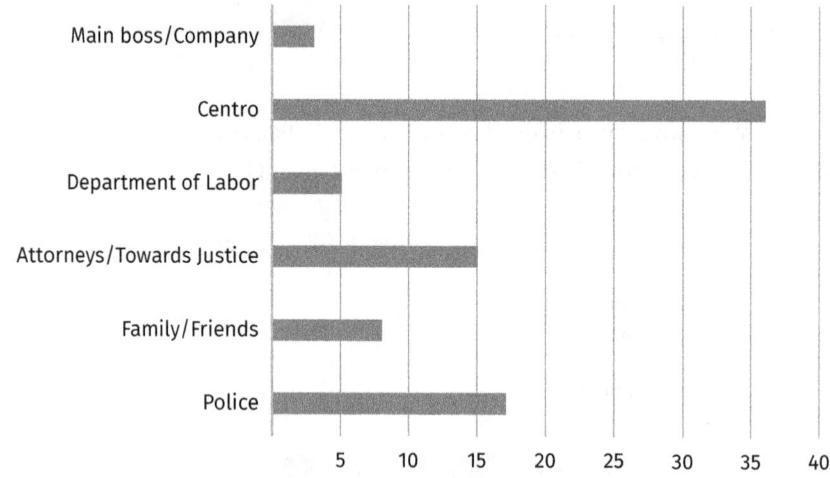

Note: $N = 90$: workers who sought help for a wage theft incident. Open-ended questions allowed multiple answers per informant.

FIGURE 23: Who helped you? Originally published in Galemba (2021).

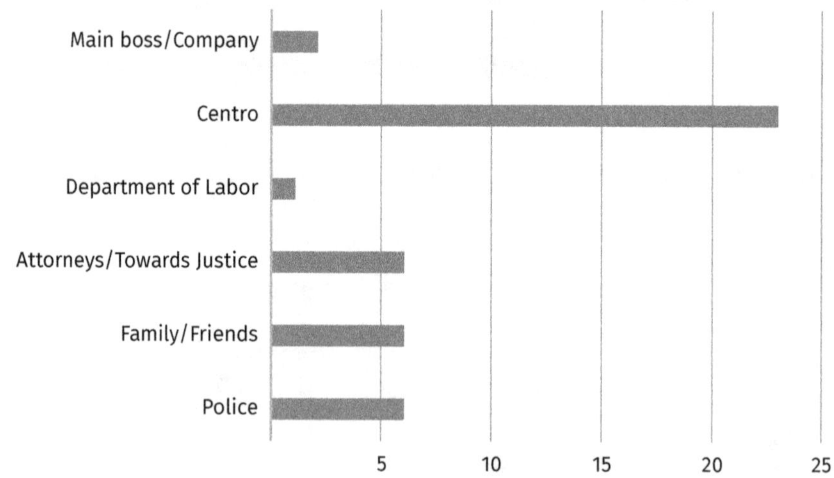

Note: $N = 48$. Of the 90 workers who sought assistance, 48 reported receiving help. Open-ended questions allowed multiple answers per informant.

Notes

Introduction: Stolen Wages on Stolen Land

1. Portions of "Claudio's story" appear in Galemba and Kuhn 2021 and Galemba 2017.

2. I use the actual names of advocates, students, union organizers, and attorneys with their permission and to credit them for their work. Workers' names are pseudonyms to protect their anonymity, with the exceptions of Davor, Diana, and Severiano, who gave permission to use only their first names. I use pseudonyms for employers and companies to avoid any potential liabilities.

3. Pressure to keep earning and stigma may motivate workers to work through, or not report, injuries (Horton 2016a; Saxton and Stuesse 2018, 69; Unterberger 2018).

4. Valenzuela et al. 2006.

5. Ibid., 9; Ordóñez 2015.

6. Peck and Theodore 2012, 744; Theodore 2007, 251.

7. Valenzuela et al. 2006; Peck and Theodore 2012; Ordóñez 2015.

8. Valenzuela et al. 2006; Theodore et al. 2008; Theodore 2007, 2017, 2020. Meléndez et al. 2014; Valdez et al. 2019; Walter et al. 2002.

9. Gomberg-Muñoz and Nussbaum-Barberena 2011.

10. Shannon Gleeson (2016, 7) argues that lack of legal status acts as a "precarity multiplier" by providing extra assurance to employers that they will likely get away with exploitation.

11. Doussard 2013; Apostolidis 2019.

12. Ollus et al. 2016.

13. Farrell et al. 2020.

14. Leighton 2019; Davies 2018; Lloyd et al. 2020.

15. Davies 2019, 305; Lloyd et al. 2020, 6, cited in Galemba 2021, 93. See Doussard 2013.

16. Labban 2013; Marx 1977.

17. Ibid.

18. Ollus et al. 2016.

19. Doussard 2013; Labban 2013.

20. Chauvin and Garcés-Mascareñas 2014; De Genova 2002; Espiritu 2003.

21. De Genova 2002, 2013; Espiritu 2003; Chauvin and Garcés-Mascareñas 2014.

22. Doussard 2013.

23. Smith-Nonini 2011, 464; Walia 2021; Segrave 2017.

24. Quesada, Hart, and Bourgois 2011; Quesada et al. 2014.

25. Quesada, Hart, and Bourgois 2011, 340; Galtung 1975, 173.

26. Quesada, Hart, and Bourgois 2011, 341.

27. Quesada et al. 2014.

28. Menjívar and Abrego 2012.

29. Haro et al. 2020; Theodore et al. 2006, 2008; Valenzuela et al. 2006; Bobo 2011; Organista, Arreola, and Neilands 2017; Walter et al. 2002; Walter, Bourgois, and Loinaz 2004; Quesada et al. 2014; Duke, Bourdeau, and Hovey 2010; Boyas, Valera, and Ruiz 2018.

30. Bourdieu 2003; Quesada, Hart, and Bourgois 2011; Ordóñez 2015.

31. Ibid.

32. Ordóñez 2015; Quesada et al. 2014; Holmes 2013.

33. See an exception in Stuesse's (2016) ethnography, which explores how activist research can contribute to organizing across difference among Mississippi poultry workers. Also see Apostolidis 2019.

34. See the critiques in Horton 2016a and Tuck 2009 (thanks to Emily Yates-Doerr for recommending Tuck's work).

35. Scott 1985; see Stuesse (2016, 156–157) on how Latino immigrant poultry workers tend to acquiesce to their working conditions to "get ahead" instead of deploying tactics of resistance more commonly used by their African American coworkers.

36. Scott 1985.

37. Bayat 2013.

38. Tuck 2009, 413; hooks 1990.

39. Tuck 2009, 409.

40. Golash-Boza 2012.

41. For California, see Quesada et al. 2014; Duke, Bourdeau, and Hovey 2010; Ordóñez 2015; Gleeson 2016; Holmes 2013; Horton 2016a; Zlolniski 2003, 2006; Milkman 2006. See Doussard (2013) on Chicago and Bernhardt et al.'s (2009) comparative study of low-wage workers in Los Angeles, New York, and Chicago. See also Fine and Gordon (2010) for strategic enforcement in New York and Los Angeles.

42. Heyman 1998; Theodore 2017, 2020. Also see Crotty 2014, 2017, 2018 for Southern California, another traditional border reception area.

43. See Armenta 2017.

44. Stuesse 2016.

45. Fussell 2011; Waren 2014; Schneider 2018.

46. World Population Review 2021; Daum et al. 2011.

47. Daum et al. 2011, 3; Fermanich 2011.

48. Berardi 2014.

49. Daum et al. 2011.

50. Ibid.; Berardi 2014.

51. Berardi 2014, 1. In 2013, Colorado repealed SB90 and approved measures to provide access to driver's licenses and in-state college tuition for undocumented residents (Martínez 2014).

52. Taft 1966.

53. Sealover 2017; Colorado Department of Labor and Employment Labor Peace Act, Title 3, Article 8.

54. Moore 2011, 226; Bell Policy Center 2017.

55. Goetz and Boschmann 2018.

56. Ibid., 4.

57. Zuñiga and Hernández León 2005, 6; Ngai 2004.

58. Goetz and Boschmann 2018, 7.

59. Riosmena and Massey 2012; Zúñiga and Hernández-Leon 2005, xiv.

60. Zúñiga and Hernández-Leon 2005, xiv.

61. Daum et al. 2011, 11; Pew Research Center 2014.

62. Goetz and Boschmann 2018.

63. Daum et al. 2011, 2.

64. Ibid., 2; Goetz and Boschmann 2018.

65. I appreciate Sarah Horton's suggestion to include this example.

66. Gledhill 1998, 280.

67. Varsanyi 2020, 13.

68. Goetz and Boschmann 2018, 4.

69. Ibid., 41.

70. Ibid., 4, 41.

71. Clemmer-Smith et al. 2014.

72. See Goodstein on the history of the Five Points neighborhood, once a center of Denver's Black community with a vibrant business center and jazz scene (Goodstein 2014, 148). However, the area became increasingly overcrowded with deteriorating living conditions, especially because racist housing and lending policies limited the mobility of African Americans until the legislature passed the Fair Housing Act in 1959 (ibid., 156, 160). In the 1950s and 1960s, as many African Americans moved out and urban renewal projects ignored the neighborhood, it began to suffer from decay, disinvestment, crime, and poor public services (ibid., 160). In 2012, a large section was declared "blighted" to pave the way for urban renewal (ibid., 170). Many residents and local businesses opposed the plans, arguing that "urban renewal programs had invariably strengthened the rich while displacing the poor" and constituted plans to "drive poor African-Americans from the neighborhood . . . to transform the area into a white yuppie annex of the central business

district" (ibid.). Recently, downtown redevelopment has made Five Points one of the hottest new housing areas.

73. Goldberg 1981, xi.

74. Vigil 1999, 18.

75. Ibid.

76. Goldberg 1981, 30.

77. These industrial neighborhood attracted Eastern European and Jewish immigrants in the nineteenth century to work in smelting and meatpacking. When they moved out, the neighborhoods became increasingly Latino (History Colorado).

78. Information from my project, Building a More Robust and Diverse Construction Trades in the Denver Metro Area IRB 1321935 with Singumbe Muyeba. Interview conducted by Jack Becker with CREA Results, Carrie DuLaney, and Emily Spahn, February 26, 2020.

79. Galvin 2016, 330.

80. Stiffler 2014.

81. Ibid.

82. This included conversations with others who became key players in the immigrant and workers' rights movements, including Julien Ross, founding Executive Director of the Colorado Immigrant Rights Coalition (CIRC), who had led the Workers Defense Project in Texas, and attorney Hillary Ronen. Others note the role of the National Interfaith Committee on Worker Justice, predecessor to Interfaith Worker Justice, in popularizing the term in the 1990s (Monforton and Von Bergen 2021, 220).

83. Other recruitment sites may exist, but I was not aware of any other substantial ones. Sites were identified by Centro and workers at other sites. Employers come to these sites to recruit workers from throughout Colorado and even other states.

84. Who Is Aurora 2016.

85. Goodstein 2014, 146.

86. Rinehart and Robinson 2007.

87. Fine 2006, 2, 14.

88. Monforton and Von Bergen 2021.

89. Fine 2006; Theodore 2017, 2020; Meléndez et al. 2014.

90. "Centro Humanitario: Employment Program."

91. Ibid.

92. See Fine (2006, 11) on how the centrality of work for new immigrants led organizations to first brand themselves as worker centers.

93. Although the donor donated the building and land to Centro in 2005, the organization had to pay a monthly annuity.

94. We received a Public Good Grant and IRISE Grant from the University of Denver for our collaboration and continued until Raja left DU in 2017.

95. Low and Engle Merry 2010.

96. Stuesse 2016, 235, 237; also Hale 2006, 2007; Gordon 1991; Bejarano et al. 2019.

97. Janes 2016; Berry et al. 2017.

98. TallBear 2014, 2; also Bejarano et al. 2019.

99. TallBear 2014, 4.

100. Ibid.; Janes 2016, 84.

101. See Stuesse 2016.

102. Seligman, Galemba, and the Southwest Regional Council of Carpenters 2018.

103. See Stuesse 2016.

104. O'Brien 2020.

105. See https://dujustwagesproject.wordpress.com/.

106. Although they note the tensions, Monforton and Von Bergen (2021) hone in on worker centers and Apostolidis (2019) based his research with worker centers in Seattle and Portland. In contrast, Ordóñez, who centers his work on a large street corner site during the Great Recession, and Camou (2009, 2012), who studied Centro but at its early stages, are more circumspect.

107. Gleeson 2016.

108. Horton 2016b, 2016c.

109. Rappaport 2007.

110. Diana, Severiano, Abbey, and Alex are credited as coauthors of the interludes and were paid for their time.

111. I edited the interviews for inclusion, and Abbey and Alex verified them with the workers.

112. Janes 2016, 84; also see Bejarano et al. 2019.

Chapter 1: Stealing Immigrant Work

1. Meixell and Eisenbrey 2014, 2. Other analyses, extrapolated from findings in the ten most populous states, put the total around $15 billion (Cooper and Kroeger 2017), but the amount is still significant and difficult to pinpoint because wage theft is vastly underreported.

2. Bobo 2011, 43–44, 21.

3. Ibid., 21.

4. Meixell and Eisenbrey 2014, 2.

5. Bernhardt et al. 2008; Bobo 2011; Theodore 2017.

6. Bobo 2011; Bernhardt et al. 2009; Cooper and Kroeger 2017; Gordon et al. 2012.

7. Bernhardt et al. 2009, 43.

8. Bobo 2011.

9. Visser 2017; Standing 2011; Walia 2021.

10. Visser 2017, 783; Goldring and Landolt 2012; Peck and Theodore 2008, 2012.

11. Besteman 2019; Walia 2021.

12. Walia 2013, 38.

13. Ibid.

14. Sassen 1990.

15. Nevins 2008.

16. Ibid.

17. Walia 2013, 2021; Ferguson and McNally 2015.

18. Ferguson and McNally 2015; Quesada, Hart, and Bourgois 2011; Walia 2021; Nevins 2008; De Genova 2002; Golash-Boza 2015; Smith-Nonini 2011; Gledhill 1998.

19. Linder 1986, 1336; Perea 2011, 99.

20. Migdal 2015.

21. Perea 2011, 99.

22. Ngai 2004, 136.

23. Menjívar and Abrego 2012; Fernández-Esquer et al. 2021.

24. Hondagneu-Sotelo 2007.

25. Standing 2011; Gleeson 2016; Bernhardt et al. 2008.

26. Milkman 2020, 68; Zlolniski 2003.

27. Fine 2006, 31.

28. Milkman 2020, 68; Standing 2011; Kalleberg 2012.

29. Kalleberg 2012; Bernhardt et al. 2008.

30. Kalleberg 2012; Standing 2011; Bernhardt 2012.

31. Weil 2018, 440.

32. Ibid. Also see Bernhardt 2012.

33. Weil 2018. Weil (2019, 158 and 2018, n. 18) connects workplace fissuring to the rise in earnings inequality. Under Weil's leadership of the DoL's Wage and Hour Division under the Obama administration, the division sought to more proactively address fissuring through strategic enforcement.

34. Weil 2018, 440.

35. Bobo 2011; Weil 2011, 2018.

36. Bernhardt 2012, 362.

37. Weil 2011, 42.

38. Weil 2018; Bobo 2011.

39. Weil 2018, 3.

40. Bernhardt 2012; Weil 2018.

41. Weil 2011, 42. Weil used Wage and Hour Division investigations conducted between 2006 and 2008 as well as 2006 data from the US Bureau of the Census report on *County Business Patterns* (ibid., 51n6).

42. Bernhardt 2012, 363.

43. Weil 2018, 4; Weil 2010, 3; Bernhardt 2012, 363.

44. Smith, Avendaño, and Ortega 2009, 9.

45. Bobo 2011, 178.

46. Ibid., 76; Weil 2018; Galvin 2016.

47. Walia 2021, 23; Ngai 2004; Gledhill 1998.

48. Montoya 2002.

49. Ngai 2004, 132; Varsanyi 2020, 8.

50. Ngai 2004, 129.

51. Milkman 2020, 13.

52. Ngai 2004, 7.

53. Durand 2007, 26.

54. Ngai 2004, 132.

55. Ibid., 138. The program was originally initiated through a binational treaty with Mexico, and although it was initially intended to be temporary, it was renewed yearly during the 1940s. In 1951, under pressure from growers during the Korean War, Congress passed Public Law 78 and reached an agreement with Mexico, the Migrant Labor Agreement, that provided the program with a "permanent statutory basis" and guided the program until its termination in 1964 (Massey et al. 2002, 37; Ngai 2004, 139; see also Horton 2016a, 205n3).

56. Calavita 2010. Massey et al. (2002, 36) argue that Mexico's rapid population growth made it difficult for its economic boom to otherwise generate sufficient jobs. While Mexico pursued an ambitious program of land reform during the 1930s, households needed financial inputs to invest for the land to be productive.

57. Ngai 2004, 137.

58. Durand 2007.

59. Ngai 2004, 137–138.

60. Calavita 2010, 17.

61. García 1980.

62. Ngai 2004, 140. See Ngai (2004, 146) on how Mexico lost some of its control over these processes.

63. Ibid., 143–144.

64. Ibid., 142; also see Loza 2016. Some braceros even participated in strikes and protests. See Ngai 2004, 145.

65. Massey et al. 2002; Balderrama and Rodríguez 2006; Ngai 2004.

66. Ngai 2004, 147–148.

67. The Texas Proviso was repealed under the Immigration Reform and Control Act in 1986 (Massey et al. 2002, 36, 90).

68. Ngai 2004, 153.

69. Ibid.

70. Ibid., 139.

71. See Loza (2016, 11) and on the Bracero Justice Movement.

72. Ibid.

73. De Genova 2002.

74. Massey et al. 2002, 41.

75. Ibid.; Ngai 2004.

76. De Genova 2002, 439.

77. Heyman 2014; Chauvin and Garcés-Mascareñas 2014; De Genova 2002.

78. Horton 2016c.

79. Espiritu 2003, 211.

80. Lung 2019, 295.

81. Ibid.

82. Ibid., 296. See also Horton 2016b.

83. Massey and Gentsch 2014, 496.

84. See Horton 2016b; Phillips and Massey 1999; Milkman 2008, 2020.

85. Massey and Gentsch 2014, 496.

86. When workers are hired by subcontractors, lines of responsibility are murkier, and it is more challenging for workers to report violations and bargain. It has also resulted in lower wages (Gentsch and Massey 2011, 882; Phillips and Massey 1999).

87. Phillips and Massey 1999, 243.

88. Ibid.; Gentsch and Massey 2011, 892.

89. Lung 2019, 301; Nessel 2001, 320; Gordon 1995, 414n17.

90. Gordon 1995; Lung 2019; Smith, Avendaño, and Ortega 2009.

91. Smith, Avendaño, and Ortega 2009, 7.

92. Lung 2019.

93. Ibid., 309.

94. Ibid., 306.

95. Ibid., 308.

96. Espiritu 2003, 211; Chauvin and Garcés-Mascareñas 2014; De Genova 2002, 2013; Calavita 2005; Cacho 2012; Horton 2017.

97. Smith, Avendaño, and Ortega 2009, 4.

98. Costa 2019.

99. Smith, Avendaño, and Ortega 2009.

100. US Immigration and Customs Enforcement 2021.

101. Ibid.

102. Chauvin and Garcés-Mascareñas 2014; De Genova 2002.

103. Calavita 2010.

104. Chávez 2013; Nevins 2008; Quesada, Hart, and Bourgois 2011.

105. Loza 2016, 6.

106. De Genova 2002; García 1980; Loza 2016; Balderamma and Rodríguez 2006.

107. Fernández-Esquer et al. 2021, 345; also see Quesada et al. 2011.

108. Gomberg-Muñoz 2011; Walia 2021. See Smith-Nonini (2011, 466) on how employers devalue workers as little more than "embodied energy."

109. For example, recent US Supreme Court decisions and the proliferation of forced arbitration agreements make class action cases more difficult and benefit firms over workers. Courts continue to grapple over guidance around employee versus independent contractor designations and joint and multiple liabilities. Despite some exclusions, the introduction of the Protecting the Right to Organize (PRO Act) in 2021 would represent a transformative shift toward bolstering rights to organize and workers' rights that have otherwise eroded over the past four decades.

Chapter 2: Boomtown: Construction and Immigration in the Mile High City

1. Scopelliti 2014. The bubble period was marked by overbuilding in many areas of the country. See Baker 2018.

2. Wallace 2016.

3. Scopelliti 2014.

4. Goetz and Boschmann 2018.

5. Ibid.

6. Ibid.

7. Hickey 2015; Svaldi April 26, 2016; Goetz and Boschmann 2018, 11.

8. Fine et al. 2020, 11. See also Ordóñez's ethnography of day labor in the San Francisco Bay Area during the Great Recession.

9. Doussard 2013. See Reich, Gordon, and Edwards (1973) on labor market segmentation within the context of monopoly capitalism. In addition to "systemic forces" that fuel segmentation of the labor market into primary sectors (also with upper and lower segments) with high wages, decent benefits and working conditions, and mobility and a secondary sector where these are lacking (Piore 1972, 2), Reich, Gordon, and Edwards (1973, 361) show how employers cultivated labor market segmentation to " 'divide and conquer' the labor force" to exert control amid rising worker proletarianization and organizing in the early twentieth century. Employers manipulated "race, ethnic, and sex antagonisms to undercut unionism and break strikes," as well as to create such segmentation (Ibid., 362).

10. Bernhardt et al. 2008.

11. Valenzuela 2003; Doussard 2013, 12.

12. Doussard 2013, 149.

13. Ibid.

14. Theodore et al. 2016; Visser 2016; Doussard 2013.

15. Bernhardt et al. 2008; Theodore et al. 2006, 2008; Doussard 2013.

16. See Stuesse (2016) on parallels in poultry processing.

17. Schneider (2018) also points to the transnational nature of construction by revealing the opportunities for international construction and investment firms and the industry's heavy reliance on immigrant labor.

18. Doussard 2013, 149; Erlich and Grabelsky 2005.

19. Western and Rosenfeld 2011; Erlich 2021.

20. Vidal and Kusnet 2009; Theodore et al. 2008, 93; Erlich and Grabelsky 2005, 424–425; US Bureau of Labor Statistics 2021.

21. Milkman 2020, 77–78; 2008, 70.

22. Erlich 2021, 1224; Allen 1994; Milkman 2006, 2020; Doussard 2013.

23. Doussard 2013.

24. Ibid.; Erlich 2021.

25. Erlich 2021, 1207; see also Doussard 2013.

26. Ibid.

27. Doussard 2013, 164; Theodore 2019.

28. Doussard 2013.

29. Ibid., 167; Erlich and Grabelsky 2005.

30. Theodore et al. 2015.

31. Milkman 2008, 66.

32. Bernhardt et al. 2008; Milkman 2008, 2020; Theodore et al. 2008.

33. Theodore et al. 2008, 94.

34. Milkman 2008.

35. Ibid.

36. Milkman 2020, 78; Rabourn 2008, 16.

37. CPWR 2018.

38. Doussard 2013; Erlich 2021; Passel and Cohn 2016.

39. CPWR 2011–2019.

40. Doussard 2013, 157.

41. Ibid.

42. Ibid., 158–159.

43. Milkman 2008, 72.

44. Erlich 2021, 1215.

45. Data compiled by Abbey Vogel.

46. Theodore et al. 2008; Doussard 2013; Theodore 2019.

47. Schneider 2018, 103; Piore 1972.

48. Ibid.; Doussard 2013.

49. Valenzuela et al. 2006; see Theodore et al. 2008, 98, on changes.

50. Valenzuela et al. 2006, 17.

51. Ibid.

52. Ibid., 20.

53. Ibid. Because the NDLS sample was overall composed of recent immigrants, it is difficult to tell whether these transitions indeed occurred.

54. Galemba and Kuhn 2021.

55. Meléndez et al. 2016; see Galemba and Kuhn 2021. It is possible that the individuals we surveyed could be among the same ones captured by the NDLS in 2004 when they were recent immigrants.

56. See Boyas, Valera, and Ruiz 2018; Crotty 2014; Organista, Arreola, and Neilands 2017; Theodore 2017, 2020; Valdez et al. 2019; Fernández-Esquer et al. 2021.

57. Hall, Greenman, and Yi 2019.

58. Valenzuela et al. 2006.

59. Galemba and Kuhn 2021; Valenzuela et al. 2006. This hovers individuals around the poverty line.

60. Passel and Cohn 2019.

61. See Massey et al. 2002; Andreas 2011.

62. Many immigrants sent for their family members, who increasingly settled in the United States (Massey, Durand, and Pren 2016b). Those who did not, especially those who were unable to adjust their status via IRCA, spent more time distanced from their families.

63. Heyman 1998.

64. Subcontracting was already well honed to control costs and employer obligations in industries like construction and janitorial services when IRCA provided an additional incentive to sidestep sanctions (Phillips and Massey 1999; Milkman 2020; Zlolniski 1994, 2003; Horton 2016a, 2016b; Stuesse 2016).

65. Zlolniski 2003; 1994; Horton 2016b; Phillips and Massey 1999; Milkman 2008; 2020.

66. Ibid.

67. Horton 2016b; Gomberg-Muñoz and Nussbaum-Barberena 2011; Gomberg-Muñoz 2016; Inda and Dowling 2013.

68. Inda and Dowling 2013; Stumpf 2006; Golash-Boza 2015; Gomberg-Muñoz 2016; Coleman 2007.

69. Horton 2016c.

70. Ibid.; see also Stumpf 2006; Inda and Dowling 2013; Golash-Boza 2015.

71. Golash-Boza 2012.

72. Ibid.

73. Patler and Golash-Boza 2017, 5. When DHS was created in 2003, the duties of the INS were assigned to the US Citizenship and Immigration Services, US Customs and Border Protection, or US Immigration and Customs Enforcement.

74. Coleman 2007; Armenta 2017; Golash-Boza 2015.

75. Golash-Boza and Hondagneu-Sotelo 2013, 277.

76. Rosas 2006; Coleman 2007; Menjívar 2014.

77. The Social Security Administration sends no-match letters when an employer's records do not match theirs, but errors can occur for various reasons and are not intended to be used for immigration enforcement purposes.

78. Menjívar and Abrego 2012; Horton 2016a; Gomberg-Muñoz and Nussbaum-Barberena 2011; Gomberg-Muñoz 2016; NILC 2020; Coleman 2007; Stuesse 2010, 2016; Lee 2014; Goldstein and Bejarano 2017; Coleman and Stuesse 2014; Golash-Boza 2012.

79. Golash-Boza 2015.

80. See Smith, Avendaño, and Ortega 2009; Gomberg-Muñoz 2016; Fussell 2011; Coleman and Stuesse 2014; Stuesse 2018; Golash-Boza 2012; Lung 2019.

81. Ibid.

82. Gomberg-Muñoz 2016; Stuesse 2010; Goldstein and Bejarano 2017.

83. See Horton 2016a, 2016b.

84. Erlich 2021; Stuesse 2018.

85. Golash-Boza and Hondagneu-Sotelo 2013; Valdez et al. 2019.

86. Valdez et al. 2019.

87. Ordóñez 2015; see also Crotty 2017.

88. Martínez 2008.

89. Ibid.

90. Massey, Durand, and Pren 2016a.

91. Ibid.; Gonzalez-Barrera 2021.

92. Gonzalez-Barrera 2021.

93. Doussard 2013.

94. Interview by Camden Bowman, June 25, 2015, Federal and 19th.

95. These arrangements rarely hold legal water. However, Nico would be unlikely to figure this out on his own and unlikely to find an attorney who was willing to take such a small case with a small fee.

96. Capece 2021, 2.

97. Ibid.

98. Doussard 2013, 159; Milkman 2006.

99. Valdez et al. 2019.

100. Ibid.

101. Ibid.

102. Valdez et al. 2019, 229.

103. Denver Channel 2021.

104. Page and Ross 2017, 1295.

105. Ibid.

106. DURA 2018.

107. Doussard 2013, 172.

108. Interview by Becky Hostetler and Patrick Garrett.

109. Development Research Partners. February 2015, accessed by Patrick Garrett, Laura Scharmer, Becky Hostetler, Caitlin Trent, and Nicky Mades.

110. Gleeson 2016, 38.

111. Theodore et al. 2008, 93

112. Ibid., 93–94; and Gabelsky 2005, 426; Milkman 2020.

113. Schneider (2018, 97) shows how the building boom in post-Katrina New Orleans prompted employers to further leverage race and immigration status to segment the labor force. Yet characteristics of jobs with poor working conditions expanded to characterize the plight of all workers, including US-born white workers who "previously enjoyed moderately better treatment."

114. Quoted from Gustavo Maldonado in Smith 2016.

115. Fritz-Mauer 2022, 17–18. I thank Fritz-Mauer for sharing his interview write-up with Jeff García from Denver Labor on January 11, 2022, and the data he obtained from the Denver Auditor's Office.

116. Fritz-Mauer 2022, 18.

117. In 2020, with an additional mandate to enforce minimum wage and overtime, as well as prevailing wage violations, Denver Labor collected just over $1 million, an impressive feat for its relatively small office. Thanks to Matt Fritz-Mauer. See the Denver Auditor's Office 2021 Annual Report.

118. I appreciate insights from attorney David Seligman here.

119. See Doussard (2013) on Chicago during the early 2000s construction boom.

120. Ibid., 157; Valdez et al. 2019.

121. Stiffler 2014, 3–4.

Chapter 3: Dreaming for Friday

1. I featured this case in my TEDxMileHigh Uncharted talk, March 20, 2021.

2. Also see Castrejón (2017, 9) on how employers may strand workers when they insist on compensation.

3. Valenzuela et al. 2006.

4. The post-Katrina reconstruction climate led Latino day laborers to experience wage violation rates that were twice that of other cities with established day labor markets servicing the construction industry (Waren 2014, 738).

5. Theodore et al. 2006.

6. Gordon et al. 2012; from Immigrants' Rights/International Human Rights Clinic 2011.

7. Workers Defense Project 2013.

8. Doussard 2013; Ordóñez 2015.

9. Interview by Natalie Southwick and Kaylee Dolen, October 8, 2015.

10. I appreciate information here from Matthew Fritz-Mauer.

11. This delay, aggravated by the slow response of enforcement agencies, dampens deterrence because the timeliness of agency response, rather than its severity, has been shown to more likely alter an employer's cost calculus to risk withholding wages (Gutzman and Soto 2018).

12. Theodore 2017, 6.

13. Doussard 2013.

14. Gomberg-Muñoz 2011; Ordóñez 2015.

15. Theodore 2017, 6.

16. Zatz 2008; Gleeson 2016.

17. Zatz 2008; Erlich 2021.

18. Erlich 2021, 1212.

19. Ibid., 1203; Jacobs et al. 2022.

20. Erlich 2021, 1225; Ormiston et al. 2020.

21. Erlich 2021; Bobo 2011.

22. Erlich 2021, 1217; Carré and Wilson 2004.

23. Erlich 2021, 1210; Ormiston et al. 2020.

24. For example, former President Trump's Department of Labor attempted to change the federal guidance to determine whether an individual is an independent contractor or employee, which President Biden blocked when he came into office.

25. Erlich 2021; Bobo 2011.

26. House Bill 09-1310 Colorado Department of Labor and Employment Staff, June 2, 2011, cited and compiled by Capece 2022, 12.

27. Ibid., exhibit A, cited in Capece 2022, 12.

28. Erlich 2021.

29. Ibid.

30. Ibid.

31. Ibid., 1212.

32. Ibid., 1217.

33. Even if employers insist that they cannot pay because workers never provided paperwork, they must still pay 76 percent of the owed wages. The other 24 percent is taxes otherwise due to the IRS. Information compiled by Annemarie Parsons; see IRS Topic No. 307 Backup Withholding.

34. Horton 2016b; Lung 2019.

35. Gleeson 2016; Holmes 2013.

36. Horton 2016c; Stuesse 2016.

37. Smith, Avendaño, and Ortega 2009, 4, 10–11.

38. Doussard 2013, xiv, 26.

39. Doussard 2013.

40. See Gleeson 2016.

41. Gleeson 2021 shows how wage claims come to stand in for, as well as offer one of the few means to recognize, the multiple forms of workplace suffering experienced by low-wage workers.

42. Gleeson 2016, 83; Doussard 2013.

43. Ollus et al. 2016; Davies 2019; Leighton 2018; Levin 2021; Lloyd et al. 2020.

44. Haro et al. 2020; Negi 2013; Organista et al. 2017.

45. Meléndez 2014; Hagan, Hernández-León, and Demonsant 2015.

46. Menjívar and Abrego 2012; Portes and Rumbaut 2001; Galemba and Kuhn 2021, 1226. I appreciate Aaron Schneider's suggestions here.

47. Díaz-Fuentes et al. 2016; Meléndez et al. 2014.

48. Galemba and Kuhn 2021.

49. Doussard (2013) also finds low wages to be an insufficient indicator.

50. Worby 2002; Díaz-Fuentes et al. 2016.

51. Labban 2013.

Chapter 4: A Day Worked Is a Day Paid

1. Case cited in Galemba and Kuhn 2021.

2. Ordóñez 2015; Doussard 2013.

3. Zemans 1982; Galemba 2021.

4. See also Ordóñez 2015.

5. This image is an English version used during the survey in 2017. Most cards were in Spanish, but we made English versions available. We updated the cards in coordination with Centro to reflect different community partners and the rising Colorado minimum wage over time. I appreciate Yessenia Prodero's assistance with producing this version.

6. Theodore 2017, 6; Castrejón 2017.

7. Case detailed in Galemba and Kuhn 2021.

8. Fussell 2011; Valdez et al. 2019; Crotty 2018.

9. Field notes by Amy Czulada, December 4, 2015, Dayton and Colfax.

10. Díaz-Fuentes et al. 2016, 479; Worby 2002.

11. Doussard 2013.

12. Theodore et al. 2008, 104.

13. Ibid.; Ordóñez 2015.

14. Camou 2009.

15. Ibid., 40.

16. Ibid.

17. Interview by Camden Bowman, Federal and 19th, February 2, 2015.

18. Ibid.

19. Interview by Amy Czulada, Centro, December 2, 2015.

20. Interview by Max Spiro, Federal and 19th, August 4, 2015.

21. I appreciate Angela Stuesse's suggestion to examine these internal dilemmas.

22. Interview by Max Spiro, August 25, 2015; see Ordóñez 2015.

23. Camou 2009, 45, 47.

24. Ibid., 45; Camou 2012; Ordóñez 2015.

25. Camou 2012, 54.

26. See, e.g., Monforton and Von Bergen 2021; Apostolidis 2019; see Meléndez et al. 2014 on associated benefits.

27. The U visa is a nonimmigrant visa that can be granted to noncitizens who are victims of crimes and collaborate with law enforcement. It allows individuals to stay and work in the country and can provide a pathway to permanent residency after three years.

28. Quesada et al. 2014; Ordóñez 2015; Gleeson 2016; Zemans 1982; Black 1973; Alexander and Prasad 2015.

29. Trautner et al. 2013.

30. Theodore 2017, 2020; Meléndez et al. 2014, 2016.

31. See Stuesse 2018, 82; Horton 2016a.

32. Monforton and Von Bergen 2021, 157.

33. Data scored and analyzed by Randall Kuhn; see Galemba and Kuhn 2021.

34. Gleeson 2016.

35. See Zemans 1982. Twenty percent of the Unregulated Work survey's sample of four thousand low-wage workers reported that they did not issue a complaint during the past year despite experiencing a labor violation, discrimination, or unsafe working conditions because they feared being fired, worried that their hours would be reduced, or believed that resolution was unlikely (Bernhardt et al. 2009, 24).

36. See statistics in Galemba and Kuhn 2021.

37. Theodore 2017, 2020; Meléndez et al. 2014, 2016.

38. In contrast, other studies found that worker center members had lower exposure to wage theft than their informal counterparts (Theodore 2019).

39. Camou 2009, 41.

40. Ibid., 42, 61.

41. Stuesse 2016.

42. Ordóñez 2015.

43. Ibid. See also Ngai (2004) on a history of distancing between Mexican Americans and more recently arrived Mexican immigrants.

44. Interview by Natalie Southwick.

45. See also Ordóñez 2015, 136.

46. Ordóñez 2015.

47. Gomberg-Muñoz 2011; Golash-Boza and Hondagneu-Sotelo 2013.

48. Stuesse 2016; Ordóñez 2015.

49. Stuesse 2016, 96.

50. Ibid.; Lipsitz 2006, 3. See Gledhill (1998, 281) on differentiation within the Mexican migrant population. Such contrasts may help one group uplift itself from

broader negative stereotypes but are conducive to capitalist exploitation that thrives off of such divisions.

51. Stuesse 2016; Lipsitz 2006.

52. See Glaser 2020.

53. See Zemans 1982.

54. Interview conducted by Sarah Horton, August 12, 2015.

55. Camou 2009; Ordóñez 2015.

56. Zemans 1982.

57. Some of the following cases are in Galemba 2021.

58. Fussell 2011.

59. Ordóñez 2015.

60. Theodore 2017, 7.

61. Ordóñez 2015.

62. Galemba and Kuhn 2021.

63. Ibid.

64. Ibid.; Díaz-Fuentes et al. 2016.

65. Camou 2012, 54.

Chapter 5: Failure to Pursue

1. Galvin 2016; Bobo 2011; Levin 2021.

2. Levin 2021, 13; Lee and Smith 2019.

3. Galvin 2016.

4. Interview by Sarah Friend and Otilia Enica, fall 2015.

5. Zemans 1982; Felstiner, Abel, and Sarat 1980–1981; Alexander and Prasad 2014; Fritz-Mauer 2021, 2022.

6. Fritz-Mauer 2021, 772; see also Alexander and Prasad 2014.

7. Interview with attorney by Brianna Klipp and Kat Englert, February 7, 2022.

8. Green 2019.

9. Ibid.

10. Ibid.

11. Alexander and Prasad 2014; Weil and Pyles 2005; Lee and Smith 2019.

12. Alexander and Prasad 2014, 1073.

13. Fritz-Mauer 2021, 771n187, 772; Alexander and Prasad 2014.

14. CDLE 2019; Galemba 2021.

15. CDLE 2019; Bernhardt et al. 2009, 42–43.

16. Galvin 2016.

17. Kim and Allmang 2021; Bobo 2011; Galvin 2016.

18. Lee and Smith 2019, 794–795.

19. Ibid.

20. Interview by Sarah Friend with assistance from Mary Kohrman, Andrew Johnson, Ryan Lowry, and Otilia Enica, October 7, 2015.

21. Interview by Sarah Friend and Otilia Enica, November 6, 2015.

22. Interview by Stacy Shomo and Kate Castenson, May 7, 2015.

23. Interview by Sarah Friend and Otilia Enica, November 6, 2015.

24. Levin 2021.

25. Leighton 2018.

26. Gerstein and Seligman 2018.

27. Ibid.

28. Galvin 2016, 338, 341.

29. As of March 2021, the backlog had improved to three to four months for cases to proceed to determination.

30. Information from a CDLE data request November 2020. Time lines began to speed up under Scott Moss's leadership after 2019, which led the DAT to debate adding filing CDLE claims back into its tool kit.

31. Towards Justice Tri-Annual report, 2014–2016.

32. If organizations that help individuals file claims do not receive transparent follow-through, they may lose credibility with workers, leading them to perceive engaging with the state to be a last resort (Fine 2017, 366; Weil and Pyles 2005).

33. Gleeson 2016, 2021.

34. This requirement can be difficult for workers to understand given the pervasiveness of employer practices to misclassify workers to evade liability.

35. Bobo 2011, 189.

36. Gleeson 2016; Erlich 2020.

37. Bernhardt 2012.

38. Ibid.; Gleeson 2021.

39. Fritz-Mauer (2021, 777) demonstrates that even for state and local agencies like Washington DC's Department of Employment Services that can address retaliation in the district, the processes are frequently too slow to counteract the damage. Even when available, penalties for retaliation are rarely applied (Lee and Smith 2019, 790).

40. Lee and Smith 2019, 790.

41. Case cited in Galemba 2021.

42. Just under 60 percent had ever experienced homelessness.

43. Ordóñez (2015, 88) observed that day laborers in Berkeley tended to account for their wages and hours only when jobs lasted multiple days.

44. Bobo 2011, 191.

45. Gleeson 2016.

46. Colorado Wage Protection Act Rules 2021, 10.

47. Ibid.

48. Interview by Rachel Kerstein, Liz Shaw, and Ayesha Hamza, April 21, 2017.

49. See Gleeson 2016, 2021.

50. Warren 2010, 115. See Gleeson 2016; Hull 2012.

51. Gleeson (2016, 79) shows how legal aid clinics and volunteers assist workers by "taking the subjective experience . . . and repackaging it in an evidence-based arsenal of documents that will help the client plead his or her case."

52. Fritz-Mauer 2021

53. Ibid.; Weil 2010, 2018.

54. Interview by Rachel Kerstein, Liz Shaw, and Ayesha Hamza, April 21, 2017.

55. Gleeson 2021.

56. As a state agency, the CDLE has available remedies to collect its own fines, but not for workers. This shortcoming was targeted in new legislation, which passed in the spring of 2022.

57. CDLE data request received on June 1, 2021, from Elizabeth Funk.

58. Cho, Koonse, and Mischel 2013, 2

59. See Fritz-Mauer 2022, 3.

60. Interview by Brianna Klipp and Kat Englert, February 7, 2022.

61. Fritz-Mauer 2022. See Chapter 2.

62. Seligman, Galemba, and Southwest Region Council of Carpenters 2018.

63. I appreciate Matthew Fritz-Mauer and David Seligman sharing these ideas. Lee and Smith (2019, 798–800) note that such liability expansions can be more effective if they clearly define who can be held be responsible and put the onus on agencies, rather than workers, to investigate where to direct the "blame."

64. Phillips 2021. Six other states and the District of Columbia passed similar legislation.

65. Here, I appreciate assistance from Nina DiSalvo.

66. See descriptions in Felstiner, Abel, and Sarat 1980–1981; Alexander and Prasad 2014; Zemans 1982.

67. Ibid. See critiques in Alexander and Prasad 2014; Lee and Smith 2019; and Fritz-Mauer 2021, 2022.

68. Black 1973, 126.

69. Also Fritz-Mauer 2021.

70. Gleeson 2016.

71. Hoag 2011, 82; Menjívar and Abrego 2012; Stuesse 2018.

72. Davies 2019.

73. Gleeson 2021; Segrave 2017.

74. Ibid.

75. Levin 2021; Lee 2014.

76. Menjívar and Abrego 2012; Lee 2014.

77. CDLE Employment Verification Law.

78. Stuesse (2018; see also Menjívar and Abrego 2012) also considers this a type of legal violence that layers upon the legal violence waged by immigration law.

79. Fine and Gordon 2010; Fine 2017; Lee and Smith 2019.

80. See also Lee and Smith 2019.

Chapter 6: God's Justice

1. Peace Corps 2004; Freire 1970.

2. Monforton and Von Bergen 2021, 17–18. Also see Apostolidis (2019) on a more grounded approach to popular education models.

3. Ordóñez 2015; Quesada et al. 2014, 44; Holmes 2013; Bourgois 1995.

4. Interview by Laurel Hayden with Elayna McCall, Stout Street, May 4, 2015.

5. Fernández-Esquer et al. 2021, 347.

6. Also see Ordóñez 2015.

7. Interview by Camden Bowman, April 9, 2015.

8. Ordóñez 2015.

9. Interview by Nikky Mades, April 15, 2015.

10. Glaser 2020, 196–197.

11. Ibid., 207.

12. Ibid., 199.

13. Bayat 2013, 16.

14. Field notes by Natalie Southwick, November 4, 2015.

15. Bobo 2011, xi.

16. Ibid., xiii.

17. Ibid.

18. There is, however, a growing number who identify with Protestant/evangelical groups, especially more recent arrivals from southern Mexico and Central America.

19. Mahadev 2019, 425.

20. Mills 2013, 21–22.

21. Ibid., 22.

22. Bourdieu 2003; Mahadev 2019.

23. Interview by Camden Bowman, 2015.

24. Duke, Bourdeau, and Hovey 2010.

25. Boyas, Valera, and Ruiz 2018.

26. Negi et al. 2021.

27. Camou (2012) describes how some workers felt ashamed to impose on family members.

28. Menjívar 1994, 1995.

29. Ibid.; Camou 2012.

30. Camou 2012.

31. Statistic by Randall Kuhn.

32. Hood et al. 2013.

33. Galemba and Kuhn 2021, 1215.

34. Haro et al. 2019; Boyas, Valera, and Ruiz 2018; Organista et al. 2017; Duke, Bourdeau, and Hovey 2010; Negi 2013; Negi et al. 2021.

35. Duke, Bourdeau, and Hovey 2010; Walter et al. 2004, 1160.

36. Interview by Natalie Southwick and Kaylee Dolen, October 8, 2015.

37. Boyas, Valera, and Ruiz 2018.

38. Interview by Camden Bowman, 2015.

39. Walter et al. 2004, 1161–1162.

40. Ibid., 1162; see also Horton 2016a; Flynn 2018.

41. Walter et al. 2004; Gomberg-Muñoz 2011.

42. Bowman 2015.

43. See Millar 2018.

44. Gomberg-Muñoz 2011.

45. Fernández-Esquer et al. (2021, 354) did not find a significant association between wage theft and mental health, but identified "wage theft as a stressor that stems from conditions reflecting structural racism, making workers vulnerable to poorer health" and injury.

46. Gomberg-Muñoz 2011.

47. Walter et al. 2004, 1166.

48. Quoted in Galemba 2021.

49. Apostolidis 2019.

50. Quesada et al. 2014.

51. Interview by Avalon Guarino and Brittny Parsells-Johnson, February 13, 2019.

52. Fernández-Esquer et al. 2021; Díaz-Fuentes et al. 2016; Gomberg-Muñoz 2011; Flynn 2018; Unterberger 2018; Horton 2016a.

53. Interview by Max Spiro; see Spiro 2017.

54. A social determinant of health lens critiques divisions between work-related and non-work-related injuries and illnesses (Flynn 2018, 17; from Bambra 2011).

55. See Horton 2016a; Saxton and Stuesse 2018; Stuesse 2018; Holmes 2013. Unterberger 2018 illustrates how employers, providers, and insurers underplay injuries and whether they are work related.

56. Unterberger 2018; Stuesse 2018.

57. Quesada et al. 2011.

58. Kovic 2008; Quesada et al. 2011.

59. Unterberger 2018; Stuesse 2018; Smith-Nonini 2011. In Ordóñez's (2015, xx) ethnography, day laborers understood their own commodification as *un leibor*, a Spanish term to denote being seen as a "unit of labor."

60. Quoted in Galemba and Kuhn 2021. See Smith-Nonini (2011) on the commoditization and exhaustion of Mexican migrant labor. Unterberger (2018) demonstrates how workplace injuries and illnesses incurred in the United States reverberate home, posing implications in both the United States and Mexico.

61. Interview by Natalie Southwick and Kaylee Dolen, October 8, 2015.

62. Crotty 2018, 625.

63. Ibid.

64. See Crotty 2017.

65. Ibid.; Crotty 2018.

66. Crotty 2018, 626.

67. Interview by Camden Bowman, Federal and 19th.

68. *Compañeros* is difficult to translate because of its many uses. It can be used for more distant peers like coworkers or to express alignment with those who share a similar social position. However, it can also refer to closer companions. Day laborers often used *compañeros* to more generally refer to fellow immigrant workers, whether at the corner or those who might work similar jobs.

69. Ordóñez 2015.

70. See Pribilsky 2004.

71. Apostolidis (2019, 201–202) also finds that conviviality is forged through shared experiences of suffering even as it coexists with self-interested competition for work, but he does not deal with these more guarded aspects.

72. Camou 2009.

73. Monforton and Von Bergen 2021, 50.

74. Crotty 2018, 625; Massey 2005; Apostolidis 2019, 215.

75. Interview by Stephanie-Renteria Perez, Dayton and Colfax, May 10, 2018.

76. Crotty 2018, 626.

77. Student presentation by Abbey Vogel, Stephanie Renteria-Perez, Sierra Amon, Pam Encinas, and Cecily Bacon, June 1, 2018. Interview by Stephanie Renteria-Perez, Dayton, and Colfax, May 10, 2018.

78. Interview by Brittny Parsells-Johnson and Avalon Guarino, Dayton and Colfax, February 13, 2019.

Chapter 7: The DAT

1. See Coutin 1993, 45.

2. As mentioned earlier, Newman is currently the Legal Director and General Counsel at NDLON.

3. Bejarano et al. 2019, 5.

4. Ibid.

5. Ibid.

6. Ibid.

7. Bejarano et al. 2019, 4, 82.

8. Haiven and Khasnabish 2014, 11.

9. Gordon 2007.

10. Ibid.

11. See Brown and Jackson 2013, 12.

12. Janes 2016, 79; Srivastava and Francis 2006; Hartman 1997.

13. Coutin 1993, 65–66, 83n1.

14. Camou 2009.

15. Clawson 2021.

16. Interview by Avalon Guarino and Brittny Parsells-Johnson, February 22, 2019.

17. Haiven and Khasnabish 2014.

18. Graeber 2009, 4, 19.

19. Ibid.

20. Ibid., 10–11; Graeber 2004.

21. Carney 2021, 113.

22. See Rubio 2021.

23. Coutin 1993.

Conclusion: *Sí, se puede*

1. Interview by Mary Kohrman and field notes by Sarah Friend, October 28, 2015.

2. Fultonberg 2018. Some of this case is in Galemba 2020.

3. Towards Justice (Nina DiSalvo), University of Denver, and Sturm College of Law Clinical Programs, April 6, 2018.

4. Fine 2017.

5. Ibid.; Fine and Gordon 2010; Lee and Smith 2019.

6. Fine 2017, 366–367.

7. Monforton and Von Bergen 2021, 228.

8. Apostolidis 2019, 104.

9. Vigil 1999.

10. Excerpt by Nancy Rosas and shared by Sarah Shikes.

11. Walia 2021.

12. Doussard 2013. See Apostolidis (2019) for an excellent discussion of the wider impacts, and politics of, precaritization.

13. Fine 2006, 33.

14. Ibid.

15. Erlich 2020; see also Jacobs et al. 2022.

16. Erlich 2020.

17. See also Apostolidis 2019.

18. Standing 2011; Bernhardt et al. 2008.

19. Jacobs et al. 2022; shared and compiled by Capece 2022.

20. Ibid.

21. Walia 2013, 2021.

22. Ordóñez 2015.

23. Tuck 2009, 411–412.

24. Janes 2016; Tuck 2009, 411–412; Bejarano et al. 2019.

25. See also Monforton and Von Bergen 2021, 82.

26. TallBear 2014, 6.

27. Perez 2008.

28. See op-eds by Chapter 7 coauthor Amy Czulada: Czulada January 9, 2021, and May 15, 2021.

29. Field and Fox 2007; Gupta and Ferguson 1997.

30. Janes 2016.

31. Berry et al. 2017, 538.

32. Tuck 2009, 412. See also Coleman and Collins 2006, 5.

33. Bejarano et al. 2019; Gupta and Ferguson 1997. Berry et al. (2017, 539–540) note how fieldwork continues to be positioned as a "masculinist rite of passage" marked by racial and class privilege.

34. Gupta and Ferguson 1997, 8.

35. See Jobson 2020; Gomberg-Muñoz 2018; Horton 2021, 104; Berry et al. 2017, 546.

36. See Stuesse 2016.

37. Abrego 2021. See also Nuñez-Janes and Ovalle 2016; Duncan 2018; Yarris 2021.

38. Duncan 2018.

39. Nuñez-Janes and Ovalle 2016, 193; Tomlinson and Lipsitz 2013.

40. Nuñez-Janes and Ovalle 2016, 191.

41. Ahmed 2004, 189.

42. Carney 2021, 121.

43. Ibid., 122.

44. Duncan 2018.

45. See also Nuñez-Janes and Ovalle 2016.

46. Ahmed 2004.

47. See Stuesse 2016.

48. Abrego 2021, 2.

49. Ibid., 13.

50. Welch 2000, 41.

51. Fine et al. (2020) point to similar trends during prior recessions. See also Horton 2021.

52. Duncan and Horton 2020.

53. Interview with Centro staff member by Sarala Pradhan and Brianna Klipp, February 22, 2022.

54. For example, after previous failures, the Colorado legislature passed the Healthy Families and Workplaces Act in July 2020, which obligated employers to provide general paid sick leave to their employees and expanded COVID-19-related sick leave, which took effect on January 1, 2021. Colorado voters approved the Paid Medical and Family Leave Act via ballot initiative in November 2020. In 2022, Colorado also passed the Unemployment Compensation Act, which extends unemployment benefits to undocumented immigrants if their status was the only impediment to their eligibility by creating a Benefit Recovery Fund.

55. See Horton (2021) on pandemic privilege; Duncan and Horton 2020.

56. Horton 2021, 101.

57. Duncan 2018.

58. See Horton 2021; Jobson 2020; Gomberg-Muñoz 2018.

59. Janes 2016, 82.

Methodological Supplement

1. Bernard 2017.

2. REDCap, see Harris et al. 2009.

3. Valenzuela et al. 2006. See further explanation of the survey methodology in Galemba and Kuhn 2021.

4. Galemba and Kuhn 2021, 1210.

5. Some individuals attempted to fill out a duplicate form when they had not already taken the survey, perhaps because we were offering a half incentive of a $5 grocery card for duplicates. After realizing some of these problems, we discontin-

ued the half incentives for duplicates. Other individuals, however, took the survey more than once without disclosing. Yet surveyors were often able to recall and minimize these errors in the field by double-checking with each other.

6. Galemba and Kuhn 2021, 1210–1211.

7. Ibid.

8. Ibid.

9. Ibid.

10. We could not assess, but it is possible, that the election of Donald Trump one month into the survey could have intensified distrust. However, the qualitative interviews revealed that day laborers has long distrusted legal organizations, social services, and researchers (see Ordóñez 2015). Fear of immigration consequences was far from new.

11. See Galemba and Kuhn 2021.

Bibliography

Abrego, Leisy. 2021. "Research as Accompaniment: Reflections on Objectivity, Ethics, and Emotions." October 2020 draft in preparation for volume, *Out of Place, Power, Person, and Difference in Socio-Legal Research*. Edited by Lynnette Chua and Mark Massoud. UCLA, 1–18. https://escholarship.org/uc/item/34v2g837.

Ahmed, Sara. 2004. *Cultural Politics of Emotion*. New York: Routledge.

Alexander, Charlotte S., and Arthi Prasad. 2014. "Bottom-Up Workplace Law Enforcement: An Empirical Analysis." *Indiana Law Journal* 89 (3): 1069–1132.

Allen, Steven G. 1994. "Developments in Collective Bargaining in Construction in the 1980s and 1990s." NBER working paper No. 4674. Cambridge, MA: National Bureau of Economic Research.

Andreas, Peter. 2011. *Border Games*. Ithaca, NY: Cornell University Press.

Apostolidis, Paul. 2019. *The Fight for Time: Migrant Day Laborers and the Politics of Precarity*. New York: Oxford University Press.

Armenta, Amada. 2017. *Protect, Serve, and Deport: The Rise of Policing as Immigration Enforcement*. Oakland: University of California Press.

Baker, Dean. September 2018. *The Housing Bubble and the Great Recession: Ten Years Later*." Washington, DC: Center for Economic and Policy Research. https://cepr.net/images/stories/reports/housing-bubble-2018-09.pdf.

Balderrama, Francisco E., and Raymond Rodríguez. 2006. *Decade of Betrayal: Mexican Repatriation in the 1930s*, rev. ed. Albuquerque: University of New Mexico Press.

Bambra, Clare. 2011. "Work, Worklessness and the Political Economy of Health Inequalities." *Journal of Epidemiology & Community Health* 65 (9): 746–750.

Bayat, Asef. 2013. *Life as Politics: How Ordinary People Change the Middle East, 2nd Edition*. Stanford, CA: Stanford University Press.

Bejarano, Carolina Alonso, Lucia López Juárez, Mirian A. Mijangos García, and Daniel M. Goldstein. 2019. *Decolonizing Ethnography: Undocumented Immigrants and New Directions in Social Science*. Durham, NC: Duke University Press.

Bell Policy Center Staff. 2017. "TABOR: Restrictive Tax Policy Holds Colorado Back." Bell Policy Center. https://www.bellpolicy.org/2017/11/08/colorados-tabor/.

Berardi, Gayle K. 2014. "The Changing Nature of Colorado Immigration Laws: 2006–2013." *Journal of Social Science for Policy Implications* 2 (4): 1–29.

Bernard, H. Russell. 2017. *Research Methods in Anthropology: Qualitative and Quantitative Approaches*. Lanham, MD: AltaMira Press.

Bernhardt, A., R. Milkman, N. Theodore, D. Heckathorn, M. Auer, J. DeFilippis, A. L. González, et al. 2009. "Broken Laws, Unprotected Workers: Violations of Employment and Labor Laws in America's Cities." Center for Urban Economic Development, National Employment Law Project and UCLA Institute for Research on Labor and Employment.

Bernhardt, Annette. 2012. "The Role of Labor Market Regulation in Rebuilding Economic Opportunity in the United States." *Work and Occupations* 39 (4): 354–375.

Bernhardt, Annette, Heather Boushey, Laura Dresser, and Chris Tilly. 2008. "An Introduction to the 'Gloves-Off' Economy." In *The Gloves-off Economy: Workplace Standards at the Bottom of America's Labor Market*, edited by Annette Bernhardt, Heather Boushey, Laura Dresser, and Chris Tilly, 1–30. Champaign: Labor and Employment Relations Association, University of Illinois at Urbana-Champaign.

Berry, Maya J., Claudia Chávez Argüelles, Shanya Cordis, Sarah Ihmoud, and Elizabeth Velásquez Estrada. 2017. "Toward a Fugitive Anthropology: Gender, Race, and Violence in the Field." *Cultural Anthropology* 32 (4): 537–65.

Besteman, Catherine. 2019. "Militarized Global Apartheid." *Current Anthropology* 60 (S19): S26–S38.

Black, Donald J. 1973. "The Mobilization of Law." *Journal of Legal Studies* 2 (1): 125–149.

Bobo, Kim. 2011. *Wage Theft in America: Why Millions of Working Americans Are Not Getting Paid—and What We Can Do About It*. New York: New Press.

Bourdieu, Pierre. 2003. "Symbolic Violence." In *Beyond French Feminisms: Debates on Women, Culture, and Politics in France, 1980–2001*, edited by Roger Célestin, Eliane DalMolin, and Isabelle Courtivron, 23–26. New York: Palgrave Macmillan.

Bourgois, Philippe. 1995. *In Search of Respect: Selling Crack in El Barrio*. Cambridge: Cambridge University Press.

Bowman, Camden Ryan. 2015. "A Fair Day's Wages: Liberty, Legality, and Liability Among Denver's Day Laborers." Master's thesis, Josef Korbel School of International Studies, University of Denver.

Boyas, Javier F., Pamela Valera, and Erika Ruiz. 2018. "Subjective Well-Being

Among Latino Day Laborers: Examining the Role of Religiosity, Social Networks, and Cigarette Use." *Health Promotion Perspectives* 8 (1): 46–53.

Brown, Kevin, and Darrell D. Jackson. 2013. "The History and Conceptual Elements of Critical Race Theory." In *Handbook of Critical Race Theory in Education*, edited by Adrienne D. Dixson and Marvin Lynn, 29–42. New York: Routledge.

Cacho, Lisa Marie. 2012. *Social Death: Racialized Rightlessness and the Criminalization of the Unprotected*. New York: NYU Press.

Calavita, Kitty. 2005. "Law, Citizenship, and the Construction of (Some) Immigrant Others." *Law and Social Inquiry* 30 (2): 401–420.

———. 2010. *Inside the State: The Bracero Program, Immigration, and the INS*. New Orleans: Quid Pro Books.

Camou, Michelle. 2009. "Synchronizing Meanings and Other Day Laborer Organizing Strategies: Lessons from Denver." *Labor Studies Journal* 34 (1): 39–64.

———. 2012. "Capacity and Solidarity: Foundational Elements in the Unionization Strategy for Immigrant Day Labourers." *International Migration* 50 (2): 41–64.

Carney, Megan A. 2021. *Island of Hope: Migration and Solidarity in the Mediterranean*. Oakland: University of California Press.

Capece, Matthew F., Esq. 2021, July 16. "Memo: Fraudulent Schemes and Violations of Employment, Tax, and Other Laws in the Construction Industry." Representative of the General President, United Brotherhood of Carpenters and Joiners of America.

———. 2022, January 31. "Size and Cost of Construction Industry Tax Fraud: Survey of National and State Studies." Representative of the General President, United Brotherhood of Carpenters and Joiners of America.

Carré, Françoise, and Randall Wilson. 2004. *The Social and Economic Costs of Employee Misclassification in Construction*. Boston: Center for Social Policy, McCormack Graduate School of Policy Studies, University of Massachusetts, Boston.

Castrejón, J. Adrian. 2017. "Voces de la Esquina: Migrant Workers Counteracting Wage Theft, Wage Deduction, and Underpayment." *Justice Policy Journal* 14 (2): 1–17.

Centro Humanitario para los Trabajadores. n.d. "Centro Humanitario: About Us." http://www.centrohumanitario.org/about-us/. Accessed June 7, 2021.

———. n.d. "Centro Humanitario: Employment Program." http://www.centrohumanitario.org/programs/employment/.

———. n.d. "Centro Humanitario: Women's Program." http://www.centrohumanitario.org/programs/womens-program/.

———. n.d. "Centro Humanitario: Worker Center." http://www.centrohumanitario.org/programs/membershipworkforce-development/.

Chauvin, Sébastien, and Blanca Garcés-Mascareñas. 2014. "Becoming Less Illegal: Deservingness Frames and Undocumented Migrant Incorporation." *Sociology Compass* 8 (4): 422–432.

Chávez, Leo Ralph. 2013. *The Latino Threat: Constructing Immigrants, Citizens, and the Nation*, Second Edition. Stanford, CA: Stanford University Press.

Cho, Eunice Hyunhye, Tia Koonse, and Anthony Mishel. 2013. "Hollow Victories: The Crisis in Collecting Unpaid Wages for California's Workers." Los Angeles: National Employment Law Project, UCLA Labor Center.

City of Aurora. 2016. "Who Is Aurora: 2016 Demographic Report: Current Census Data, Key Areas, and Comparisons." Planning and Development Services Department, Aurora, CO. https://www.auroragov.org/UserFiles/Servers/Server_1881137/Image/City%20Hall/About%20Aurora/Date%20&%20Demographics/Who%20is%20Aurora%202016%20FINAL%2040MB.pdf/.

Clawson, Laura. 2021, February 3. "Amazon to Pay Huge Settlement in Wage Theft Case." *Workplace Fairness*. https://www.workplacefairness.org/blog/2021/02/03/amazon-to-pay-huge-settlement-in-wage-theft-case/.

Clemmer-Smith, Richard, Alan Gilbert, David Fridtjof Halaas, Billy J. Stratton, George E. Tinker, Nancy D. Wadsworth, and Steven Fisher. 2014. "Report of the John Evans Study Committee University of Denver." Denver: University of Denver.

Coleman, Mathew. 2007. "Immigration Geopolitics Beyond the Mexico-US Border." *Antipode* 39 (1): 54–76.

Coleman, Simon, and Peter Collins. 2006. "Introduction: 'Being . . . Where?' Performing Fields on Shifting Grounds." In *Locating the Field: Space, Place, and Context in Anthropology*, edited by Simon Coleman and Peter Collins, 1–22. New York: Berg.

Colorado Department of Labor and Employment. 2016. Employment Verification Law. https://cdle.colorado.gov/employment-eligibility-laws/employment-verification-law%20Accessed%20August%2012.

———. 2019. Wage and Hour Claims Monthly Report. Division of Labor Standards and Statistics.

———. 2021. Wage Protection Rules. Division of Labor Standards and Statistics. https://cdle.colorado.gov/sites/cdle/files/7%20CCR%201103-7%20Wage%20Protection%20Rules_0.pdf.

———. n.d. "Colorado Labor Peace Act: Title 8, Article 3 CRS." Division of Labor Standards and Statistics. https://cdle.colorado.gov/sites/cdle/files/Labor%20Peace%20Act%20%28C.R.S.%208-3-101%2C%20et%20seq%29.pdf. Accessed June 7, 2021.

Cooper, David, and Teresa Kroeger. 2017, May 10. "Employers Steal Billions from Workers' Paychecks Each Year." Washington, DC: Economic Policy Institute. https://www.epi.org/publication/employers-steal-billions-from-workers-paychecks-each-year/.

Cornelius, Wayne A. 2001. "Death at the Border: Efficacy and Unintended Consequences of US Immigration Control Policy." *Population and Development Review* 27 (4): 661–685.

Costa, Daniel. 2019, June 20. "Immigration Enforcement Is Funded at a Much Higher Rate Than Labor Standards Enforcement—and the Gap Is Widening." Washington, DC: Economic Policy Institute. https://www.epi.org/blog/

immigration-enforcement-is-funded-at-a-much-higher-rate-than-labor-standards-enforcement-and-the-gap-is-widening/.

Coutin, Susan Bibler. 1993. *The Culture of Protest: Religious Activism and the US Sanctuary Movement*. Boulder, CO: Westview Press.

———. 2003. *Legalizing Moves: Salvadoran Immigrants' Struggle for US Residency*. Ann Arbor: University of Michigan Press.

CPWR: Center for Construction Research and Training. "Hispanic Employment Dashboards. Hispanic Construction Workers, 2011–2019." https://www.cpwr.com/research/data-center/data-dashboards/hispanic-employment-dashboard/.

———. 2018. "Chart Book (6th edition): Labor Force Characteristics—Hispanic Workers in Construction and other Industries." https://web.archive.org/web/20200805024436/; https://www.cpwr.com/research/data-center/the-construction-chart-book/chart-book-6th-edition-labor-force-characteristics-hispanic-workers-in-construction-and-other-industries/.

Crotty, Sean. 2014. "The Social Geography of Day Labor: Informal Responses to the Economic Downturn." *Yearbook of the Association of Pacific Coast Geographers* 76: 22–48.

———. 2017. "Can the Informal Economy Be 'Managed'?: Comparing Approaches and Effectiveness of Day-Labor Management Policies in the San Diego Metropolitan Area." *Growth and Change* 48 (4): 909–941.

———. 2018. "Strategic Visibility and the Production of Day-Labor Spaces: A Case Study from the San Diego Metropolitan Area." *Urban Affairs Review* 54 (3): 593–631.

Czulada, Amy. 2021, January 9. "If Biden Represents the Working Class, He Should Cancel All Student Debt." *The Hill*. https://thehill.com/opinion/education/532984-if-biden-represents-the-working-class-he-should-cancel-all-student-debt.

———. 2021, May 15. "Debt Is a Tool of Oppression." *The Hill*. https://thehill.com/opinion/finance/553643-debt-is-a-tool-of-oppression.

Daum, Courtenay W., Robert J. Duffy, Kyle Saunders, and John A. Straayer. 2011. "Introduction: State of Change: Colorado Politics in the Twenty-First Century." In *State of Change: Colorado Politics in the Twenty-First Century*, edited by Courtenay W. Daum, Robert Duffy, and John A. Straayer, 1–18. Boulder: University Press of Colorado.

Davies, Jon. 2019. "From Severe to Routine Labour Exploitation: The Case of Migrant Workers in the UK Food Industry." *Criminology and Criminal Justice* 19 (3): 294–310.

De Genova, Nicholas. 2002. "Migrant 'Illegality' and Deportability in Everyday Life." *Annual Review of Anthropology* 31 (1): 419–47.

———. 2013. "Spectacles of Migrant 'Illegality': The Scene of Exclusion, the Obscene of Inclusion." *Ethnic and Racial Studies* 36 (7): 1180–1198.

Denver Auditor's Office. 2021. "2021 Annual Report." https://www.denvergov.org/files/assets/public/auditor/documents/audit-services/annual-reports/english/2021-annual-report-digital.pdf.

Denver Channel. 2021, June 30. "Investors Pour Money into Build-to-Rent Projects in Colorado." Denver Channel. https://www.thedenverchannel.com/news/local-news/investors-pour-money-into-build-to-rent-projects-in-colorado.

Development Research Partners. 2015. "2015 Economic Forecast for Metro Denver." Littleton, CO: Denver Metro Chamber of Commerce.

Díaz Fuentes, Claudia M. Leonardo Martínez Pantoja, Meshawn Tarver, Sandy A. Geschwind, and Marielena Lara. 2016. "Latino Immigrant Day Laborer Perceptions of Occupational Safety and Health Information Preferences." *American Journal of Industrial Medicine* 59 (6): 476–485.

Doussard, Marc. 2013. *Degraded Work: Industry Restructuring, Immigration and the New Low-Wage Labor Market.* Minneapolis: University of Minnesota Press.

Duke, Michael R., Beth Bourdeau, and Joseph D. Hovey. 2010. "Day Laborers and Occupational Stress: Testing the Migrant Stress Inventory with a Latino Day Laborer Population." *Cultural Diversity and Ethnic Minority Psychology* 16 (2): 116.

Duncan, Whitney L. 2018, January 31,. "Acompañamiento/Accompaniment." Hot Spots, *Fieldsights.* https://culanth.org/fieldsights/acompa%C3%B1amiento-accompaniment.

Duncan, Whitney L., and Sarah B. Horton. 2020, April 18. "Serious Challenges and Potential Solutions for Immigrant Health During COVID-19." *Health Affairs Blog.* https://www.healthaffairs.org/do/10.1377/hblog20200416.887086/full/.

DURA Renew Denver. 2018, December 19. "DURA Creates Thoughtful Redevelopment Through Affordable Housing." DURA Renew Denver. https://renewdenver.org/dura-creates-thoughtful-redevelopment-through-affordable-housing/.

Durand, Jorge. 2007. "The Bracero Program (1942–1964): A Critical Appraisal." *Migración y Desarrollo* 2 (2): 25–40.

Erlich, Mark. 2021. "Misclassification in Construction: The Original Gig Economy." *ILR Review* 74 (5): 1202–1230.

Erlich, Mark, and Jeff Grabelsky. 2005. "Standing at a Crossroads: The Building Trades in the Twenty-First Century." *Labor History* 46 (4): 421–445.

Espiritu, Yen Le. 2003. *Home Bound: Filipino American Lives across Cultures, Communities, and Countries.* Berkeley: University of California Press.

Farrell, Amy, Katherine Bright, Ieke de Vries, Rebecca Pfeffer, and Meredith Dank. 2020. "Policing Labor Trafficking in the United States." *Trends in Organized Crime* 23 (1): 36–56.

Felstiner, William, Richard L. Abel, and Austin Sarat. 1980–1981. "The Emergence and Transformation of Disputes: Naming, Blaming, Claiming . . . (1980–1)." *Law and Society Review* 15 (3–4): 631–654.

Ferguson, Susan, and David McNally. 2015. "Precarious Migrants: Gender, Race and the Social Reproduction of a Global Working Class." *Socialist Register* 51: 1–23.

Fermanich, Mark. 2011. "Colorado's Fiscal Future: We Get What We Pay For." Fiscal Policy Series Report 2011-100-01. Denver: School of Public Affairs, University of Colorado at Denver.

Fernández-Esquer, Maria Eugenia, Lynn N. Ibekwe, Rosalia Guerrero-Luera,

Yesmel A. King, Casey P. Durand, and John S. Atkinson. 2021. "Structural Racism and Immigrant Health: Exploring the Association Between Wage Theft, Mental Health, and Injury Among Latino Day Laborers." *Ethnicity and Disease* 31 (Suppl.): 345–356.

Field, Les W., and Richard G. Fox. 2007. "Introduction: How Does Anthropology Work Today?" In *Anthropology Put to Work*, 1–19, edited by Les W. Field and Richard G. Fox. Oxford, UK: Berg.

Fine, Janice Ruth. 2006. *Worker Centers: Organizing Communities at the Edge of the Dream*. Ithaca, NY: Cornell University Press.

———. 2017. "Enforcing Labor Standards in Partnership with Civil Society: Can Co-Enforcement Succeed Where the State Alone Has Failed?" *Politics and Society* 45 (3): 359–388.

Fine, Janice, Daniel J. Galvin, Jenn Round, and Hana Shepherd. 2020, September. "Maintaining Effective US Labor Standards Enforcement through the Coronavirus Recession." Report: Labor. Washington, DC: Washington Center for Equitable Growth. https://equitablegrowth.org/wp-content/uploads/2020/09/090320-labor-enforcement-report.pdf.

Fine, Janice, and Jennifer Gordon. 2010. "Strengthening Labor Standards Enforcement Through Partnerships with Workers' Organizations." *Politics and Society* 38 (4): 552–585.

Flynn, Michael A. 2018. "Im/migration, Work, and Health: Anthropology and the Occupational Health of Labor Im/migrants." *Anthropology of Work Review* 39 (2): 116–123.

Freire, Paulo. 1970. *Pedagogy of the Oppressed*. New York: Seabury Press.

Fritz-Mauer, Matthew. 2016. "Lofty Laws, Broken Promises: Wage Theft and the Degradation of Low-Wage Workers." *Employment Rights and Employment Policy Journal* 20 (1): 71–128.

———. 2021. "The Ragged Edge of Rugged Individualism: Wage Theft and the Personalization of Social Harm." *University of Michigan Journal of Law Reform* 54: 735–799.

———. 2022, March 14. "Naming, Blaming, and Just Plain Giving Up." https://papers.ssrn.com/sol3/papers.cfm?abstract_id=4029827/.

Fultonberg, Lorne. 2018, April 5. "Students Score Big Win in Wage-Theft Case." *University of Denver: News, In the Community*. https://www.du.edu/news/students-score-big-win-wage-theft-case.

Fussell, Elizabeth. 2011. "The Deportation Threat Dynamic and Victimization of Latino Migrants: Wage Theft and Robbery." *Sociological Quarterly* 52 (4): 593–615.

Galemba, Rebecca B. 2017, October 4. "Claudio's Story." *The DU Just Wages Project@Korbel*. https://dujustwagesproject.wordpress.com/2017/10/04/claudio/.

———. 2020, May 22. "Anthropology of Wage Theft in Colorado." *Anthropology News: Society for Economic Anthropology*. https://anthropology-news.org/index.php/2020/05/22/anthropology-of-wage-theft-in-colorado/.

———. 2021. "'They Steal Our Work': Wage Theft and the Criminalization of Immigrant Day Laborers in Colorado, USA." *European Journal on Criminal Policy and Research* 27 (1): 91–112.

Galemba, Rebecca, and Randall Kuhn. 2021. "'No Place for Old Men': Immigrant Duration, Wage Theft, and Economic Mobility Among Day Laborers in Denver, Colorado." *International Migration Review* 55 (4): 1201–1230.

Galtung, Johan. 1975. *Peace: Research, Education, Action.* Copenhagen: C. Ejlers. Essays in Peace Research.

Galvin, Daniel J. 2016. "Deterring Wage Theft: Alt-Labor, State Politics, and the Policy Determinants of Minimum Wage Compliance." *Perspectives on Politics* 14 (2): 324.

García, Juan Ramon. 1980. *Operation Wetback: The Mass Deportation of Mexican Undocumented Workers in 1954.* Westport, CT: Greenwood Press.

Gentsch, Kerstin, and Douglas S Massey. 2011. "Labor Market Outcomes for Legal Mexican Immigrants Under the New Regime of Immigration Enforcement." *Social Science Quarterly* 92 (3): 875–893.

Gerstein, Terri, and David Seligman. 2018, April 20. "A Response to 'Rethinking Wage Theft Criminalization.'" On Labor: Workers, Unions, Politics. https://onlabor.org/a-response-to-rethinking-wage-theft-criminalization/.

Glaser, Alana Lee. 2020. "Collective Complaint: Immigrant Women Caregivers' Community, Performance, and the Limits of Labor Law in New York City." *PoLAR: Political and Legal Anthropology Review* 43 (2): 195–210.

Gledhill, John. 1998. "The Mexican Contribution to Restructuring US Capitalism." *Critique of Anthropology* 18 (3): 279–296.

Gleeson, Shannon. 2016. *Precarious Claims: The Promise and Failure of Workplace Protections in the United States.* Oakland: University of California Press.

———. 2021. "Labor Precarity, Immigration, and the Challenges of Accessing Worker Rights." In *Precarity and Belonging: Labor, Migration, and Noncitizenship*, edited by Catherine S. Ramírez, Sylvanna M. Falcón, Juan Poblete, Steven C. McKay, and Felicity Amaya Schaeffer, 131–144. New Brunswick, NJ: Rutgers University Press.

Goetz, Andrew R., and E. Eric Boschmann. 2018. *Metropolitan Denver: Growth and Change in the Mile High City.* Philadelphia: University of Pennsylvania Press.

Golash-Boza, Tanya. 2012. *Due Process Denied: Detentions and Deportations in the United States.* New York: Routledge.

———. 2015. *Deported: Immigrant Policing, Disposable Labor, and Global Capitalism.* New York: New York University Press.

Golash-Boza, Tanya, and Pierrette Hondagneu-Sotelo. 2013. "Latino Immigrant Men and the Deportation Crisis: A Gendered Racial Removal Program." *Latino Studies* 11 (3): 271–292.

Goldberg, Robert Alan. 1981. *Hooded Empire: The Ku Klux Klan in Colorado.* Urbana: University of Illinois Press.

Goldring, Luin, and Patricia Landolt. 2012. "Caught in the Work–Citizenship

Matrix: The Lasting Effects of Precarious Legal Status on Work for Toronto Immigrants." In *Migration, Work and Citizenship in the New Global Order*, edited by Luin Goldring and Patricia Landolt, 85–102. New York: Routledge.

Goldstein, Daniel M., and Carolina Alonso-Bejarano. 2017. "E-Terrify: Securitized Immigration and Biometric Surveillance in the Workplace." *Human Organization* 76 (1): 1.

Gomberg-Muñoz, Ruth. 2011. *Labor and Legality: An Ethnography of a Mexican Immigrant Network*. New York: Oxford University Press.

———. 2016. "Criminalized Workers: Introduction to Special Issue on Migrant Labor and Mass Deportation." *Anthropology of Work Review* 37 (1): 3–10.

———. 2018. "The Complicit Anthropologist." *Journal for the Anthropology of North America* 21 (1): 36–37.

Gomberg-Munoz, Ruth, and Laura Nussbaum-Barberena. 2011. "Is Immigration Policy Labor Policy?: Immigration Enforcement, Undocumented Workers, and the State." *Human Organization* 70 (4): 366–375.

Gonzalez-Barrera, Ana. 2021, July 9. "Before COVID-19, More Mexicans Came to the U.S. Than Left for Mexico for the First Time in Years." *Pew Research Center*. https://www.pewresearch.org/fact-tank/2021/07/09/before-covid-19-more-mexicans-came-to-the-u-s-than-left-for-mexico-for-the-first-time-in-years/.

Goodstein, Phil. 2014. *Curtis Park, Five Points, and Beyond: The Heart of Historic East Denver*. Denver, CO: New Social Publication.

Gordon, Colin, Matthew Glasson, Jennifer Sherer, and Robin Clark-Bennett. 2012. "Wage Theft in Iowa." Iowa City: Iowa Policy Project.

Gordon, Edmund T. 1991. "Anthropology and Liberation." In *Decolonizing Anthropology: Moving Further Towards an Anthropology for Liberation*, edited by Faye V. Harrison, 149–167. Arlington,VA: American Anthropological Association.

Gordon, Jennifer. 1995. "We Make the Road by Walking: Immigrant Workers, the Workplace Project, and the Struggle for Social Change." *Harvard Civil Rights-Civil Liberties Law Review* 30 (2): 407–450.

———. 2007. "Lawyer Is Not the Protagonist: Community, Campaigns, Law, and Social Change, The Symposium: Race, Economic Justice, and Community Lawyering in the New Century: Concluding Essay." *California Law Review* 95: 2133–2145.

Graeber, David. 2004. *Fragments of an Anarchist Anthropology*. Chicago: Prickly Paradigm Press.

———. 2009. *Direct Action: An Ethnography*. Oakland, CA: AK Press.

Green, Llezlie L. 2019. "Wage Theft in Lawless Courts." *California Law Review* 107 (4): 1303–1344.

Gupta, Akhil, and James Ferguson. 1997. "Discipline and Practice: 'The Field' as Site, Method, and Location in Anthropology." In *Anthropological Locations: Boundaries and Grounds of a Field Science*, edited by Akhil Gupta and James Ferguson, 1–46. Berkeley: University of California Press.

Guzman, Jesus, and Caleb Soto. 2018. "El Pan de Cada Dia: A Review of Wage Theft Policies." *Harvard Journal of Hispanic Policy* 30: 11–17.

Hagan, Jacqueline, Rubén Hernández-León, and Jean-Luc Demonsant. 2015. *Skills of the Unskilled: Work and Mobility among Mexican Migrants*. Oakland: University of California Press.

Haiven, Max, and Alex Khasnabish. 2014. *The Radical Imagination: Social Movement Research in the Age of Austerity*. London: Zed Books.

Hale, Charles R. 2006. "Activist Research v. Cultural Critique: Indigenous Land Rights and the Contradictions of Politically Engaged Anthropology." *Cultural Anthropology* 21 (1): 96–120.

———. 2007. "In Praise of 'Reckless Minds': Making a Case for Activist Anthropology." In *Anthropology Put to Work*, edited by Les W. Field and Richard G. Fox, 103–127. Oxford, UK: Berg.

Hall, Matthew, Emily Greenman, and Youngmin Yi. 2019. "Job Mobility Among Unauthorized Immigrant Workers." *Social Forces* 97 (3): 999–1028.

Haro, Alein Y., Randall Kuhn, Michael A. Rodriguez, Nik Theodore, Edwin Melendez, and Abel Valenzuela. 2020. "Beyond Occupational Hazards: Abuse of Day Laborers and Health." *Journal of Immigrant and Minority Health* 22 (6): 1172–1183.

Harris, Paul A., Robert Taylor, Robert Thielke, Jonathon Payne, Nathaniel Gonzalez, and Jose G. Conde. 2009. "Research Electronic Data Capture (REDCap)—a Metadata-Driven Methodology and Workflow Process for Providing Translational Research Informatics Support." *Journal of Biomedical Informatics* 42 (2): 377–381.

Hartman, Saidiya V. 1997. "Innocent Amusements: The Stage of Sufferance." In *Scenes of Subjection: Terror, Slavery and Self-Making in 19th Century America*, edited by S. Hartman, 17–48. New York: Oxford University Press.

Heyman, Josiah M. 1998. "State Effects on Labor Exploitation: The INS and Undocumented Immigrants at the Mexico-United States Border." *Critique of Anthropology* 18 (2): 157–180.

———. 2014. "'Illegality' and the US-Mexico Border: How It Is Produced and Resisted." In *Constructing Immigrant "Illegality": Critiques, Experiences, and Responses*, edited by Cecilia Menjívar and Daniel Kanstroom, 111–135. New York: Cambridge University Press.

Hickey, Chuck. 2015, April 14. "Study: Denver Apartment Rent Increases to Be Largest in US This Year." *KDVR: FoxDenver 31 & Channel 2*. https://kdvr.com/news/study-denver-apartment-rent-increases-to-be-largest-in-u-s-this-year/.

History Colorado. n.d. "Globeville-Elyria-Swansea Memory Project." https://www.historycolorado.org/globeville-elyria-swansea-memory-project.

Hoag, Colin. 2011. "Assembling Partial Perspectives: Thoughts on the Anthropology of Bureaucracy." *PoLAR: Political and Legal Anthropology Review* 34 (1): 81–94.

Holmes, Seth M. 2013. *Fresh Fruit, Broken Bodies: Migrant Farmworkers in the United States*. Berkeley: University of California Press.

Hood, Kenny, Monica Petersen, and Ashley Williamson. 2013. "Social Networks and Denver Labors: An Investigation of Social Networks Among Day Laborers at El Centro Humanitario Para Los Trabajadores." Graduate student paper submitted to Rebecca Galemba's Qualitative Research Methodologies course, University of Denver.

hooks, bell. 1990. "Postmodern Blackness." *Postmodern Culture* 1 (1).

Horton, Sarah B. 2016a. *They Leave Their Kidneys in the Fields: Illness, Injury, and Illegality Among US Farmworkers.* Oakland: University of California Press.

———. 2016b. "Ghost Workers: The Implications of Governing Immigration Through Crime for Migrant Workplaces." *Anthropology of Work Review* 37 (1): 11–23.

———. 2016c. "From 'Deportability' to 'Denounce-Ability': New Forms of Labor Subordination in an Era of Governing Immigration Through Crime." *PoLAR: Political and Legal Anthropology Review* 39 (2): 312–326.

———. 2017. "Diverted Retirement." *The US-Mexico Transborder Region: Cultural Dynamics and Historical Interactions,* edited by Carlos G. Vélez-Ibáñez and Josiah Heyman, 322–341. Tucson: University of Arizona Press.

———. 2021. "On Pandemic Privilege: Reflections on a 'Home-Bound Pandemic Ethnography.'" *Journal for the Anthropology of North America* 24 (2): 98–107.

Hull, Matthew S. 2012. "Documents and Bureaucracy." *Annual Review of Anthropology* 41: 251–267.

Immigrants' Rights/International Human Rights Clinic. 2011. "All Work and No Pay: Day Laborers, Wage Theft, and Workplace Justice in New Jersey." Newark, NJ: Center for Social Justice, Seton Hall University School of Law.

Inda, J. X., and J. A. Dowling. 2013. "Introduction: Governing Migrant Illegality." In *Governing Immigration Through Crime: A Reader,* edited by J. A. Dowling and J. X. Inda, 1–36. Stanford, CA: Stanford University Press.

IRS. 2021, March 12. "IRS: Topic No. 307 Backup Withholding." IRS. https://www.irs.gov/taxtopics/tc307#:~:text=When%20it%20applies%2C%20backup%20withholding,dividend%2C%20or%20patronage%20dividend%20income.

Jacobs, Ken, Kuichih Huang, Jenifer MacGilvary, and Enrique Lopezlira. 2022, January. "The Public Cost of Low-Wage Jobs in the US Construction Industry." UC Berkeley Labor Center. https://laborcenter.berkeley.edu/the-public-cost-of-low-wage-jobs-in-the-us-construction-industry/.

Janes, Julia E. 2016. "Democratic Encounters? Epistemic Privilege, Power, and Community-Based Participatory Action Research." *Action Research* 14 (1): 72–87.

Jobson, Ryan Cecil. 2020. "The Case for Letting Anthropology Burn: Sociocultural Anthropology in 2019." *American Anthropologist* 122 (2): 259–271.

Kalleberg, Arne L. 2012. "Job Quality and Precarious Work: Clarifications, Controversies, and Challenges." *Work and Occupations* 39 (4): 427–448.

Kim, Joy Jeounghee, and Skye Allmang. 2021. "Wage Theft in the United States: Towards New Research Agendas." *The Economic and Labour Relations Review* 32 (4): 534–551.

Kovic, Christine. 2008. "Jumping from a Moving Train: Risk, Migration and Rights at NAFTA's Southern Border." *Practicing Anthropology* 30 (2): 32–36.

Labban, Mazen. 2013, August 23. "Wage Theft, Wage as Theft." *Monthly Review.* https://mronline.org/2013/08/23/labban230813-html/#_edn24.

Lee, Jennifer J., and Annie Smith. 2019. "Regulating Wage Theft." *Washington Law Review* 94 (2): 759–822.

Lee, Stephen. 2014. "Policing Wage Theft in the Day Labor Market." *University of California Irvine Law Review* 4 (2): 655–678.

Leighton, Paul. 2018. "No Criminology of Wage Theft: Revisiting 'Workplace Theft' to Expose Capitalist Exploitation." In *Revisiting Crimes of the Powerful: Marxism, Crime and Deviance*, edited by Steven Bittle, Laureen Snider, Steve Tombs, and David Whyte, 188–201. New York: Routledge.

Levin, Benjamin. 2021. "Wage Theft Criminalization." *University of California Davis Law Review* 54 (3): 1429–1506.

Linder, Marc. 1986. "Farm Workers and the Fair Labor Standards Act: Racial Discrimination in the New Deal." *Texas Law Review* 65: 1335.

Lipsitz, George. 2006. *The Possessive Investment in Whiteness: How White People Profit from Identity Politics*. Philadelphia: Temple University Press.

Lloyd, Anthony, Georgios A. Antonopoulos, and Georgios Papanicolaou. 2020. "'Illegal Labour Practices, Trafficking and Exploitation': An Introduction to the Special Issue." *Trends in Organized Crime* 23 (1): 1–6.

Low, Setha M., and Sally Engle Merry. 2010. "Engaged Anthropology: Diversity and Dilemmas: An Introduction to Supplement 2." *Current Anthropology* 51 (S2): S203–S226.

Loza, Mireya. 2016. *Defiant Braceros: How Migrant Workers Fought for Racial, Sexual, and Political Freedom*. Chapel Hill, NC: UNC Press Books.

Lung, Shirley. 2019. "Criminalizing Work and Non-Work: The Disciplining of Immigrant and African American Workers." *University of Massachusetts Law Review* 14: 290–348.

Mahadev, Neena. 2019. "Karma and Grace: Rivalrous Reckonings of Fortune and Misfortune." *HAU: Journal of Ethnographic Theory* 9 (2): 421–438.

Martínez, Lisa M. 2008. "'Flowers from the Same Soil': Latino Solidarity in the Wake of the 2006 Immigrant Mobilizations." *American Behavioral Scientist* 52 (4): 557–579.

———. 2014. "Dreams Deferred: The Impact of Legal Reforms on Undocumented Latino Youth." *American Behavioral Scientist* 58 (14): 1873–1890.

Massey, Doreen B. 2005. *For Space*. London: Sage.

Massey, Douglas S., Jorge Durand, and Nolan J. Malone. 2002. *Beyond Smoke and Mirrors: Mexican Immigration in an Era of Economic Integration*. New York: Russell Sage Foundation.

Massey, Douglas S., Jorge Durand, and Karen A. Pren. 2016a. "The Precarious Position of Latino Immigrants in the United States: A Comparative Analysis of Ethnosurvey Data." *Annals of the American Academy of Political and Social Science* 666 (1): 91–109.

———. 2016b. "Why Border Enforcement Backfired." *American Journal of Sociology* 121 (5): 1557–1600.

Massey, Douglas S., and Kerstin Gentsch. 2014. "Undocumented Migration to the United States and the Wages of Mexican Immigrants." *International Migration Review* 48 (2): 482–499.

Meixell, Brady, and Ross Eisenbrey. 2014, September 11. "An Epidemic of Wage Theft Is Costing Workers Hundreds of Millions of Dollars a Year." Washington, DC: Economic Policy Institute. https://files.epi.org/2014/wage-theft.pdf.

Meléndez, Edwin J., M. Anne Visser, Nik Theodore, and Abel Valenzuela Jr. 2014. "Worker Centers and Day Laborers' Wages." *Social Science Quarterly* 95 (3): 835–851.

Meléndez, Edwin, M. Anne Visser, Abel Valenzuela, and Nik Theodore. 2016. "Day Labourers' Work Related Injuries: An Assessment of Risks, Choices, and Policies." *International Migration* 54 (3): 5–19.

Menjívar, Cecilia. 1994. "Salvadorian Migration to the United States in the 1980s." *International Migration* 32 (3): 371–401.

———. 1995. "Kinship Networks Among Immigrants." *International Journal of Comparative Sociology* 36 (3–4): 219–232.

———. 2014. "Immigration Law Beyond Borders: Externalizing and Internalizing Border Controls in an Era of Securitization." *Annual Review of Law and Social Science* 10: 353–369.

Menjívar, Cecilia, and Leisy J. Abrego. 2012. "Legal Violence: Immigration Law and the Lives of Central American Immigrants." *American Journal of Sociology* 117 (5): 1380–1421.

Migdal, Ariela. 2015, May 6. "Home Health Care Workers Aren't Guaranteed Minimum Wage or Overtime, and the Legacies of Slavery and Jim Crow Are the Reason Why." https://www.aclu.org/blog/womens-rights/womens-rights-workplace/home-health-care-workers-arent-guaranteed-minimum-wage-or.

Milkman, Ruth. 2006. *LA Story: Immigrant Workers and the Future of the US Labor Movement*. New York: Russell Sage Foundation.

———. 2008. "Putting Wages Back into Competition: Deunionization and Degradation in Place-Bound Industries." In *The Gloves Off Economy: Workplace Standards at the Bottom of America's Labor Market*, edited by Annette Bernhardt, Heather Boushey, Laura Dresser, and Chris Tilly, 65–90. Champaign: University of Illinois at Urbana-Champaign.

———. 2020. *Immigrant Labor and the New Precariat*. Hoboken, NJ: Wiley.

Millar, Kathleen M. 2018. *Reclaiming the Discarded: Life and Labor on Rio's Garbage Dump*. Durham, NC: Duke University Press.

Mills, Martin A. 2013. "The Opposite of Witchcraft: Evans-Pritchard and the Problem of the Person." *Journal of the Royal Anthropological Institute* 19 (1): 18–33.

Monforton, Celeste, and Jane M. Von Bergen. 2021. *On the Job: The Untold Story of Worker Centers and the New Fight for Wages, Dignity, and Health.* New York: The New Press.

Montoya, María E. 2002. *Translating Property: The Maxwell Land Grant and the Conflict over Land in the American West, 1840–1900.* Berkeley: University of California Press.

Moore, Scott. 2011. "Financial Architecture of Post-Republican Colorado." In *State of Change: Colorado Politics in the Twenty-First Century*, edited by Courtenay W. Daum, Robert Duffy, and John A. Straayer, 217–234. Boulder: University Press of Colorado.

Negi, Nalini Junko. 2013. "Battling Discrimination and Social Isolation: Psychological Distress Among Latino Day Laborers." *American Journal of Community Psychology* 51 (1), 164–174.

Negi, Nalini Junko, Jennifer L. Siegel, Priya B. Sharma, and Gabriel Fiallos. 2021. "'The Solitude Absorbs and It Oppresses': 'Illegality' and Its Implications on Latino Immigrant Day Laborers' Social Isolation, Loneliness and Health." *Social Science and Medicine* 273. https://doi.org/10.1016/j.socscimed.2021.113737.

Nessel, Lori A. 2001. "Undocumented Immigrants in the Workplace: The Fallacy of Labor Protection and the Need for Reform." *Immigration and Nationality Law Review* 22: 303–336.

Nevins, Joseph. 2008. *Dying to Live: A Story of US Immigration in an Age of Global Apartheid.* San Francisco: City Lights Books.

New York State Nail Salon Industry Enforcement Task Force. n.d. "Nail Salon Wage Bond Coverage FAQs." New York Department of State. https://dos.ny.gov/system/files/documents/2021/03/wage-bond-faqs.pdf.

Ngai, Mae. 2004. *Impossible Subjects: Illegal Aliens and the Making of Modern America.* Princeton: Princeton University Press.

NILC (National Immigration Law Center). 2020. "Worksite Immigration Raids." https://www.nilc.org/issues/workersrights/worksite-raids/.

Nuñez-Janes, Mariela and Mario Ovalle. 2016. "Organic Activists: Undocumented Youth Creating Spaces of Acompañamiento." *Diaspora, Indigenous, and Minority Education* 10 (4): 189–200.

O'Brien, Megan. 2020. "Women and Wage Theft." *DU Immigrant and Refugee Rights Colectivo Digest.* https://ducolectivo.wordpress.com/women-and-wage-theft-the-historical-context-and-manifestation-of-devaluation-and-exploitation/.

Ollus, Natalia, Anne Alvesalo-Kuusi, and Anniina Jokinen. 2016. *From Forced Flexibility to Forced Labour: The Exploitation of Migrant Workers in Finland.* Helsinki: European Institute for Crime Prevention and Control, .

Ordóñez, Juan Thomas. 2015. *Jornalero: Being a Day Laborer in the USA.* Oakland: University of California Press.

Organista, Kurt C., Sonya G. Arreola, and Torsten B. Neilands. 2017. "Depression and Risk for Problem Drinking in Latino Migrant Day Laborers." *Substance Use and Misuse* 52 (10): 1320–1327.

Ormiston, Russell, Dale Belman, and Mark Erlich. 2020. "An Empirical Methodology to Estimate the Incidence and Costs of Payroll Fraud in the Construction Industry." *Report.* http://stoptaxfraud. net/wp-content/uploads/2020/03/National-Carpenters-Study-Methodology-for-Wage-and-Tax-Fraud-Report-FINAL. pdf.

Page, Brian, and Eric Ross. 2017. "Legacies of a Contested Campus: Urban Renewal, Community Resistance, and the Origins of Gentrification in Denver." *Urban Geography* 38 (9): 1293–1328.

Passel, Jeffrey S., and D'Vera Cohn. 2016. "Size of US Unauthorized Immigrant Workforce Stable After the Great Recession." Pew Research Center. https://www.pewresearch.org/hispanic/2016/11/03/size-of-u-s-unauthorized-immigrant-workforce-stable-after-the-great-recession/.

———. 2019, June 12. "Mexicans Decline to Less Than Half the US Unauthorized Immigrant Population for the First Time." Pew Research Center. https://www.pewresearch.org/fact-tank/2019/06/12/us-unauthorized-immigrant-population-2017/.

Patler, Caitlin, and Tanya Maria Golash-Boza. 2017. "The Fiscal and Human Costs of Immigrant Detention and Deportation in the United States." *Sociology Compass* 11 (11). https://doi-org.du.idm.oclc.org/10.1111/soc4.12536.

Peace Corps. 2004. "Nonformal Education Manual." Washington, DC: Peace Corps. https://files.peacecorps.gov/multimedia/pdf/library/M0042.pdf.

Peck, Jamie, and Theodore Nik. 2008. "Carceral Chicago: Making the Ex-Offender Employability Crisis. *International Journal of Urban and Regional Research*, 32 (2): 251–281.

———. 2012. Politicizing Contingent Work: Countering Neoliberal Labor Market Regulation . . . From the Bottom Up?" *South Atlantic Quarterly* 111 (4): 741–761.

Perea, Juan F. 2011. "The Echoes of Slavery: Recognizing the Racist Origins of the Agricultural and Domestic Worker Exclusion from the National Labor Relations Act." *Ohio State Law Journal* 72 (1): 95–138.

Perez, Teresita. 2008, September 22. " 'Sí Se Puede': A Phrase with a Rich History." *Center for American Progress.* https://www.americanprogress.org/issues/race/news/2008/09/22/4950/si-se-puede/.

Pew Research Center. 2014. "Demographic and Economic Profiles of Hispanics by State and County, 2014. Colorado. Pew Research Center. https://www.pewresearch.org/hispanic/states/state/co.

Phillips, Julie A., and Douglas S. Massey. 1999. "The New Labor Market: Immigrants and Wages After IRCA." *Demography* 36 (2): 233–246.

Phillips, Zachary. 2021, June 8. "New York State Legislature Passes Construction Wage Theft Bill." *Construction Dive.* https://www.constructiondive.com/news/new-york-state-legislature-passes-construction-wage-theft-bill/601450/.

Piore, Michael J. 1972. "Notes for Theory of Labor Market Stratification." Working Paper 95. Cambridge, MA: Department of Economics, MIT..

Portes, Alejandro, and Rubén G. Rumbaut. 2001. *Legacies: The Story of the Immigrant Second Generation.* Berkeley: University of California Press.

Pribilsky, Jason. 2004. "'Aprendemos A Convivir': Conjugal Relations, Co-Parenting, and Family Life Among Ecuadorian Transnational Migrants in New York and the Ecuadorian Andes." *Global Networks* 4 (3): 313–334.

Quesada, James, Sonya Arreola, Alex Kral, Sahar Khoury, Kurt C. Organista, and Paula Worby. 2014. "'As Good As It Gets': Undocumented Latino Day Laborers Negotiating Discrimination in San Francisco and Berkeley, California, USA." *City and Society* 26 (1): 29–50.

Quesada, James, Laurie Kain Hart, and Philippe Bourgois. 2011. "Structural Vulnerability and Health: Latino Migrant Laborers in the United States." *Medical Anthropology* 30 (4): 339–362.

Rabourn, Mike. 2008. "Organized Labor in Residential Construction." *Labor Studies Journal* 33 (1): 9–26.

Rappaport, Joanne. 2007. "Anthropological Collaborations in Colombia." In *Anthropology Put to Work*, edited by Les W. Field and Richard G. Fox, 21–43. Oxford, UK: Berg.

Reich, Michael, David M. Gordon, and Richard C. Edwards. 1973. "A Theory of Labor Market Segmentation." *American Economic Review* 63 (2): 359–365.

Rinehart, Ted, and Tony Robinson with Emily Lennon, Payaam Kharimkhani, and Refugio Perez. 2007. "El Centro Humanitario: Denver's Humanitarian Center for Day Laborers." Denver: El Centro Humanitario. https://www.centrohumanitario.org/wp-content/uploads/2013/02/El-Centro-Story-1.pdf.

Riosmena, Fernando, and Douglas S, Massey. 2012. "Pathways to El Norte: Origins, Destinations, and Characteristics of Mexican Migrants to the United States 1." *International Migration Review* 46 (1): 3–36.

Rosas, Gilberto. 2016. "The Border Thickens: In-Securing Communities after IRCA." *International Migration* 54 (2): 119–130.

Rubio, Elizabeth Hanna. 2019. "'We Need to Redefine What We Mean by Winning': NAKASEC's Immigrant Justice Activism and Thinking Citizenship Otherwise." *Amerasia Journal* 45 (2): 157–172.

Sassen, Saskia. 1990. *The Mobility of Labor and Capital: A Study in International Investment and Labor Flow.* Cambridge: Cambridge University Press.

Saxton, Dvera I., and Angela Stuesse. 2018. "Workers' Decompensation: Engaged Research with Injured Im/migrant Workers." *Anthropology of Work Review* 39 (2): 65–78.

Schneider, Aaron. 2018. *Renew Orleans?: Globalized Development and Worker Resistance After Katrina.* Minneapolis: University of Minnesota Press.

Scopelliti, Demetrio M. 2014, September. "Housing: Before, During, and After the Great Recession." Washington, DC: US Bureau of Labor Statistics. https://www.bls.gov/spotlight/2014/housing/pdf/housing.pdf.

Scott, James C. 1985. "Weapons of the Weak." *Everyday Forms of Peasant Resistance.* New Haven: Yale University Press.

Sealover, Ed. 2017, February 14. "Colorado Senate Passes Bill to Become 'Right-to-Work' State." https://www.bizjournals.com/denver/news/2017/02/14/colorado

-senate-passes-bill-to-become-right-to.html.

Segrave, Marie. 2017. "Labour Trafficking and Illegal Markets." In *The Routledge Handbook of Crime and International Migration*, edited by S. Pickering and J. Ham, 302–315. London: Routledge.

Seligman, David, Rebecca Galemba, and the Southwest Regional Council of Carpenters. 2018. "Combating Wage Theft in Denver: How the City of Denver Can Protect the Safety and Dignity of Workers." Denver. https://d3n8a8pro7vhmx.cloudfront.net/towardsjustice/pages/345/attachments/original/1521739712/2018.03.21_Combating_Wage_Theft_White_Paper_FINAL..pdf?1521739712.

Smith, Jerd. 2016, April 22. "Colorado Wage Complaints Surge Amid Claims of Payroll Fraud, Abuse of Workers." *Daily Camera*. http://www.dailycamera.com/boulder-business/ci_29802278/wage-complaints-surge-amid-labor-protests-over-claims.

Smith, Rebecca, Ana Avendaño, and Julie Martínez Ortega. 2009. "Iced Out: How Immigration Enforcement Has Interfered with Workers' Rights." AFL-CIO, American Rights at Work Education Fund, and National Employment Law Project. https://ecommons.cornell.edu/bitstream/handle/1813/88125/afl_cio16_Iced Out_report.pdf?sequence=1.

Smith-Nonini, Sandy. 2011. "The Illegal and the Dead: Are Mexicans Renewable Energy?" *Medical Anthropology* 30 (5): 454–474.

Spiro, Max. 2017, September 18. "The Faces of Wage Theft: David." *The DU Just Wages Project@Korbel*. https://dujustwagesproject.wordpress.com/2017/09/18/the-faces-of-wage-theft-david/.

Srivastava, Sarita, and Margot Francis. 2006. "The Problem of Authentic Experience': Storytelling in Anti-Racist and Anti-Homophobic Education." *Critical Sociology* 32 (2–3): 275–307.

Standing, Guy. 2011. *The Precariat: The New Dangerous Class*. London: Bloomsbury Academic.

Stiffler, Chris. 2014. "Wage Nonpayment in Colorado. Workers Lose $740 Million Per Year: An Analysis of Nonpayment of Wages to Colorado Workers." Colorado Fiscal Institute.

Stuesse, Angela. 2010. "What's 'Justice and Dignity' Got to Do with It?: Migrant Vulnerability, Corporate Complicity, and the State." *Human Organization* 69 (1): 19–30.

———. 2016. *Scratching Out a Living: Latinos, Race, and Work in the Deep South*. Oakland: University of California Press.

———. 2018. "When They're Done with You: Legal Violence and Structural Vulnerability Among Injured Immigrant Poultry Workers." *Anthropology of Work Review* 39 (2): 79–93.

Stuesse, Angela, and Mathew Coleman. 2014. "Automobility, Immobility, Altermobility: Surviving and Resisting the Intensification of Immigrant Policing." *City and Society* 26 (1): 51–72.

Stumpf, Juliet. 2006. "The Crimmigration Crisis: Immigrants, Crime, and Sovereign Power." *American University Law Review* 56 (2): 367–420.

Svaldi, Aldo. 2016, April 26. "Metro Denver Rent Gains at Triple U.S. Average in January." *Denver Post.* https://www.denverpost.com/2015/02/20/metro-denver-rent-gains-racing-at-triple-u-s-average-in-january/.

TallBear, Kim. 2014. "Standing with and Speaking as Faith: A Feminist-Indigenous Approach to Inquiry." *Journal of Research Practice* 10 (2): 1–7.

Taft, Philip. 1966. "Violence in American Labor Disputes." *The Annals of the American Academy of Political and Social Science* 364 (1): 127–140.

Theodore, Nik. 2007. "Closed Borders, Open Markets: Immigrant Day Laborers' Struggle for Economic Rights." In *Contesting Neoliberalism: Urban Frontiers*, edited by Helga Leitner, Jamie Peck, and Eric Sheppard, 250–265. Minneapolis: University of Minnesota Press.

———. 2017. "After the Storm: Houston's Day Labor Markets in the Aftermath of Hurricane Harvey." Chicago: University of Illinois at Chicago.

———. 2020. "Regulating Informality: Worker Centers and Collective Action in Day-Labor Markets." *Growth and Change* 51 (1): 144–160.

Theodore, Nik, Derick Blaauw, Catherina Schenck, Abel Valenzuela Jr., Christie Schoeman, and Edwin Meléndez. 2015. "Day Labor, Informality and Vulnerability in South Africa and the United States." *International Journal of Manpower* 36 (6): 807–823.

Theodore, Nik, Edwin Meléndez, Abel Valenzuela, and Ana Luz Gonzalez. 2008. "Day Labor and Workplace Abuses in the Residential Construction Industry: Conditions in the Washington, DC Region." In *The Gloves-off Economy: Workplace Standards at the Bottom of America's Labor Market*, edited by Annette Bernhardt, Heather Boushey, Laura Dresser, and Chris Tilly, 91–109. Champaign: University of Illinois at Urbana-Champaign.

Theodore, Nik, Abel Valenzuela Jr., and Edwin Meléndez. 2006. "La Esquina (the Corner): Day Laborers on the Margins of New York's Formal Economy." *WorkingUSA* 9 (4): 407–423.

Tomlinson, Barbara, and George Lipsitz. 2013. "American Studies as Accompaniment." *American Quarterly* 65 (1): 1–30.

Towards Justice. 2014–2016. *Tri-Annual Report.* https://towardsjustice.org/who-we-are/annual-reports/2017-03-23-final-tj-tri-annual-report-1/.

Trautner, Mary Nell, Erin Hatton, and Kelly E. Smith. 2013. "What Workers Want Depends: Legal Knowledge and the Desire for Workplace Change Among Day Laborers." *Law and Policy* 35 (4): 319–340.

Tuck, Eve. 2009. "Suspending Damage: A Letter to Communities." *Harvard Educational Review* 79 (3): 409–428.

Unterberger, Alayne. 2018. "'No One Cares if You Can't Work': Injured and Disabled Mexican-Origin Workers in Transnational Life Course Perspective." *Anthropology of Work Review* 39 (2): 105–115.

US Bureau of Labor Statistics. 2021. "Economic News Release: Table 3. Union Affiliation of Employed Wage and Salary Workers by Occupation and Industry." https://www.bls.gov/news.release/union2.t03.htm#union_a03.f.2.

US Immigration and Customs Enforcement. 2021, May 18. "Worksite Violations: Targeting Employers Involved in Criminal Activity and Labor Exploitation." US Department of Homeland Security. https://www.ice.gov/investigations/worksite.

Valdez, Zulema, Nancy Plankey-Videla, Aurelia Lorena Murga, Angelica C. Menchaca, and Cindy Barahona. 2019. "Precarious Entrepreneurship: Day Laborers in the US Southwest." *American Behavioral Scientist* 63 (2): 225–243.

Valenzuela Jr., Abel, Nik Theodore, Edwin Meléndez, and Ana Luz Gonzalez. 2006. "On the Corner." In *Day Labor in the United States: Report of the Center for Study or Urban Poverty*. Los Angeles: University of California.

Varsanyi, Monica W. 2020. "Hispanic Racialization, Citizenship, and the Colorado Border Blockade of 1936." *Journal of American Ethnic History* 40 (1): 5–39.

Vidal, Matt, and David Kusnet. 2009. "Organizing Prosperity." *Union Effects on Job Quality, Community Betterment, and Industry Standards*. Washington, DC: Economic Policy Institute.

Vigil, Ernesto B. 1999. *The Crusade for Justice: Chicano Militancy and the Government's War on Dissent*. Madison: University of Wisconsin Press.

Visser, M. Anne. 2017. "A Floor to Exploitation? Social Economy Organizations at the Edge of a Restructuring Economy." *Work, Employment and Society* 31 (5): 782–799.

Walia, Harsha. 2013. *Undoing Border Imperialism*. Chico, CA: AK Press.

———. 2021. *Border and Rule: Global Migration, Capitalism, and the Rise of Racist Nationalism*. Chicago: Haymarket Books.

Wallace, Alicia. 2016, April 21. "Amid Colorado Construction Boom, Workers Are Scarce, Contractors Say." *Denver Post*. https://www.denverpost.com/2015/09/10/amid-colorado-construction-boom-workers-are-scarce-contractors-say/.

Walter, Nicholas, Philippe Bourgois, and H. Margarita Loinaz. 2004. "Masculinity and Undocumented Labor Migration: Injured Latino Day Laborers in San Francisco." *Social Science and Medicine* 59 (6): 1159–1168.

Walter, Nicholas, Philippe Bourgois, H. Margarita Loinaz, and Dean Schillinger. 2002. "Social Context of Work Injury among Undocumented Day Laborers in San Francisco." *Journal of General Internal Medicine* 17 (3): 221–229.

Waren, Warren. 2014. "Wage Theft Among Latino Day Laborers in Post-Katrina New Orleans: Comparing Contractors with Other Employers." *Journal of International Migration and Integration* 15 (4): 737–751.

Warren, Kay. 2010. "The Illusiveness of Counting 'Victims' and the Concreteness of Ranking Countries: Trafficking in Persons from Colombia to Japan." In *Sex, Drugs, and Body Counts: The Politics of Numbers in Global Crime and Conflict*, edited by Peter Andreas and Kelly M. Greenhill, 110–126. Ithaca, NY: Cornell University Press.

Weil, David. 2010. "Improving Workplace Conditions through Strategic Enforcement." Boston University School of Management Research Paper, no. 2010–20.

———. 2011. "Enforcing Labour Standards in Fissured Workplaces: The US Experience." *Economic and Labour Relations Review* 22 (2): 33–54.

———. 2018. "Creating a Strategic Enforcement Approach to Address Wage Theft: One Academic's Journey in Organizational Change." *Journal of Industrial Relations* 60 (3): 437–460.

———. 2019. "Understanding the Present and Future of Work in the Fissured Workplace Context." *RSF: The Russell Sage Foundation Journal of the Social Sciences* 5 (5): 147–165.

Weil, David, and Amanda Pyles. 2005. "Why Complain: Complaints, Compliance, and the Problem of Enforcement in the US Workplace." *Comparative Labor Law & Policy Journal* 27 (1): 59–92.

Welch, Sharon D. 2000. *A Feminist Ethic of Risk*, revised edition. Minneapolis: Fortress Press.

Western, Bruce, and Jake Rosenfeld. 2011. "Unions, Norms, and the Rise in US Wage Inequality." *American Sociological Review* 76 (4): 513–537.

Worby, Paula. 2002. "Occupational Health and Latino Migrant Day Laborers: A Preliminary Exploration." Berkeley: Institute for Labor and Employment, University of California.

Workers Defense Project. 2013. "Build a Better Texas: Construction Working Conditions in the Lone Star State." Workers Defense Project in collaboration with the Division of Diversity and Community Engagement at the University of Texas at Austin. https://workersdefense.org/wp-content/uploads/2020/10/research/Build%20a%20Better%20Texas.pdf.

World Population Review. 2021. "Median Household Income by State." https://worldpopulationreview.com/state-rankings/median-household-income-by-state.

Yarris, Kristin Elizabeth. 2021. "ICE Offices and Immigration Courts: Accompaniment in Zones of Illegality." *Human Organization* 80 (3): 214–223.

Zatz, Noah. 2008. "Working Beyond the Reach or Grasp of Employment Law." In *The Gloves-Off Economy: Problems and Possibilities at the Bottom of America's Labor Market*, edited by Annette Bernhardt, Heather Boushey, Laura Dresser, and Chris Tilly, 31–64. Champaign: Labor and Employment Relations Association, University of Illinois at Urbana-Champaign,.

Zemans, Frances Kahn. 1982. "Framework for Analysis of Legal Mobilization: A Decision-Making Model." *Law and Social Inquiry* 7 (4): 989–1071.

Zlolniski, Christian. 2003. "Labor Control and Resistance of Mexican Immigrant Janitors in Silicon Valley." *Human Organization* 62 (1): 39–49.

———. 2006. *Janitors, Street Vendors, and Activists: The Lives of Mexican Immigrants in Silicon Valley*. Berkeley: University of California Press.

Zúñiga, Víctor, and Rubén Hernández-León. 2005. *New Destinations: Mexican Immigration in the United States*. New York: Russell Sage Foundation.

Index